Today, at one and the same time, scholarly publishing is drawn in two directions. On the one hand, this is a time of the most exciting theoretical, political and artistic projects that respond to and seek to move beyond global administered society. On the other hand, the publishing industries are vying for total control of the ever-lucrative arena of scholarly publication, creating a situation in which the means of distribution of books grounded in research and in radical interrogation of the present are increasingly restricted. In this context, MayFlyBooks has been established as an independent publishing house, publishing political, theoretical and aesthetic works on the question of organization. MayFlyBooks publications are published under Creative Commons license free online and in paperback. MayFlyBooks is a not-for-profit operation that publishes books that matter, not because they reinforce or reassure any existing market.

1. Herbert Marcuse, *Negations: Essays in Critical Theory*
2. Dag Aasland, *Ethics and Economy: After Levinas*
3. Gerald Raunig and Gene Ray (eds), *Art and Contemporary Critical Practice: Reinventing Institutional Critique*
4. Steffen Böhm and Siddhartha Dabhi (eds), *Upsetting the Offset: The Political Economy of Carbon Markets*
5. Peter Armstrong and Geoff Lightfoot (eds), *'The Leading Journal in the Field': Destabilizing Authority in the Social Sciences of Management*
6. Carl Cederström and Casper Hoedemaekers (eds), *Lacan and Organization*
7. Félix Guattari and Antonio Negri, *New Lines of Alliance, New Spaces of Liberty*
8. Gerald Raunig, Gene Ray and Ulf Wuggenig (eds), *Critique of Creativity: Precarity, Subjectivity and Resistance in the 'Creative Industries'*
9. Michał Kozłowski, Agnieszka Kurant, Jan Sowa, Krystian Szadkowski and Jakub Szreder (eds), *Joy Forever: The Political Economy of Social Creativity*

JOY FOREVER

Joy Forever:
The Political Economy of Social Creativity

Michał Kozłowski, Agnieszka Kurant, Jan Sowa, Krystian
Szadkowski and Jakub Szreder (eds)

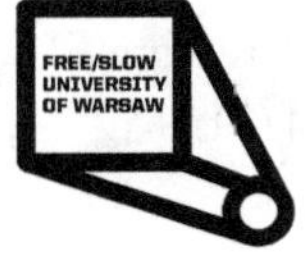

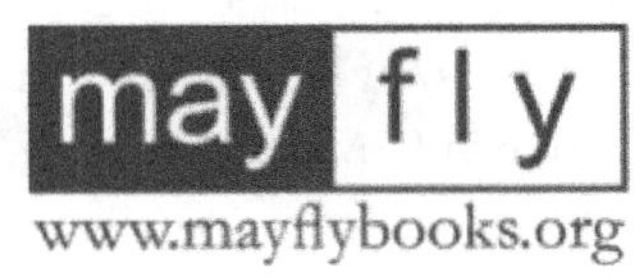

www.mayflybooks.org

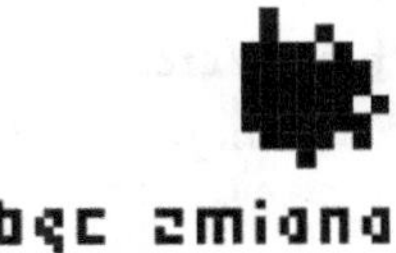

This work was originally published in Polish as an outcome of the international conference *The Labour of the Multitude? The Political Economy of Social Creativity* held in Warsaw, 20-22 of October 2011. Organisers of the conference were: Free/Slow University of Warsaw, Bęc Zmiana Foundation, University of Warsaw, Ministry of Culture and National Heritage of the Republic of Poland.

The publishers of Polish edition are: Free/Slow Univeristy of Warsaw (www.wuw-warsaw.pl) and Bęc Zmiana Foundation, Warsaw (www.beczmiana.pl).

First published in English by MayFlyBooks in paperback in London and free online at www.mayflybooks.org in 2014.

Cover design: Grzegorz Laszuk, Anna Hegman, Książki i Strony, www.kis11.pl

Proofreading and translations: Marsha Bradfield, Jason Francis McGimsey, Daniel Malone

Coordination and editorial assistance: Szymon Żydek

CC: The editors & authors 2014

ISBN (Print) 978-1-906948-19-1
ISBN (PDF) 978-1-906948-18-5

Contents

Contributors

Hans Abbing is an economist and visual artist. He is Professor Emeritus of Sociology of Art at the University of Amsterdam. He wrote the book *Why are Artists Poor: The Exceptional Economy of the Arts*. In 2016, his new book will be published, *The Art Period: Will Art become Common after Two Hundred Years of Splendor?*

Joanna Bednarek is an independent/precarious researcher and lecturer at Adam Mickiewicz University (Poznań, Poland). Author of several articles and a book titled *Polityka poza formą: Ontologiczne uwarunkowania poststrukturalistycznej filozofii polityki (Politics Beyond Form: Ontological determinations of poststructuralist political philosophy)*. Her research interests include relations between ontology and political theory, autonomist marxism, feminist theory and posthumanism.

Luc Boltanski is the leading figure in the new 'pragmatic' school of French sociology. He is a Professor at the École des Hautes Etudes en Sciences Sociales, Paris, and the founder of the Groupe de Sociologie Politique et Morale. He contributed to the start of the "political and moral sociology" framework. Political and moral sociology has gradually developed as a research programme — in the sense proposed by Imre Lakatos — around a conceptual nucleus looking to construct a theory of action based on Émile Durkheim's theory of moral fact, revising the inheritance of 'methodological structuralism' from the point of view of dynamics and processes. The research program stresses how, in many conflicts, the characteristics of the disputants change during the course of the conflict. His work has significantly influenced sociology, political economy and social and economic history.

Isabelle Bruno is a lecturer in Political Science at the University of Lille (France). She is working on neoliberal governmentality and managerial technology of government, more specifically on the genealogy of benchmarking in the U.S. industry and its current use in the European Union (research policy and the fight against social exclusion). She has published a book in French on the European Research Area (*À vos marques®, prêts… cherchez ! La stratégie européenne de Lisbonne, vers un marché de la recherche*, Éditions du Croquant, 2008) and a recent article in "Minerva" titled *The "Indefinite Discipline" of Competitiveness Benchmarking as a Neoliberal Technology of Government* (47/3, September 2009, 261-280).

Neil Cummings was born in Wales and lives in London. He is Professor of Theory and Practice at the CCW Graduate School, Chelsea College of Art and Design, a member of Critical Practice and on the editorial board of Documents of Contemporary Art. See www.neilcummings.com.

Diedrich Diederichsen is an author, journalist, cultural critic and a Professor at the University of Fine Arts in Vienna. He is one of Germany's most renowned intellectual writers at the crossroads of arts, politics, and pop culture.

Dave Beech, Andy Hewitt and Mel Jordan work collectively as the **Freee Art Collective**. Freee is concerned with the publishing and dissemination of ideas and the formation of opinion, or what Jürgen Habermas describes as the 'public sphere'. Freee's practice combines and links a number of key art historical elements; the use of text (as slogan), print, sculptural props, installation, video photography and montage – developing speech act theory and theories of art's social turn. Freee attempts to complicate the notion of the convivial in social practice by using witnesses instead of participants and develops theories of place and space from radical geography, theories of hegemony and the multitude, the theory of the philistine and the political theory of parrhesia in its projects. In 2011 Beech, Hewitt and Jordan established the journal Art and the Public Sphere. Freee's recent exhibitions include: 'We are Grammar', Pratt Manhattan Gallery, New York, 2011,

'Touched', Liverpool Biennial, Liverpool, 2010; 'When Guests Become Hosts', Culturgest, Porto, Portugal, 2010. Freee have recently contributed chapters to two forthcoming books: *Manifesto Now! Instructions for Performance, Philosophy, Politics*, (eds) Laura Cull & Will Daddario, published by Intellect Book and *New Interactive Practices in Contemporary Art*, (ed) Kathryn Brown, Publisher I.B.Tauris. For more information on Freee's Projects go to: www.freee.org.uk.

Isabelle Graw is Professor of the History of Art and Art Theory at Staatliche Hochschule für Bildende Künste (Städelschule), where she co-founded the Institut für Kunstkritik in 2003. She is an art critic, co-founder of "Texte zur Kunst", and the author of several books, including *Die bessere Hälfte. Künstlerinnen im 20. und 21. Jahrhundert* (2003), *High Price: Art between the Market and Celebrity Culture* (2009) and *Texte zur Kunst. Essays, Rezensionen, Gespräche* (2011).

Michal Kozłowski is Associate Professor at Philosophy Department at University of Warsaw (Poland). His work concerns the problem of subjectivity, history and historicity, capitalism and art. He extensively uses the concepts of Foucault, Bourdieu, Marx, Spinoza and the first generation operaismo. He is chef editor of Bez Dogmatu (quarterely review on politics and culture published since 1993) and co-editor of Le Monde Diplomatique. Edycja Polska. Published *Les contre-pouvoirs de Foucault* (Paris, 2011), *Sprawa Spinozy* (Cracow, 2011)

Agnieszka Kurant is an artist and writer. Her practice is related to the concepts of phantom capital, invisible labor, hybrid authorship and the harvesting of surplus value in society unbeknownst to the workers. Kurant's work has been exhibited at museums worldwide including Palais de Tokyo, Paris; Tate Modern, London; MoMA PS1, New York; Witte de With, Rotterdam; Stroom den Haag; Moderna Museet; Sculpture Center and most notably, at the Polish Pavilion during the 2010 Venice Biennale. In 2009 she was shortlisted for the International Henkel Art Award (Mumok, Vienna). Her work was also included in Frieze Projects; Performa Biennial; Bucharest Biennale, and Moscow Biennale. Sternberg Press published her monograph

Unknown Unknown in 2008. The artist has an upcoming commission for the Guggenheim Museum (June 2015). Kurant has lectured at universities and art academies including: The Vera List Center for Art and Politics at The New School, Otis College of Art and Design; USC Roski School of Fine Arts, Rhode Island School of Art; Rice University, Houston; Ecole de Beaux Art in Lyon and Goldsmith College, London.

Alexander Neumann is a senior researcher living in Paris where he obtained his PhD and his 'Habilitation à diriger des recherches' (CNRS). He wrote several books about conceptual and empirircal aspects of the Frankfurt School: *Conscience de casse*; *Kritische Arbeitssoziologie*; *Après Habermas*; and *Le principe Hartz* (to be published). He is currently directing a UE funded project about French-German cross border development.

The Precarious Workers Brigade is a growing group of precarious workers in culture and education. The group reaches out in solidarity with all those struggling to make a living in the climate of instability and enforced austerity. Its members have come together not to defend what was, but to demand, create and reclaim:

EQUAL PAY: no more free labour, guaranteed income for all

FREE EDUCATION: all debts and future debts cancelled now

DEMOCRATIC INSTITUTIONS: cut unelected, unaccountable and unmandated leaders

THE COMMONS: shared ownership of space, ideas and resources

John Roberts is Professor of Art & Aesthetics at the University of Wolverhampton, and the author of a number of books, including: *Philosophizing the Everyday: Revolutionary Praxis and the Fate of Cultural Theory* (Pluto 2006), *The Intangibilities of Form: Skill and Deskilling in Art After the Readymade* (Verso 2007) and *The Necessity of Errors* (Verso 2011). He has also contributed to a wide range of journals, including "Radical Philosophy", "Historical Materialism", "New Left Review", "Third Text", "Oxford Art Journal" and "New Literary History and Philosophy of Photography".

Gigi Roggero is a precarious researcher and a militant of the collectives: edu-factory and Uninomade, participates in The Knowledge Liberation Front network, and is a regular contributor to "Il Manifesto." Among his publications, he is the author of *The Production of Living Knowledge: The Crisis of the University and the Transformation of Labor in Europe and North America.*

Martha Rosler is an artist living in Brooklyn, New York. As an artist and activist, Rosler aims to engage people as citizens. Her concerns often center on the public sphere and landscapes of everyday life, especially as they affect women. She has worked extensively on questions of housing, homelessness, and the built environment. Her work in video, photomontage, public posters, and collaborative actions often takes on and challenges the national security state. In November 2012, she conducted the *Meta-Monumental Garage Sale* at MoMA, New York, almost 40 years after her initial presentation of the Garage Sale in Southern California.

Stevphen Shukaitis is a lecturer at the University of Essex and a member of the Autonomedia editorial collective. Since 2009, he has coordinated and edited Minor Compositions (http://www.minorcompositions.info). He is the author of *Imaginal Machines: Autonomy & Self-Organization in the Revolutions of Everyday Life* (2009, Autonomedia) and editor (with Erika Biddle and David Graeber) of *Constituent Imagination: Militant Investigations // Collective Theorization* (AK Press, 2007). His research focuses on the emergence of the collective imagination in social movements and the changing compositions of cultural and artistic labour.

Jan Sowa (born 1976) studied literature, philosophy and psychology at the Jagiellonian University in Kraków, Poland and University Paris VIII in Saint-Denis, France. He holds a Ph.D. in sociology and a habilitation in cultural studies. He is Associate Professor at the Chair of Anthropology of Literature and Cultural Studies at the Jagiellonian University. Member of Board of the Polish National Programme for the Development of Humanities. He edited and authored several books (recently: *Fantomowe ciało króla. Peryferyjne zmagania z nowoczesną formą*, 2012) and published around 100 articles in Poland and abroad (recently: with Jakub Majmurek and Kuba Mikurda, *Un événement dans* *la glacière: le Carnaval de Solidarnosc (1980-81) comme jaillissement de l'imagination politique* in: A. Badiou, S. Žižek, *L'idée du communisme II*, Paris 2012 and *Un giro inesperado de la ideología. Neoliberalismo y el colapso del Bloque Soviético*, "Metapolítica", Marzo 2013). Jan Sowa is currently working on a book exploring links between the 20[th] century artistic and political vanguard movements. Contact: jan.sowa[at]uj.edu.pl.

Krystian Szadkowski (born 1986) – marxist and higher education researcher, PhD candidate at the Institute of Philosophy of Adam Mickiewicz University of Poznań and researcher at the UNESCO Chair UNESCO Chair in Institutional Research and Higher Education Policy AMU. He is finishing his PhD thesis entitled *W strone uniwersytetu jako instytucji dobra wspólnego. Filozoficzne podstawy krytycznych badań nad szkolnictwem wyń szym* [*Towards the University as an Institution of the Common. Philosophical Foundations of Critical Higher Education Research*]. Editor-in-chief of peer-reviewed academic journal "Praktyka Teoretyczna/Theoretical Practice".

Kuba Szreder is a graduate at the sociology department of Jagiellonian University (Krakow). He works as a curator of interdisciplinary projects. As part of his curatorial practice he organizes research projects, seminars and conferences, writes articles and edits publications which coalesce critical reflection with art theory and sociological analysis of contemporary art field. In the fall of 2009 he started his PhD research at Loughborough University School of the Arts, where he scrutinizes the apparatus of project making and its relation to the independent curatorial practice.

Massimiliano Tomba teaches Political Philosophy at the University of Padua. He has published several texts on the political philosophy of Kant, Hegel, the post-Hegelians, Marx and Walter Benjamin. He is the author of *Krise und Kritik bei Bruno Bauer. Kategorien des Politischen im nachhegelschen Denken* (Frankfurt am Main: Peter Lang, 2005); *La vera politica. Kant e Benjamin: la possibilità della giustizia* (Macerata: Quodlibet, 2006); with D. Sacchetto, *La lunga accumulazione originaria. Politica e lavoro nel mercato mondiale* (Verona: Ombre Corte, 2008); *Marx's Temporalities* (Leiden: Brill, 2013).

Marina Vishmidt is a London-based writer occupied mainly with questions around art, labour and the value-form. She has just completed a PhD at Queen Mary, University of London on *Speculation as a Mode of Production in Art and Capital.* Research posts have included the Montehermoso Research Grant (2011/12), critic-in-residence at the FRAC Lorraine (2009) and a fellowship at the Jan van Eyck Academie (2007/8). She holds an MA from the Centre for Research in Modern European Philosophy. Co-editor of *Uncorporate Identity* (2010) with Metahaven, and *Media Mutandis: Art, Technologies and Politics* (NODE. London, 2006). She is a frequent contributor to catalogues, edited collections and journals such as "Mute", "Afterall", "Parkett" and "Texte zur Kunst". She also takes part in the collective projects Unemployed Cinema, Cinenova and Signal: Noise. She is currently writing a book with Kerstin Stakemeier on the politics of autonomy and reproduction in art.

The **Carrot Workers Collective** is a London-based group of current or ex interns, mainly from the creative and cultural sectors, as well as workers within the arts and education sectors that meet regularly to think together about the conditions of free labour in contemporary societies. They are currently undertaking a participatory action research around voluntary work, internships, job placements and compulsory unpaid work – AKA, workfare – in order to understand the impact they have on material conditions of existence, life expectations and sense of self, together with their implications in relation to education, lifelong training, exploitation, and class interest.

Acknowledgements

Every act of creativity is always a collective endeavour. This book in particular is a direct result of the international conference 'Labour of the Multitude? Political Economy of Social Creativity', convened in Warsaw in October 2011. We would like to thank all people and institutions engaged in facilitating the intellectual exchange that eventually resulted in *Joy Forever*.

We would like to express our sincere thanks especially to Bogna Świątkowska, Szymon Żydek and Ela Petruk who together with the team of Bęc Zmiana Foundation organised and facilitated the conference.

We would like to thank all the participants of the conference, whose presentations, comments and statements has contributed to the intellectual process that lead to the creation of this tome: Hans Abbing, Marsha Bradfield, Luc Boltanski, Neil Cummings, Diedrich Diederichsen, Isabelle Graw, Matteo Pasquinelli, John Roberts, Gigi Roggero, Martha Rosler, Hito Steyerl, Joanna Bednarek, Isabelle Bruno, Dusan Grlja, Precarious Workers Brigade, Johsua Simon, Stevphen Shukaitis, Britta Timm Knudsen, Ewa Majewska, Jason Francis McGimsey, Vlad Morariu, Yiannis Mylonas, Alexander Neumann, Bojana Romic, Massimiliano Tomba, Marina Vishmidt and Patricia Reed.

We would like to thank dr hab. Piotr Żuk for reviewing the Polish version of *Joy Forever* and the team of translators, editors and designers who participated in the production process of the Polish book: Paweł Michał Bartolik, Joanna Bednarek, Iwona Bojadżijewa, Anna Hegman, Piotr Juskowiak, Mateusz Karolak, Agnieszka Kowalczyk, Grzegorz Laszuk, Wiktor Marzec, Maciej Mikulewicz, Aniela Pilarska, Mikołaj Ratajczak, Paulina Sieniuć, Maciej Szlinder and Anna Wojczyńska.

We express our gratitude to partners and funders of the conference: the Faculty of Philosophy and Sociology of University of Warsaw (especially professor Jacek Migasinski), the interdisciplinary team of cooperation between the University of Warsaw and EHESS (especially professor Morgane Labbe from EHESS Paris), the Austrian Cultural Forum in Warsaw and the programme Observatory of Culture initiated by the National Centre for Culture.

Special thanks go to Armin Beverungen, one of the editors of MayFly Books, whose patience and engagement made the release of this book finally happen, and to Marsha Bradfield, Jason McGimsey and Daniel Malone, whose editorial support enabled completion of the book.

Since the time of releasing Polish edition of *Joy Forever*, the English versions of some of the texts featured here have been published in other volumes and journals. We would like to thank several publishers for their cooperation and kind permission to reprint the following texts in the English version of our volume: Isabelle Graw, "The Value of Painting: Notes on Unspecificity, Indexicality, and Highly Valuable Quasi-Persons", reprinted from tome edited by Isabelle Graw, Daniel Birnbaum and Nikolaus Hirsch *Thinking through Painting – Reflexivity and Angency beyond the Canvas*, published by Sternberg Press in 2012; Martha Rossler, "The Artistic Mode of Revolution: From Gentrification to Occupation", first published online in *e-flux* journal, volume 03 / 2012; John Roberts, "Labour, Emancipation and the Critique of Craftskill", published in *The Journal of Modern Craft*, volume 5, issue 2, July 2012.

Introduction: What Makes People Creative? Creativity as a Social Construct

Michał Kozłowski and Kuba Szreder

Creativity appears, at a first glance, to be a very trivial thing, and easily understood. Its analysis shows that it is, in reality, a very queer thing, abounding in metaphysical subtleties and theological niceties. There are indeed many good reasons for restating Marx's famous passage on commodity fetishism. Thus, not only does it seem that creativity undergoes various forms of commodification, but that it is also one of the fetishes of our times. We unavoidably tend to forget that, in a way similar to the commodity, creativity is not merely a thing, an action, a feature or a quality, but it is, above all, a social relation and, as such, it is shaped historically. We propose to reflect upon creativity not as a bond linking creator and creation, not as a quality found in one individual, but rather as a relation between a creator and other subjects involved in the creative process. The theological nuance is here. No doubt the very term 'creation' started its world-historical career with Christian theology. *Creatio ex nihilo* provides an unmediated example of a sovereign, one-sided, free, voluntary and unique productive gesture. Is not this monotheistic figure of 'the creator' echoed in parts of our contemporary imagination? Do not our present-day creative classes and individuals partake in the divine aura of the original creator? Or maybe they relate more to the pagan concept of praxis, which Aristotle defined as an action undertaken by a free man as virtuous conduct, without any purpose other than itself, as opposed to *poiesis,* an action guided by sheer necessity? The concept of praxis as self contained activity – being the goal in itself, not driven by mundane obligations – takes us to the ultra-modern Schillerian concept of art as an action freed from worldly utility and therefore from necessity. For Schiller, art 'throws a veil over physical necessity, offending a free mind by its coarse nudity, and dissimulating our degrading parentage with matter by a delightful illusion of freedom' (Schiller, 1794: Letter IV). The sweet burden of creation, however, is not for all but only for a few. 'We see that remarkable people uniting at once fullness of form and fullness of substance, both philosophising and creating, both tender and energetic, uniting a youthful fancy to the virility of reason in a glorious humanity' (Schiller, 1974: Letter XXVI). Schiller establishes the connection between creative action and the redemption of humankind; he forges this link in the privileged zone of artistic autonomy. This very connection explains to a great extent the fact that in order to look for a political and social economy of creativity, this volume extensively discusses creativity in art. Not for the sake of art itself, but rather seeking to exploit it as a polygon where creativity, power and freedom are closely intertwined.

However, it is not only *la bohème* that is ascribed such a fundamental role in creativity. A young Karl Marx didn't perhaps count on creativity as an emancipatory force but, conversely, he thought human creativity was something that should itself be emancipated in a revolutionary process.

> Yet the productive life is the life of the species. It is life-engendering life. The whole character of a species, its species character, is contained in the character of its life-activity; and free, conscious activity is man's species character. (Marx, 1988: 76)

This creative character of human beings is for now suppressed, suspended or rather alienated through capitalistic exploitation. Thus the worker 'surrenders its creative power, like Esau his birthright for a mess of pottage' and 'the creative power of his labour establishes itself as the power of capital, as an alien power confronting him' (Marx, 1973: 307). So, creativity is to be freed as praxis in the ancient sense of the term (as 'free conscious activity') while, at the same time, it already is an alienating force of the capitalist world as we know it. This suppressed though still thriving creativity as real labour power, is the hidden secret of alienated labour. But this somewhat dialectical account of creativity didn't save Marx from severe criticism, issued by later generations of his eminent followers.

Raoul Vaneigem, one of the protagonists of the Internationale Situationiste *(IS),* wrote in an afterword to a new edition of *The Communist Manifesto*:

> 'It is creation, not labour, that is specific to human beings. The transformation of life force into labour force represses and inverts this aspiration for self-enjoyment that demands the combined creation of the world and individual destiny. A universe transformed by labour only achieves the modernity of its fundamental inhumanity because it implies the transformation of man into labourer, his negation as a living and desiring being. By basing emancipation on the collective management of the means of production, Marx and Engels turned liberty into the flag of universal oppression.' (Vaneigem, 1996: 76)

Obviously in this passage Vaneigem refers less to Marx's early writings than to the policies and dogmas of those Marxists (the vast majority) who considered productive labour and toil the inevitable destiny of mankind. But his arguments are representative of the movement, around 1968, as he dissented with the disciplinary system of what we now call 'capitalistic Fordism'. The refusal of the assembly line's debilitating conditions was at least partially driven by the notions of free, non-alienated and creative life. Although Vaneigem and his colleagues from the IS never missed a chance to scorn the official art scene, they nevertheless promoted the surrealists' uncompromised legacy, one that bravely struggled to merge art and life while redeeming the 'poetry of the everyday' (Vaneigem, 1982), from the alienated regimes of capitalistic dullness. As Boltanski and Chiapello point out such 'artistc critique' of capitalism contrasted tedious bourgeois ways of life with 'the freedom of artists, … their refusal of any form of subjection in time and space and, in its extreme forms, of any kind of work' (Boltanski and Chiapello, 2005: 38). This type of critique tapped into the mythology of artistic avant-gardes that considered artistic creation as a paradigmatic example of unalienated labour, of what Bruno Gulli identifies as 'neither productive nor unproductive' activity (Gulli, 2005: 1). To its apologists and propagators, art formed an autonomous exception to capitalistic regimes of disciplined labour and instrumental reason.

But as Luc Boltanski and Eve Chiapello argue, eventually such 'artistic critique' and reasonable refusal of objectified existence was co-opted and utilized in the 'new spirit of capitalism', which evolved in response to the upheavals of the 1960s and 1970s. The popular desire to lead an unbridled creative life cushioned the progress into what David Harvey calls a new regime of flexible accumulation. Sadly, it soon followed that freedom was not awarded to working populations but rather to capital flows that, unrestrained from stiff labour arrangements, could roam the globe in search of the highest profit rates.

In this new regime, human creativity became just another resource to be harvested by a variety of 'mechanisms of capture', to use Christian Marazzi's (2010b) term. The forces of creation, instead of defying capitalistic pursuits for profit, are captured as intellectual property, framed as lifestyles and consumer preferences and utilized as a means for accumulating capital.

In the 1990s and 2000s, creativity became cherished as a stimulant of productivity, a way to maintain competitive advantages and safeguard the fading dominance of the developed West. This explains the incredible progress that the 'creative industries' have made over the last three decades. A long time had already passed since Thedore Adorno and Max Horheimer wrote that the 'culture industry endlessly cheats its consumers from what it endlessly promises' (Adorno and Horkheimer, 2002: 131). With genuine contempt, they criticized the culture industry as a mechanism designed to manufacture ideological docility, mass deception and false reconciliation. Quite contrarily, proponents of the creative industries presented their industry as salvation for 'Cool Britannia' (a term coined in the late 1990s in circles surrounding British New Labour), from the vices of globalization and deindustrialization that had been wreaking havoc in the West since the 1980s. The discourse of industrialized creativity, promoted by, among many others, the British think-tank Comedia and the American consultant guru Richard Florida, was unapologetically capitalistic, treating creativity as a resource to be tapped for a variety of uses. Creativity acquired an almost supra-natural status, being both a magical treatment for social ills and a managerial snake oil to keep companies or cities competitive. The notions of 'creative cities' and a 'creative class' were founded on the success of what Sharon Zukin had already called the Artistic Mode of Production in early 1980s, which 'by an adroit manipulation of urban forms … transfers urban space from the "old" world of industry to the "new" world of finance, or from the realm of productive economic activity to that of nonproductive economic activity' (Zukin, 1989: 178). The blueprints for culture-led regeneration and creative gentrification were replicated in numerous cities around the world, more or less dutifully imitating so called 'Soho effect'. Countless municipalities, reacting to the their financial calamities, strove to attract cohorts of hipsters and legions of *bourgeois-bohèmes* to their otherwise derelict districts in the hopes of using their creative revalorisation. Obviously, these creative dreams were shattered by the recent financial crisis, which revealed what creative makeup attempted to hide: the structural instabilities of contemporary capitalism.

However, the critical interest in creativity did not lose its momentum, as the term turns up in many discourses that are not necessarily related to the art scene, holding its enchanted grasp on policymakers and creative practitioners alike. Through its complex genealogies, the term 'creativity' acquired a bundle of meshed and frequently conflicting meanings. Creativity intertwines and semantically merges with other terms like artistic creation, innovation, self-fulfillment, spontaneity, vocational involvement, freedom and flexibility. Instead of following foundationalist phantasms to pin down the essence of creativity, our publication pursues a different strategy. It features authors who are critically concerned with dissecting the semantic opaqueness of creativity, focusing their attention on a variety of social, economic and political uses and abuses of this notion. Their arguments, uncompromising in their complexity and specificity, could be categorized into three general registers, each tackling creativity from varied perspectives:

1. Creativity as discourse and ideology. The two are distinct but closely related. Ideology consists of grand narratives about creativity, combining axiology, philosophy, historiosophy and eschatology. It saturates the contemporary *Zeitgeist* in particular theories and various forms of cultural representation with common, naturalised wisdoms about creativity, originality, genius and expression. Discourses about creativity are less coherent but more practical; they are concerned with creativity in terms of management techniques and schemes of the division of labour, justifications concerning the share of profit and working conditions, rationales for public services, grounds for setting new social distinctions (creative vs. non-creative) and modes of subjectivisation and subjection etc.

2. Creativity as a productive force. There is a feeling or a belief that, in the current phase of capitalism, an enormous amount of creativity is being suppressed, wasted or exploited – possibly all three. How, if at all, did the 'creative turn' in capitalism's evolution transform the power relations in our societies? What are the new forms of exploitation and seizure of profit that

take into account the diffused creativity and dispersed labour of the 'social factory'? Subsequently, where are the new lines of labour struggle, its new frontiers and stakes, located?

3. Creativity as critique. On the one hand, we asked ourselves whether it is still possible to deliver a coherent and binding social critique from the position of creativity (as Vaneigem intended). On the other hand, we simply wanted to know how and what men and women who think of themselves as creative (or are considered creative by others) actually critique. Putting these two questions together it seemed could prove particularly relevant and, we believe, it has.

We don't want, in any way, to assimilate the texts included in this volume to this somewhat arbitrary tripartite division. Nonetheless, as the reader will see, each of them contributes to enrich at least one of these registers and most contribute to all three. We were looking to dissect the social uses of creativity and we hope that, thanks to our authors, much light has been cast on its shadows and blind spots. For better or worse, we were not able to utterly disenchant the appeal that creativity still holds. Moreover, we are unsure whether such disenchantment would be the right thing to achieve, since the question to what extent capitalism's abuse of creativity is playing with fire remains unanswered.

PART ONE:
THE ART OF SPECULATION

1

From Object to Œuvre. The Process of Attribution and Valorization of Objects

Luc Boltanski

[translated by Jason McGimsey, reviewed by Daniel Malone]

Capitalism and Aura

In 'The Work of Art in the Age of Mechanical Reproduction', an essay written in 1935, Walter Benjamin announces 'profound changes are impending in the ancient craft of the Beautiful[1]' . This shift is caused by the 'amazing changes' created by the technical procedures that allow the unlimited reproduction of an œuvre, i.e. primarily photography and cinema (Benjamin, 2007: 217). Similarly to the other thinkers of the Frankfurt School – like Theodor Adorno or Max Horkheimer – Benjamin associates technical reproducibility with the development of a cultural industry and with the irruption of modes of production and the relevant circulation of the 'capitalistic mode of production' into the art world. These changes are interpreted in terms of 'decline'. Reproducibility removes the *uniqueness* – the main property of art – from it, the property it depends on for its *aura*, as a *unique presence* manifested in 'the here and now', which Benjamin compares to the 'unique phenomenon of a distance, however close it may be', like 'a mountain range on the horizon or a branch which casts its shadow over you' (Benjamin, 2007: 223). This aura, originally tied to the 'cult value' of an œuvre, is displaced to what Benjamin calls its 'exhibition value' (*ibid.*).

---

[1] Note from the editors: Benjamin here cites Paul Valéry.

Considered as a spatial and temporal *singularity*, an œuvre is therefore relevantly assimilated to an 'event that happens only once', so that its reappearance is a sort of reiteration or a commemoration of an original event. The example of a theatrical performance shows this, being a recreation that 'cannot be separated for the spectators from that of the actor' (Benjamin, 2007: 229). 'The poorest provincial staging of Faust', writes Benjamin, 'is superior to a Faust film in that, ideally, it competes with the first performance at Weimar (Benjamin, 2007: 243). 'The presence of the original', states Benjamin, 'is the prerequisite to the concept of authenticity' (Benjamin, 2007: 220). *Uniqueness* is what makes the 'authority of the object' (Benjamin, 2007: 221) Opposed to this uniqueness, there is what we can call *multiplicity*, comparable to 'products [put] on the market' (Benjamin, 2007: 219) by the cultural industry that abolish an œuvre by transforming it into a commodity. In short, this uniqueness of an œuvre calls to the 'empirical uniqueness of the creator' (Benjamin, 2007: 244) and, at the same time, surpasses it.

We can clearly see that these interwar critical theorists saw cinema as the paradigmatic example of capitalism's cultural invasion. In terms of production, films require important investments and management techniques that can coordinate the activity of a great number of workers in a strictly hierarchical organization, just like a factory. Likewise, regarding consumption, the film presents itself as multiple, encouraging the greatest number of copies possible so that it can be seen by a multitude of paying moviegoers. It should be noted, however, that more than 70 years since this text was written, art seems to have escaped its seemingly fatal destiny of being transformed into multiple commodities produced by a cultural industry. Works of art are still unique, most often created by individuals working alone or with a small team, like artisans, and whose fabrication doesn't require great financial means. The fact that they can be the object of monetary exchange is nothing new. Can it be deduced that the production and circulation of fine art have remained at the margins of continual capitalist expansion, extending to ever-new domains?

Using some concepts introduced by Benjamin, notably those of singularity, event, object, 'the authority of the object' and 'exposition value', we will try to propose a framework that can interpret the recent changes in the art world and the changes in capitalism, paying particular attention to the displacement of the sources of profit from the productive industry to the financial industry and the economy of singularities.

Exposition Value and Market Value

In Pierre Bourdieu's analyses (1992), we find the idea (alluded to by Frankfurt's critical philosophers) that art is inhabited by a tension between its strictly artistic value and its market value. Art's aesthetic valorization (on which the formation of an artist's 'symbolic capital' rests) is the inverse of its market value, i.e. its capacity to generate profit. This relation, quite clear in the case of multiple copies produced by the cultural industry (with, for example, the distinction between blockbusters and art films) is far from evident in the case of unique works. The current situation offers numerous contrary examples, in particular those analyzed by Isabelle Graw (2009), of contemporary artists whose prices have rapidly risen without this hurting their artistic reputation, as if the increase in market value had caused an increase in artistic value (Moulin, 1992: 70-75).

Indeed, in the case of unique works circulating in a narrow market of experts and collectors, market value builds on exposition value. It is the growth of exposition value that gives an œuvre the authority on which the growth of its market value rests. These two forms of valorization are manifested through the process of the circulation of an œuvre. Like economic assets in general, a work can only acquire value through circulation. On a theoretical level, it is therefore necessary to distinguish two processes of circulation that can, in practice, partially overlap: one that assures the creation of exposition value and another on which the creation of its market value depends. Assuming that the process of market valorization depends on the process of artistic valorization, the latter must have, in the eyes of the observer, a relatively autonomous character so that market valorization is constituted and, more importantly, stabilizes.

In the case of art, the relation between determining exposition value and market value can be compared, metaphorically, to the value established between rating agencies and trading floors in finance. Or, in another example, the relation between the 'core value' established by financial analysts (that is, as we know, fictional) as compared to daily stock quotations. If we can show that the agents who lavish advice on investors closely collaborate with those who intervene in markets, or even worse, that they are one and the same, the whole financial system tends to break down under accusations of manipulation and illegality. This effectively gives credibility to the descriptions that, revealing the absence of any supporting foundation for determining value, denounce the purely speculative character of value. In art, the degree of intricacy – variable according to the historical situation – between the process of circulation that establishes exposition value and the process of fixing market value, constitutes an important factor of stability or instability for assessment in this domain.

The Question of Attribution

When he speaks of the 'authority of the object', Benjamin implements a sort of concatenation that links two states of an object of art in the same utterance. It is, on one hand, the *object* and, on the other, a *sign* that manifests a claim to authority, in the sense that it can lend intentionality (Baxandall, 1991) and agency to it, as Alfred Gell's analyses (2009) have successfully highlighted. It is this close relation of the object and the sign that constitutes the œuvre. This is also recognized through the concept that copyright only can be claimed – as we well know – when an idea is placed on a 'support' (text, canvas, score, etc.). Consequently, a process that precedes the determination of exposition value (on an analytical level, if not necessarily in practice) exists. This process is the one through which the object is given the properties of an œuvre. This process could be described as a process of attribution.

Two uses of the term *attribution* can be found in historical and social sciences. The first, in art history, indicates the study of the way in which, especially since the 19th century, disparate objects (pieces) are compared so that they can be attributed to the same individual, to whom the 'paternity' of these objects is recognized (paternity is also the term used in copyright). This can be an individual whose identity is already known, or an individual whose uniqueness is supposed, although his identity remains unknown ('the Master of St. Bartholomew's altarpiece in Cologne'). It can even be a group, a style or a period (as when a piece is attributed to the series of 'Etruscan bronzes'). Carlo Ginzburg, in his famous essay dedicated to traces, demonstrated the importance of this process of attribution for social sciences in general

(Ginzburg, 1989: 139-180), taking particular note of the processes invented by Morelli.

Four remarks can be made regarding this process of attribution. The first is that it doesn't modify the substantial properties of the piece, but contributes in determining their sense. The second is that it doesn't settle for establishing a relation of sameness between them but concerns their identity (in accordance with the distinction established by Paul Ricoeur, 1990). The third is that it alone renders the determination of false or apocryphal works possible. The possibility that counterfeits exist thus becomes the best indicator that we are in the presence of an œuvre. Finally, the fourth remark is that this process of attribution modifies the exposition value of a piece and, consequently, its market value. The same signs, placed on the same support, see their value increase considerably if the piece can be attributed to a master (a recent example, to which the French newspaper *Le Monde* dedicated an article, concerns the lively debate over whether a portrait on vellum of a young woman from Milan can be attributed to Leonardo de Vinci, the price of which could go from $120,000 to $150 million if this attribution was recognized; see Bellet, 2011).

A second use of the term attribution was developed in the domain of social psychology, and later in cognitive sciences. In these disciplines, the theory of attribution concerns the study of the way so-called 'ordinary' people make casual hypotheses that allow them to explain events, both in the behavior of others (why did that colleague act like he didn't know me when I passed him?), and in the case of historical events (for example the attack on the World Trade Center on September 11th 2001[2]). Therefore its object is what is called 'naïve psychology' and describes the way relations of causality are understood in day-to-day life (Malle, 2004; Tilly, 2006).

Comparing these two uses allows us to see several clear similarities. In both cases, attribution takes a fact (an event is a fact in the same way as an object is a fact) and considers it a spatial-temporal singularity with the aim of giving it a sense. An event, understood as a singularity inscribed in space and time, has an immediate meaning that its physical dimensions give to it. However, in itself, it doesn't make any sense. To give sense to a singular event, a hypothesis concerning the cause of which it is an effect must be posed. This means attributing it an entity that is considered more stable over time than the event that needs explaining, and whose identity can support intentionality and agency. Some building has just collapsed. This event is a fact. It has a meaning (if it had risen toward the sky instead of falling to earth we would have talked about a 'miracle'). But to give sense to this fact, we must be able to attribute the responsibility to an entity's action: an earthquake? A dishonest owner who wanted to pocket the insurance money? A terrorist planted a bomb? Etc.

This process is precisely the one that transmutes an object into an œuvre. In order for an ordinary thing, whatever it may be – a 'commonplace object', as logicians say (Nef, 2000) – to be transmuted into an œuvre, it is necessary and sufficient to treat it like an event (to use Benjamin's term), which is given meaning by attributing it to an entity – called the cause or the author of that event – that has an identity, intentionality and agency. If an œuvre, unlike an object, can be called intentional in the sense that it contains and is, as an object, something exterior to it; and if, following Gell, its agency can be accented in the sense that it generates actions or that it provokes new events, these properties befall it only insofar as it has been assigned to an entity. In other words, generally, it is assigned to a person who has a robust and stable identity. An œuvre's intentionality and agency can thus be treated like the result of the projection of the intentionality and the agency of a person onto an object. Attribution is what allows us to give an object an *authority*.

This can best be seen in the borderline case of the 'chromos' market discussed by Raymonde Moulin in an essay that builds on a study of art gallery stores set up in malls on the outskirts of Montréal, whose clients are the newly urbanized middle class. These galleries show paintings, sold as 'originals' because they are manually painted, but produced in series, starting from pre-established formats or from photographs, by painters who give these galleries the exclusive rights to their abundant production (more than 300 paintings per year). Now, to assure 'the artistic valorization of the paintings' and to transform these standardized products into an œuvre, the galleries engage in the work of constructing authors that these objects are attributed to. Each employee-painter is given a different pseudonym corresponding more or less to the different genres (landscapes, portraits of infants, etc.) that he or she is specialized in. Individual shows, complete with private viewings and catalogues, are organized. The same article cites the case of Swedish wholesalers who oblige painters to produce 4000 to 5000 paintings per year, sometimes working on a dozen paintings at any given time. In this case also, authors are invented and individualized through pseudonyms, fictional biographies mentioning awards, honors, etc. (Moulin, 1992: 34-44).

Adorno's Desk in a Frankfurt Square

This attribution device, which probably always presides over the qualification of what we call an œuvre, revealed as the gesture typical of 20th century art, consists in taking an object, a commonplace thing, and transmuting it into an œuvre through a simple trick of displacement and signature (Fraenkel, 1992). There is an œuvre in the public square of a university neighborhood in Frankfurt: inside a transparent cube of Plexiglas different things are arranged – notably a desk and a chair. There is a lamp, some papers and various objects on the desk. A copper plaque indicates that this is the desk where Theodor Adorno wrote. This œuvre is a monument to the memory of this Frankfurt School philosopher. Let's consider the desk where I am now writing. The placement of the objects sitting on this desk has a certain order to it, and probably even a form of coherent logic that an intelligent semiologist or sociologist, having well-read (or over-read) Goffman, could reveal. But it is only an object and not an œuvre of the so-called 'installation' genre. The objects sitting on my desk are not fixed in such a way as to make their arrangement transportable without deforming it, and their fleeting combination hasn't been the subject of an aggregation susceptible to giving them the quality of a count-as-one – as Alain Badiou's ontology would have it (1988: 31-39) – that this work depends on to be qualified as art.

I'm ignoring who the author of this œuvre is and his history. But it was probably commissioned by the City of Frankfurt to some well-known artist, intended to commemorate the death of Adorno. It would have been impossible for Adorno himself, even though he was an artist in his own way (he studied, as you know, composition under the direction of Arnold Schönberg and wrote chamber music), to pretend to 'be an artist' by moving his desk to a city square. Such an act, barely thinkable, would have been interpreted as a sign of insanity. This means that this kind of *coup* that constitutes attribution – it alone being capable of giving authority to an object and transmuting it into an œuvre – is not in the hands of the person the œuvre is attributed to. Like all forms of authority, it depends on an authority granted by other people, invested with an authority that has been equally granted to them (and so on) by the intermediary of an unlimited chain of authorizations. The maker of an object can't call himself the author of an œuvre, even if he claims having fixed an idea on a support. His situation is similar to the legitimate power holder who must be granted authority by others. This is illustrated, in opposite terms, in the scandalous example of Napoleon putting the crown on his head with his own hands during his coronation as the Emperor of France. Or again, to take another example from a distant area, the situation of the Mayenne peasant studied by Jeanne Favret, who overwhelmed with woes can't declare himself bewitched and publicly accuse another person of being the guilty witch (usually a neighbor), unless there is a third announcer who occupies a supposedly neutral position in the system of witchcraft, and who has suggested this possibility to him.

In this sense, the transformation of an object into an œuvre is equivalent, not metaphorically but substantially, to the transmutation of bodily waste into a holy relic, as the fact has often been noted (and, specifically, by my brother, the artist Christian Boltanski). Imagine a man who, regarding and declaring himself a saint or God's vessel, cuts off a limb to give, or rather sell, to a group of followers? Such a gesture would be enough to disqualify his claim to sainthood. What historians of Christianity call the 'invention' of relics (a flourishing business in late antiquity and the Middle Ages) has many similarities with the transformation of an object into an œuvre. The invention consists in taking a body part, itself deprived of any value, and attributing it to a body glorified through the sufferings of martyrdom, based on the construction of a narrative that is both biographic and topographic. When this happens, which is far from always being the case, this attribution transforms the profane body part into a precious object with an incommensurable value, itself then producing value both on a mystic as well as economic level. Churches, pilgrimages, markets and all sorts of other derivative products are built around it. The relic, an object of desire *par excellence*, is the material of lucrative business and counterfeit productions that the holders of the one true specimen stubbornly unmask. Relics pass from hand to hand. But the question of knowing if we can discuss the existence of something like a relic market is problematic due to the absence of the principle of equivalence that allows objets to be ordered. There is no system of measurement that can organize Saint Celine's toe and Saint Barnabas' bones into a hierarchy. What could a little piece of bone be good for if not accomplishing miracles? The relic poses, just like an œuvre, intentionality and agency that are manifested by the intermediary of actions that we attribute to it. This unique event, the transmutation of a body part into a relic, is then the source of multiple events. A relic, like the one studied by Krzystof Pomian from Saint Mark's body, was the foundation of the authority of Venice's Doges after its arrival in 808 and is, in this sense, what produced an uninterrupted series of events such as, for example, Petrarch's 1362 decision to bequeath his books to Saint Mark. The author of *Canzoniere* is also a good *passeur* from relic to artwork if we remember that François I, traveling through Avignon, gave the city authorities a large sum of money to construct a mausoleum for the body of Laura, whose physical existence is still questionable. As Krzystof Pomian remarks, Venice was overflowing with relics, having 'probably tens of thousands of them', and whose presence played an important role in the city's wealth. It is, according to the same historian, in this image that collections were 'reinvented', starting from princely or ecclesiastic collection-treasures and then to individual collections where the 'content was principally antiques and paintings' (Pomian, 2003: 20-135).

Object, Thing, Piece, Œuvre, Icon

We can, at this point, suggest a vocabulary to indicate the different steps in the 'social life of an object' – as Arjun Appadurai says – that can be seen, in a certain moment of its itinerary, as an œuvre (1986). Let's start with any object that we can call a *thing*. This object can have little pertinence for someone (a pebble); pertinence for me, for example because of how I use it, or simply because it belongs to me (my pencil); pertinence for an indefinite number of other people (the ticket machine in the subway), etc. The object can be carried by one person (my coffee machine) or can circulate among many, for example if it is rented (a public bicycle), etc. Here, it isn't important whether this object is 'natural' or 'man-made'. Let's just say that the object in question can acquire pertinence in three ways: from someone's personal attachment to it and the attention that this person gives to it; in the function of its use, which refers to its functionality; or because it is tied to an individual or collective entity in a property relationship (usually through a contract, i.e. according to a legal principle). None of these ways require, in themselves, that the object changes, i.e. in order to become an œuvre for the purposes of our discussion.

Two intermediate steps between the thing and the œuvre can be indicated: the *object* and the *piece*. We can take for example an *object*, an object that is no longer in someone's environment, or in a relationship of attachment, nor in a relationship of functional use, nor in a relationship of property. At this point, it isn't important if it was purchased, found or stolen. In the practice of second-hand dealers – the subject of a remarkable book by Hervé Sciardet, *Les marchands de l'aube* – we can simply say that it has 'come out' or that it is no longer 'in its juice' (Sciardet, 2003). This object, momentarily lifted from its destiny as *garbage*, has found a place, for example, in the heap of things of one of those bad guys who occupy the lowest rungs in the flea market hierarchy. The ones that, at the crack of dawn, display a collection of dissimilar things that higher ranking antique dealers use as the raw material for their business, hoping to come across a 'good deal', meaning a piece of quasi-scrap whose potential value has gone unnoticed until then. Some of these things end up being garbage. Others will come to know a more desirable destiny. But this isn't important for the moment; they are nothing more than an object.

The *piece* is a thing that has been considered worthy of belonging to a *collection* (Pomian, 1987), whatever grade it may be, Chinese bronzes or keychains. Lifted from the status of quasi garbage which it still holds in flea market heaps, the thing transmutes into a piece once it is near other things with which it has a relationship of affinity. This means that the piece is a thing that has met an *amateur* or a *collector*. The collector can be called the *author* of his collection. We can attribute this transmutation of the thing into a piece to him. His œuvre, just like that of a *curator*, consists in the invention of a principle of equivalence, allowing different things to be considered in a certain relationship. The collector, just like the curator, can consider himself a creator in this sense, almost in the same way an artist does (which is often the case today). The collection, or the exposition, is thus similar to a kind of installation. The principle of equivalence under which the pieces are brought together can remain largely implicit, requiring a kind of real work of interpretation on the part of the spectator (thus elevating him to the position of a quasi critic).

In many cases, the way the thing would be considered in this relationship will be tied to an entity that we can call 'society' or 'period', or even 'style'. They are, most often, older pieces, meaning objects that have had a relationship of attachment, functionality and/or property in the past. For example, medieval spoons. It is the fact of being connected to these entities that makes them pieces and not things. Their sameness gives them, on one hand, a common meaning, and the fact of being brought to 'society', a 'period' or a 'style' gives them, on the other hand, a sense. We can note that in order to be good collection objects these pieces must be similar under a principal relationship (sameness), often established by referring to the functions that they had when they were used (as keychains, as stoups, as spoons, etc.), and different under secondary relationships in such a way that they offer the largest variety possible. Thus, when these things are gathered, they gain dignity and can, for example, be put into a *catalogue*. But they are not, in this sense, *œuvres*, even if they are well on their way.

In order for an object to be truly considered an *œuvre*, it must go through yet another change in state of matter, meaning that another kind of event intervenes. This event consists in attributing the object's origin to an identified entity, called the object's *author*. The author is the *cause* of the object. In Alfred Gell's terms (citing Pierce), the *œuvre* takes on an indexical relationship with the entity which is supposed to be its cause (Gell, 2009). In this sense, the *œuvre* can always be considered an *event*, too. In fact, it constitutes an absolute singularity whose attribution and interpretation reveal its sense. Following this change in state, the *œuvre* stands out from the backdrop of the object that now acts as a support. The canvas, virgin or uniformly covered by color, is an object. But a monochrome attributed to an author (like Malevitch, for example), is an œuvre with intentionality and agency. A doubt may remain: if, for example, a canvas is covered by something that resembles a child's scribbles. We may think it is a thing. However, attributed to Twombly, it is an *œuvre*, etc.

We can speak of *icons* (Marion, 1982: 15-38) to accent a last transformation of an object (that, like the previous transformations, is reversible). The change of state (i.e. the event) that transforms the object, the thing or the piece into an œuvre displaces the intentionality and agency of a supposedly identifiable and permanent entity (i.e. a person) to an object. But we can think that, in the case of certain, particularly famous œuvres, the œuvre itself is detached from the author and is thus invested with the identity of an intentionality and agency of its own. Thus it has the power to bring about other changes, exercised on other œuvres or other people, as if they fell under its ascendancy.

The Force of An Œuvre

We can call the force of an œuvre its capacity to bring about changes in states, i.e. in turn generate a more or less high number of events that are related to it as the original event. Certain œuvres have a very weak force (but are nevertheless œuvres). Others have considerable force. This depends on the tests that it is put to, in each moment of time, so that the force of an œuvre is never definitively stabilized and is always uncertain. It gives rise to debate. This force is gained or lost in the course of different trials of circulation that are also trials of valorisation. Some of them will increase or restrict the exposition value of an œuvre. In the course of another trial of circulation, dependent on the first, the object will be given a price. This second trial says what it is, but as an object, since it is the one that determines its market value.

In a great number of domains, the capacity of reducing uncertainty in the most ordinary situations by saying *it is what it is* (referring to 'the whatness of what is' as I explain in the book *On critique*), particularly in the case of debate, is delegated to what we call the *institution*. In *On critique*, I tried to show that what we call an institution's *semantic* task – inspired by John Searle (1998; 2005: 1-22) – is always, in our society, more or less dependent on the State, and plays a major political role, since it was linked to their quality of *beings without bodies*. Institutions are thus endowed with an authority that can resolve disagreements between corporeal beings who are always reducible to divergences in points of view, tied to their specific positions in space or time, individual interests, the unconscious, etc. But, since institutions are beings without bodies, they can only render their *qualifying* operations public through spokespersons who are, themselves, of flesh and bone like you or me. So, in this sense, they fall easily under the blade of criticism: do they really express the ideas of the institution where they, too, can only provide a point of view that depends on their own interests, under the guise of their institutional role? I call this tension the *hermeneutic contradiction* (Boltanski, 2009).

We can take a particularly successful institution, whose political role is one of the most important, as an example: the scientific institution. This institution accomplished this tour de force (to not say coup de force) in building itself a monopoly over the statements about what is while assuming the possibility of modifying them in function of its *internal* debate. The project of establishing an artistic institution based on the model of the scientific institution, attempted by the great 19th century European states, with its Academies, Grandes Écoles, National Competitions, awards and official Expositions, was never able to impose itself in a permanent way (it perhaps resurfaced in the 1970s-80s but without much success).

It would take too long to try to go further into depth regarding the reasons for its failure here. Suffice to note that, in the case of œuvres, the process of attribution, qualification and valorization can't be based, at least for living artists, on institutions with inescapable verdicts. Art is made circulating in spaces with blurred boundaries, where autonomy isn't sufficiently assured to make determinations that try to condition these spaces while immune to external forces, notably, the forces that can be attributed to capitalism. This also means that, like capitalism itself, these spaces are never safe from criticism.

One of the main tasks of what we call 'the sociology of art' is dedicated to building models that permit an awareness of the way paths of circulation are articulated as the means through which exposition value is generated and market value is established. I will now propose two programs of inquiry that aim to define the contours of two modes of articulation that have marked the 20th century or, if you will, the two ways these different trials are *arranged*. I will call the first *domestic* arrangement and the second *capitalist* arrangement.

Domestic Circulation

We can base our discussion around *Canvases and Careers*, the seminal book by Harrison and Cynthia White, written over 40 years ago, that analyses the collapse of the academic system in France at the end of the 19th century in order to roughly sketch the contours of the domestic model of circulation subsequently put into place. It by no means excludes the circulation of money, even of large in sums of money. It is not so much the fact that there is money involved in the process that is the problem. The question, rather, concerns the way that œuvres circulate and the speed of that circulation.

It is generally considered that what I call the domestic model has four agents: the artist, the dealer, the collector and the critic. It is among these four agents that the object circulates to become an œuvre and acquires a certain force. In this kind of model, the event that determines the *sense* of the œuvre passes, as always, through its attribution to an entity, in this case someone with a body – called the 'artist' – during the course of a process of circulation. This attribution, once accomplished, must be constantly maintained for the œuvre to remain efficient.

But, in the framework of a domestic mode, the way that these processes of attribution and maintenance work retains a *personal* character. The œuvre is passed around from body to body, along a chain of personal and even physical relationships. For example, the dealer, who is friends with the artist, goes to his studio. He sees the object – the future œuvre – 'in its juice' to use the flea market term from above. It is there, in the hodgepodge of the studio, near an old kettle, next to dirty rags covered in paint, a bottle of wine, etc.; traces that are a part of the artist's body and that are, in some way, an extension of it. The dealer, for a sum of money, extracts that object from the hodgepodge, snatches it from its environment and transports it to his gallery (if he has one). In the gallery, collectors will come to see what is going on. Perhaps what has become an œuvre will get their attention based on the dealer's opinion; they might even be friends with the dealer himself. They will buy the object, but most often only to show it in their apartment where the object will stay (unless they have serious financial problems), then it will be passed down in their family or bequeathed to a museum. In doing so, it is virtually the person to whom this œuvre is assigned to that makes it enter into their familiar environment. And this is probably the reason why authors whose behaviour or personal opinions are judged as too scandalous may have trouble in finding buyers.

During this circulation, the object, having become an œuvre, retains the trace of the artist's body, transported through the chain of personal relationships that tie the artist to the dealer, the dealer to collectors, etc. We can think of what Marcel Mauss says, in his The Gift, about the sale of domestic animals in traditional societies. The transmission of the beast, in exchange for a sum of money, isn't enough to separate it from its previous owner. A whole ritual of detachment – to make sure that the animal doesn't go back to who is still its veritable master – must be associated with the sale. This kind of personal attachment, which is a problem in the case of selling a cow, can be an advantage when selling a painting. It is what allows the sense of œuvre to be maintained, as a sign of the author, during the different steps in its circulation.

Now, a word on the critic who plays an essential role in this domestic mode. Most often, this mode maintains personal and friendly relationships with the artist, the dealer and collectors. They are all part of the same *circles*, almost the same family. The critic's importance lies in the fact that the 'artist' – let us remember – can't self-proclaim himself as one. More particularly, in this specific organization, he is expected, according to the romantic ideal, to not know what he is doing, in the true sense of the word. He is comparable to a sibyl who ignores the sense of the words she pronounces. Things come from him, *things* that might become *œuvres*. But he ignores the sense and the value of his œuvre (for example, hagiography would have it that he takes no care of the object that he makes, or forgets it as soon as it comes into the world, etc.). The critic occupies the place from whence the paternity (and it would be better to say, in this case, the maternity) of things that the artist makes can be attributed to him. The critic is also the one that gives them a force and that starts the process of valorization. He works by gathering different things attributed to the same artist and establishing a relation of biographical equivalence or affinity among them. He can also constitute the artificial group of œuvres that are attributed to the same entity in the form of a totality doted with sense: the Œuvre, with a capital letter. This œuvre can be, in turn, differentiated from the œuvres of other artists constituted according to the same principle.

In this way, the critic's job is an essential contribution to the attribution process. It maintains and reinforces the ties between the object and its cause, of which the œuvre is the index. Thanks to the critic, circulation can extend beyond the artist's circle of friends and personal relationships. The critic can also become, almost without wanting to, a collector. He buys œuvres or receives them as gifts. But his collection has, first of all, a dimension of memory. A whole, that can be seen as *patrimony*, is formed and this question will then arise with the issue of succession.

An essential characteristic of this mode of circulation is its sluggishness. An œuvre's path can cross multiple generations. Consequently, the temporal lapse between the moment of creation and the moment of recognition contains, in each moment in time, an uncertainty in the question of knowing which œuvres really count. The current judgment is always relativized by its comparison with a future judgment, in another possible world – a gap on which the hopes of avant-garde artists are founded. The same goes for market value, whose growth is supposed to take long enough to discourage short-term speculation. Seen from an economic point of view, accumulation therefore takes the patrimonial, rather than capitalist, form. A good that lasts – as it is said – (for example a priceless family home) is not capital. Property is revealed as capital only when it generates profit through a process of circulation that is only as effective as it is fast.

Capitalist Circulation

A new regime of circulation that has been progressively put into place over the last few decades, has the primary characteristic of an important increase in the speed of the circulation of œuvres and the area where this circulation takes place (Rosa, 2013). It multiplies exchanges and therefore the perspective for profit. It detaches the œuvre from the patrimonial sphere to push it into the sphere of capital. We can try to describe this process without getting into the thorny issue of the sheer artistic value of œuvres that concern aesthetic judgment (often accompanied by an almost ethical judgment) and not sociology, even if different modes of circulation tend to select and valorize different œuvres. A sociologist is therefore relieved of the delicate task of playing the arbiter between Alberto Giacometti and Damien Hirst, and of asking if one is more 'authentic' than the other, to use Walter Benjamin's term.

The agents of domestic circulation – artists, curators, collectors, critics – are still active in the capitalist mode of circulation. But their relative importance, like their respective roles, are modified and they have to face the rise to power of other agents operating in the media or the economic sphere, such as the now famous auction houses or sovereign wealth funds. The consequences include a concentration of galleries, an increased importance of the most financially powerful collectors for establishing exposition value and a shrinking role given to critics.

In this mode of circulation, an œuvre's market value is better assured than it was in domestic circulation. But the high degree of intricacy in the process of establishing exposition value and market value tends to throw doubt on the autonomy of judgments that the first is based on. This confusion consequently risks increasing the volatility of the latter that, as we've seen, exposition value depends on. Moreover, the increase in the speed of circulation and the area where circulation takes place modifies the attribution conditions that assure – and that must still assure – the relation between the œuvre and the person identified as its 'creator'. A few important elements to describe these changes can be found in Isabelle Graw's book High price (2009).

In domestic circulation, the paternal object-œuvre-author relationship was assured through the chains of interaction between bodies. In capitalist circulation, it must be intensified through ties of another kind, favoring faster, more distant operations. An artist's body and the œuvre's texture must be able to be substituted by aliases, supposing the intervention of a process of codification that requires the selection and stylization of traits judged pertinent. Because this process is subject to constraints of speed and distance, it tends to escape critics who work on a local level. This can be seen, for example, in œuvres in the media sphere, with the growing importance given to celebrity culture and storytelling (a technique originating from management that has also conquered the political world – see Salmon, 2007). The alias must be able to function almost as a brand that the œuvres can be attributed to. The analogy is less metaphorical than it seems at first glance if we remember that the brand, at least at its origins in the 19th century, was always associated with a signature or even a portrait, as to simulate a personal tie between products industrially produced in series and a corporeal person incarnating their origin and guaranteeing their quality.

The development of capitalist circulation tends to bend an œuvre's mode of constitution and perhaps, at the same time, modify the principles for selecting recognition postulants in function of their dispositional capacities to adjust to these new forms. We have seen that, in domestic circulation, the artist isn't supposed to control, reflexively, the sense of his œuvre; that task being assigned to the critic who, in some way, reveals it to him. In capitalist circulation, the artist has to produce not only an object that can transmute into an œuvre, but also an alias of that object that gives it sense – all of which assumes codification, as in the case of the figure of the artist himself. The object-maker must also have a sufficient level of reflexivity to anticipate the conditions that will preside over their reception. This is done to make the task of associating the alias and the object to the alias of its presumed creator easier and more fluid. He *constructs* his œuvre, in the same sense that sociology talks about *constructing reality*. This is probably the reason why artists have become, over the course of just a few years, so fond of theories, borrowed from philosophy and/or the social sciences.

In this state of things, the force of the œuvre is measured less in the number and sophistication of the interpretations, spread out over a long period, that it provokes in commentators, than in the potency of events that mark its circulation, that have a media or market dimension, or that they inscribe in the framework of expositions with near-architectural dimensions (like the 'Monumenta' expo in Paris). The figure of the post-romantic, post-impressionist or post-surrealist artist, vulgar, alcoholic, working-class and above all rebel, now disqualified, is substituted by a new figure that joins the qualities of the savant, aware of what he does and what value it has, and the *entrepreneur* able to manage the fabrication of great machines perceived as unique, even if their edification requires the participation of a great number of collaborators. The trials, in the sense of the term used in *On Justification* (Boltanski and Thévenot, 1991), that must be satisfied in order to make it in this world, have profoundly changed, as have the personal and social attitudes of those chosen by these trials.

Similarly, the roles of curators and critics have changed. The former, if they haven't been eliminated or absorbed by the process of concentration, risk being left to local niches, corresponding to secondary markets. As for the latter, they are more and more confined to the tasks of common education and popularization, destined to form the tastes of a growing number of those who, with cultural capital but without economic capital, make up the lines in front of big expositional spaces that present œuvres they will never acquire. But the effects of their advice on the choice of large collectors are probably in marked decline. They are, in this, analogous to the market analysts on mainstream media whose predictions motivate the 'little people', online traders (who are called trolls) who have but little influence on the decisions of large traders.

Two States of Capitalism

Were Walter Benjamin and the critical thinkers of the Frankfurt School right or wrong when they anticipated capitalism's hold over œuvres that, for them, was the near collapse of everything they loved and everything they called 'art' and 'beauty'? Putting these value judgments aside, and limiting ourselves to the issue of the relation between the world of creation and that of capitalist accumulation, we can say they were sometimes right and sometimes wrong.

Wrong, because they imagined capitalism as above all industrial, which explains that their apocalyptic predictions could take not only an anti-capitalist but also an antimodernist bent. But how could they have foreseen capitalism's shifts that have marked the Western world over the last few decades?

If the logic of capitalism has indeed penetrated the art world, it hasn't been through the substitution of unique works with an *aura* with mechanically reproduced multiples. It has done so, on the contrary, by assuming its own means to assure the rapid circulation of unique works, valorizing techniques and a circulation that allows the confection, manipulation and distribution of this aura. Subjected to the potency of events, including the market events that punctuate circulation, this aura can surge or evaporate according to the coups de force that break big operators onto the scene. Do we not read, in the works often written by specialized journalists, of the turpitude of the art market, for example when Charles Saatchi was able to make the value of Sandro Chia plunge by boisterously getting rid of his works that he has in his collection? Or again, when Kunstkompass, created in 1970 (one of the ancestors of the benchmarking techniques that later invaded every other domain, including the university – see Bruno, 2008), come to be considered, thirty years later (and not only by the *Wall Street Journal*), as 'the only possible yardstick of contemporary art' (Bellet, 2001: 218, 245). Who remembers the indignant diatribes that the appearance of this caused among critics and 'avant-garde' artists who even asked for their names to be taken off of the list of award winners?

Cinema's contrasting evolutions, on one hand, and the changes in fine arts, on the other, are particularly illuminating to demonstrate how these two forms that developed under Western capitalism have affected the art world.

On one hand, the enormous industrial experience, accumulated over the course of the last two centuries, largely deserted the mass production of material goods that occupied numerous workers who were difficult to control and discipline and has been delegated to poorer countries, called 'emerging countries', that in a number of cases are subject to authoritarian powers. Industrial know-how has been displaced, for the most part, toward technological research and the production of immaterial and reproducible goods, proposed on large markets to a multitude of consumers asked only for modest financial sacrifices. Cinema is a typical example of this. The art of the multiple par excellence, cinema has continued its evolution toward more and more industrial forms, characterized by enormous investments, modes of organization and coordination borrowed from management to organize the labour of huge teams and the more and more frequent use of sophisticated digital technologies.

On the other hand, there has been the development of a financial economy as well as what Lucien Karpik calls an *economy of singularities*. The latter is based on 'single-exchange and incommensurable products', which include – according to Karpik – 'personalized professional services, artwork, high cuisine, gourmet wines, luxury items,' etc. (Karpik, 2007: 9).

In conclusion, we will propose two hypotheses. The first is that the financial economy joins an industrial dimension with specific traits that bring it closer to the economy of singularities. The second is that, in the vast area of the economy of singularities, the mode of circulation of contemporary œuvres is the domain where its similarities with the financial economy's way of functioning are the most vivid.

The financial economy has developed considerably for over 20 years, transposing an industrial know-how to bond exchanges, notably by way of the organization and management of financial businesses and in the use of digital technologies and software based on mathematic models. But, in other relations, the financial economy has a number of traits in common with the economy of singularities. This is the case of derivative products called 'exotic', built for particular clients and mutually negotiated. These products, which conserve the trace of the mathematicians that created them, are largely incomprehensible to inexperienced traders. But, more generally, these financial instruments are products that, although they are supposedly 'known before purchase' as 'standard products' might be, most often hold an important component of 'mystery' so that 'every interpretation' contributes to the 'requalification of the product'. Financial markets are populated by radical uncertainty, meaning that they are unpredictable, taking on the *quality* of the products and the *strategies* of traders that can easily be suspected of *opportunism*. In these types of markets, options are oriented toward the search for information that enables the selection of the 'best product', in market conditions that are 'unpredictable and opaque'. The gap between 'the necessary knowledge and the client's competence' induces modes of profitability that are based on 'information asymmetries' that favor a limited number of experienced traders to the detriment of the masses of small buyers. All this despite the numerous directives responsible for the transparency of transactions, and despite the reference, above all in crisis situations, to a 'fundamental value' whose 'objective' character is fictional, just like the now abandoned reference to the 'criteria of beauty' is in the domain of art.

As this schematic description suggests, we can only be struck by the convergences between the evolution of financial markets and the part of the economy of singularities that constitutes the market of contemporary œuvres. In both cases, a number of common traits appear. Notably, both the difficulty of using specific criteria to break down 'indivisible realities' and to build systems of equivalence able to arrange incommensurable goods into a hierarchical order. The role given to interpretation in valorization and the similarity of agents, or supposed instances of these, determine the value of goods and those who profit from their circulation. Finally, we observe the appearance of ever-new and opaque goods and the increasing speed of operations.

Nevertheless, the evolution toward this type of economy adopts an even purer form in the case of the valorization and circulation of œuvres than it does in finance. Finding themselves emancipated from the industrial imperative, these processes can, in the case of art, systematically profit from the 'reference most radically opposed to interchangeability': the reference to 'the human being' (Karpik, 2007: 51). The relation of attribution, important in the case of finance constitutes, in the case of œuvres, the very foundation of a way to make profit based on the indissociable circulation of objects that are sometimes homogeneous and sometimes distinct, as well as names of singular people to which the creation of those objects is attributed.

Coming back to our point of departure, we will remark that it was difficult, for example, to anticipate in the 1930s the way that photography, multiple par excellence, and video art – which shares many traits with film – would sacrifice, in some way, one of their main attributes, i.e. being reproducible, in order to be treated like unique pieces, objects of collections and market speculation. It all happened as if the new opportunities of market access, made possible by changes in capitalism, had predominance over the changes in technical, or properly artistic, constraints – but at the price of maintaining and even reinforcing the relation of attribution that ties a unique piece to a unique creator. This, against many prophets who, coming from the avant-garde, announced the death of the author and the development of creations that would be the work of collective intelligence. Or even those who felt the creative possibilities contained in each human being liberated, a liberation that what would have supposedly had the effect of vaporizing art as it had been known to Western metaphysics and, consequently, the disappearance of the art market itself.

In the end, we will add that, as rereading earlier philosophers suggests, changes in capitalism have, affecting the world of arts, notably changed the situation of the social critic, when claiming to manifest itself with the aid of œuvres. During the 20th century, the *external* critique of capitalist society was almost always associated with an *internal* critique of the functioning of the art world in that, precisely, the latter was seen as threatened by the intrusion of capitalism. This critique was founded, above all, on the valorization of the artisanal as opposed to the industrial; the personal as opposed to the anonymous; the unique as opposed to the multiple. It is now struggling to affirm itself in a capitalist cosmos that not only recognizes the singularity of œuvres and their creators, but also makes that recognition a significant source of profit.

2

A Joy Forever

Neil Cummings

Act 1. Scene 1

It's Friday the 10th of July 1857, it's mid-morning, cold for the time of year and drizzling with rain. We are in a crowd approaching the entrance to the spectacular Art Treasures Exhibition at Old Trafford in Manchester. As we enter the doorway, above our heads is inscribed the first line of English poet, John Keats's *Endymion,*

A thing of beauty is a joy forever.

Inside the spectacular, temporary, cast-iron and glass structure an orchestra is playing, and fountains are cascading. The Art Treasures Exhibition is obviously inspired by The Great Exhibition of the Works of Industry of all Nations of 1851, the astonishing mid-century celebration of modern industrial technology, art, design and manufacturing. The Great Exhibition, of some one hundred thousand objects in Joseph Paxton's pre-fabricated cast-iron and glass Crystal Palace, a temporary building so vast it enclosed mature elm trees, was a perfect performance of the free trade ideal. Fourteen thousand exhibitors from all around the world competitively displayed their goods in a previously unimagined space of exhibition and leisure. The traditional distinctions between things dissolved in entertainment. The Great Exhibition was the template for every museum, department store, shopping mall and trade fair thereafter, as historian Donald Preziosi (2001) suggests, 'We have never left the Great Exhibition'.

Inside the Art Treasures galleries, dense chatter accompanies the crowds as we navigate the 16,000 paintings and sculptures on display. Between the 5th of May and the 17th of October the exhibition will attract over 1.3 million visitors; that's about four times the population of Manchester. And, I probably don't need to remind you that Manchester is the shock-city of industrialisation, a laboratory for experimentation in manufacturing, trade and finance. Friedrich Engels is here, researching and writing; he had sent a series of reports to Karl Marx that were to be published as *The Condition of the Working Class in England.* The city's increasingly wealthy cotton merchants want to celebrate its wealth and power, although not through industry: they want to celebrate through an exhibition of culture[1]. And so they convene the most spectacular collection of artworks England has ever seen, under one roof.

As we walk through the exhibition following our printed guide, the artworks seem to be organised chronologically, a literal demonstration of the historical development of art. Although the exhibition is also subdivided into smaller spaces and themed: Pictures by Ancient Masters, Pictures by Modern Masters, British Portraits and Miniatures, Water Colour Drawings, and so on. Engels will write to Karl Marx:

'Everyone up here is an art lover just now and the talk is all of the pictures at the exhibition...'

Given that most public museum collections are, at best, in a nascent state, the majority of the artworks are borrowed from over 700 private collections from Britain's wealthiest families. And many of the artworks have never been exhibited in public before.

The organization of the Art Treasures Exhibition, the interplay between private and public interests, the modes of exhibition and display of artworks have a formative influence on the public art institutions currently being

---

[1]   There had been a spectacular Exhibition of British Industrial Art in Manchester in 1845, although by 1855 there were 1,724 cotton warehouses in Manchester and only 95 cotton mills. Trade had replaced production as the city's main source of wealth.

established. For example, in London, Sir Henry Cole – one of the prime movers of the Great Exhibition – is intent on using some of the £186,000 profit to improve art and design appreciation. Land is purchased in South Kensington, and many exhibits from the Great Exhibition are acquired to form the nucleus of a public collection for the magnificent new South Kensington Museum – later to become the Victoria and Albert Museum.

At about the same time, and nearing the end of his life, Sir Henry Tate, a sugar magnate, philanthropist and major collector of Victorian art, offers his private collection as a gift to the nation. Parliament declines. Tate then offers to fund a public gallery to house his collection and to initiate a National Gallery of British Art, providing the government donate a suitable site, and undertake the gallery's administration. After much debate, Tate's offer is accepted. The site chosen is the disused Millbank Penitentiary, a huge prison near the Thames, it is demolished and the new 'palace of art' the National Gallery of British Art, is constructed. Later, the name will change to The Tate Gallery in recognition of Tate's generosity and commitment.

Act 1. Scene 2

It's Friday evening, and after a tiring day at the Art Treasures Exhibition we take a hansom cab to the Athenaeum in Mosely Street. The Athenaeum is a private institution, a club for the promotion of learning. We manage to squeeze into a packed, hot, and smoky lecture hall just in time to see the famous John Ruskin step up to the lectern to deliver the first lecture in his series of two, entitled *The Discovery and Application of Art*. The second lecture, performed the following Monday 13th is called *The Accumulation and Distribution of Art*. Combined, the marathon lectures will build a coherent, if a somewhat rambling, model of a political economy of art, later published as *A Joy Forever and Its Price in the Market* (Ruskin, 2006).

Ruskin clears his throat, and begins

Now, it seemed to me that since, in the name you have given to this great gathering of British pictures, you recognize them as Treasures – that is, I suppose, as part and parcel of the real wealth of the country – you might not be uninterested in tracing certain commercial questions connected with this particular form of wealth. Most persons express themselves as surprised at its quantity; not having known before to what an extent good art had been accumulated in England: and it will, therefore, I should think, be held a worthy subject of consideration, what are the political interests involved in such accumulations, what kind of labour they represent, and how this labour may in general be applied and economized, so as to produce the richest results. (2006: 16)

He goes on to discuss how to discover your genius. He thinks that the recently founded art schools – he calls them trial schools – are good and productive[2]. And then, how to distribute the genius you have found. Put simply, Ruskin feels we need people with money prepared to spend on contemporary art, and nurture it.

Act 1. Scene 3

It is Monday 13th, a little warmer, and we are back at the packed Athenaeum. Ruskin, stroking his beard, begins by recapping

> Our subject which remain for our consideration this evening are, you will remember, the accumulation and the distribution of works of art. Our complete inquiry fell into four divisions – first, how to get our genius; then, how to apply our genius; then, how to accumulate its results; and lastly, how to distribute them – we have tonight to examine the modes of its preservation and distribution.

Accumulation

Art should not be cheap – great works depend on the quality of attention paid to them. You need a commercial network of artists, dealers and collectors to circulate artworks. Private individuals prepared to invest time, attention and money.

---

[2] In 1835 a Select Committee is set in motion to 'Enquire into the best means of extending a knowledge of the Arts and the principles of Design among the people, especially the manufacturing population of the country'. The following year the Committee recommends that Parliament invest £1,500 to establish a central school of design in London, with further annual funding to establish a network of provincial schools in the major industrial centres of the country. The Government School of Design is established at Somerset House in London in 1837, and Art & Design becomes the first form of publicly funded education in Britain.

Distribution

And yet, he asks rhetorically, how can we bring great art within the reach of the multitude? [Ruskin's term] The answer? We need larger and more numerous public museums – to do for art what printing did to literature.

> [...] don't grumble when you hear of a new picture being bought by Government at a large price. There are many pictures in Europe now in danger of destruction, which are, in the true sense of the word, priceless; the proper price is simply that which it is necessary to give to get and to save them. (2006: 61)

While he appreciates the love and investment implicit private collections, he also recognizes the necessity of public institutions, of *curating* national wealth, and then he ends by drawing this distinction

> So then, generally, it should be the object of government, to collect the works of dead masters in public galleries, arranging them so as to illustrate the history of nations, and the progress and influence of their arts; and to encourage the private possession of the works of *living* masters. (2006: 65)

Ruskin profusely thanks the audience for their attention, and then basks in thunderous applause having sketched the foundations of a political economy for artworks. His sketch has two principle structural forces: priceless artworks (literally) by dead artists removed from the competitive market by public museum acquisition, and a competitive market circulating and evaluating artworks by living artists.

Act 2. Scene 1

We are in New York on the 18th of October 1973, an Indian Summer, it's a pleasantly warm evening.

Two years earlier, on 15th August, and without prior warning, President Richard Nixon announces in a Sunday evening televised address that America is abandoning the almost thirty-year-old Bretton Woods agreement, and removing the dollar from fixed-rate convertibility to gold. Through the Bretton Woods system, the US dollar had acted in the 20th century as gold had during Ruskin's 19th. Inflation in the United States, the escalating cost of the war in Vietnam, a growing American trade deficit and increasingly vast amounts of finance capital circulating outside of government control, are all pressurising the value of the dollar. With Bretton Woods abandoned, the dollar is allowed to 'float', that is, to fluctuate against other currencies, and exchange rates promptly recalibrate.

In the midst of this financial downturn, and on the eve of divorce, Robert and Ethel Scull decide to sell 50 artworks from their amazing collection of American pop and Abstract Expressionist art at Sotheby's auction house in New York. The Sculls had begun collecting in the mid-1950s, when there was virtually no interest, or market, for contemporary art, with funds derived from a taxicab business founded by Ethel's father.

When Jasper Johns first exhibits at the Leo Castelli Gallery in 1957, not one of the artworks sell. Castelli calls Robert Scull, he visits, and buys the whole exhibition.

At the entrance to Sotheby's on 5th Avenue, security holds back a crowd of protestors at the door, demonstrating at the obscenity of selling artworks for profit in a time of crisis. We manage to squeeze through and into the packed auction saleroom to mingle with gallerists, dealers, museum directors, wealthy collectors, celebrities, TV crews, and a drunk and irate Robert Rauchenberg. After three hours of frantic, and near hysterical bidding the sale ceases and has turned-over an astronomical $2,242,900.

Thaw, a Robert Rauschenberg combine-painting that the Sculls bought for $900 some 16 years earlier, sells for $85,000; Andy Warhol's large-canvas *Flowers,* bought for $3,500, sells for $135,000, and Jasper Johns' *Double White Map,* bought for $10,000, fetches $240,000.

The auction is a spectacular event, which ends in an awed silence and a sharp exchange as Rauchenberg shouts at Scull: 'I've been working my ass off just for you to make that profit.' Scull retorts: 'It works for you too, Bob. Now I hope you'll get even bigger prices' (Schott and Vaughn, 1973). The shock is not just from the Sculls' unbelievable profits, but also from the sudden realisation that contemporary art is a viable financial vehicle. A thing of beauty is a joy forever, and has a price in the market. A speculative market for contemporary art is both enacted and revealed, and one of the things revealed is a further bifurcation in the political economy of artworks.

ACT 3. Scene 1

Markets are a brilliant bundle of technologies, assembled to circulate *things*. All kinds of *things*. The most visible form of a market is the competitive market. A neo-classical economic model of a competitive market pictures rational individuals pursuing their own self-interest, without regard for others, as the motive force in markets. The laws of supply and demand at play amongst these rational individuals extrudes the values – often represented by a financial price – exchanged, in any transaction.

These fundamental elements – rational agents, supply and demand and price mechanisms – function in all markets everywhere; like natural laws. Like gravity.

Except of course competitive markets don't actually work like this. Or at least, only in ideological models. Principally this is because the neo-classical model is spectacularly under-socialised, and the social labour of market-making is under-researched, under-theorised and undervalued.

Enabling values to be made, and made present, is part of the work that markets do. And every value expressed as a price, is a nexus of myriad social processes. Markets are meshworks of embedded desires, needs, rules, technologies, rituals and obligations, and nowhere is this more apparent than in the markets for the circulation of contemporary art.

As in Ruskin's sketch for a political economy of art, outside of public museums, and some secretive private collections in the Freeport of Geneva, artworks circulate through competitive markets. But *how* does this circulation take place? What are these embedded desires, rules, behaviours and obligations?

The bankruptcy of art history, and the public failure of criticism and art theory has enabled the values of competitive markets to dominate our recent evaluations of contemporary art. And markets mark the things that circulate within them[3].

---

[3] That 'Markets mark the things they distribute' was a phrase political philosopher Michael Sandel deployed in the first 2009 *BBC Reith Lectures*. He used an example, derived from the USA, of paying a fee to schoolchildren to encourage them to read. By paying children to read they might begin to believe that reading is a way

ACT 3. Scene 2

Primary Market

As the Robert and Ethel Scull auction sale exposed, the circulation of contemporary artworks is structured by two competitive markets – and prices for the same assets in one are routinely half that of the other. This already makes little sense to a neo-classical economist.

The primary market is convened by gallerists who organise and manage 'commercial' galleries. Whether as small single person enterprises or vast corporate machines, what gallerists share is the desire to work directly with artists, promote their work through exhibitions, and sell their artworks to potential collectors.

To become a gallerist is easy, the start-up costs are extremely small – some enthusiasm, contacts, a small exhibition and office space, and an advertising budget. There are no formal qualifications necessary; no indemnity required, no trade association to join, and no regulatory bodies. The primary market is, for all intents and purposes, while not quite 'unregulated', certainly without a 'formal' professional structure.

It's also easy to attract a group of artists keen to exhibit; just tell them you are a gallerist, and they generally come running. Typically a gallery will 'represent' between 10 and 25 artists. To be 'represented', usually means that an artist will be offered a solo exhibition annually or bi-annually and their artworks will be included in appropriate gallery group exhibitions.

'Representation' for the gallery includes bringing the artwork to the attention of curators and collectors, and placing the artworks in curated public exhibitions, biennials, and at art fairs; nationally and internationally. They also arrange studio visits with select collectors and curators, organise private views to launch exhibitions, assemble press brunches and lunches, and choreograph lavish dinners and after-parties. The primary gallerist chooses, nurtures and develops the artists they 'represent' through creating a dense social network.

---

of earning money. Any inherent good of reading will be overwritten by the desire to financially profit.

Much of the labour of nurture is in the management of the informational prosthesis of the circulating artworks; through producing press releases and exhibition invites, buying advertising space, placing articles in newspapers and magazines, publishing catalogues, documenting and archiving artworks, and by cultivating critics, editors and publishers.

These are just some of the mechanisms through which an emergent market for artworks is convened.

And into this potential market, the gallerist introduces new artworks to collectors. Usually artworks are taken on consignment from an artist for exhibition, and it's common for the gallerist to take a 50% commission, and often more, on any sales. Sold artworks leave the artist's studio, pass through the gallery at exhibition and enter private collections. Here they remain until the collector decides to re-sell, or donate to a museum collection. Unsold artworks return to the deep-sleep of storage, while some linger in the gallery as 'stock' to be displayed to prospective collectors, or curators[4].

All 'represented' artists have a primary gallery. Any curators, public institutions or museums that want to exhibit the artists artworks have to deal with the primary gallery; and any other commercial galleries who wish to exhibit and sell the artists artworks have to do business with them too.

Gallerists talk endlessly about supporting young artists, they love visiting studios, socialising, and installing exhibitions; they love art, and prefer not to let commerce and the market 'complicate' their relationships. And yet when they discuss gallery stock, or their private collections, they know exactly how much they initially paid, the last market evaluation, any potential discounts to be offered to select collectors or museums, and of course, in the blink of an eye, are able to calculate the artwork's financial appreciation.

While primary gallerists thrive by taking risks and having confidence in their 'taste', they also seek to hedge the risks involved, through their promotional practices and by managing their network of friends and collectors into an economy of taste. To paraphrase sociologist Pierre Bourdieu: 'taste is what other people like you like'.

---

[4] Unofficially, artworks are often 'kept' by the gallery to offset un-recovered expenses in the hope of recouping costs at some later date.

If you or I were to stroll into the Foksal Gallery Foundation from the street with a pocket full of cash, fall in love with a Paulina Ołowska painting on display, and decide we really, really wanted to buy it for our home, the gallerist would not necessarily sell it to us. Even if we offered to pay over the asking price[5]. She or he will feel that we are the 'wrong' sort of person to own the artwork, or probably buying it for the 'wrong' reasons. And, if we are not already known to the gallerist, and therefore outside of their economy of taste, then definitely, we are the 'wrong' sort of person.

Nurturing the 'right' collector, and placing an artwork with them for the 'right' reason is the principle means of control of the value of an artwork through the primary competitive market in the political economy of art. Selling for the 'right' reasons include placing an artwork with a prestigious collector who will add to the evaluation of an artist and artwork – not necessarily the person prepared to pay the highest price. The 'right' collector might already have, or be in the process of building an 'important' art collection. The 'right' reasons might include the collector being prepared to sign a resale agreement, a quasi-legal document guaranteeing a 'right of first refusal' on any future sale back to the primary gallerist[6].

The 'right' reason could be encouraged if the collector promised to donate the artwork to an important public museum collection at some future date.

Gifting an artwork to a national collection removes the artwork from circulation, but also lends prestige to the artist – and therefore future artworks, the generous collector, and perceptive gallerist[7].

Through managing the circulation of artworks through economies of taste, an artwork or artist are never entirely disentangled from their producer – the gallerist. It's not surprising that relationships, and particularly long working

---

[5] If the artist is fairly prominent in the competitive market, the gallerist will sometimes pretend that there is a waiting-list to acquire an artwork. And if you are very, very lucky you will be added to the list.

[6] Resale agreements are mechanisms by which the gallerists try to insure that artworks do not spin out of their orbit, and into the less manageable secondary market.

[7] A gift distributes status, while gifting to a public museum removes an artwork from circulation. In public collections artworks cease to circulate, they become literally 'priceless'.

relationships develop into friendships between gallerists and artist, or gallerist and collector, or perhaps all three[8]. Collectors are often referred to as supporters, 'angels' or 'friends' of the gallery.

In the extraordinarily dense flow of gifts and obligations, debts and favours, loans and discounts that lubricate artworks in their circulation, economic transactions merge into relational social exchanges. A discount offered between gallerist and collector is as much a sign of mutuality as it is a display of economic of power.

Primary gallerists appear to do everything possible to delay an artwork's spiral into the secondary economy.

ACT 3. Scene 3

The Secondary Market

The secondary market for contemporary art is structured through auction houses.

Auctions are relational competitive markets, and breath-taking theatre. The twin poles of drama – the flicker between despair and euphoria – are endlessly produced, because buyers compete to establish an appropriate evaluation – when the hammer falls. The price is extruded as the auction is conducted, by the last person standing in the tournament of value[9].

Of course there are price precedents to refer to, there are reserve prices established, published estimates, and guarantees offered, and yet none of these can be taken as true. An auction has to be convened and set in motion to perform the social production of evaluation, live, and in real-time.

If the primary market relies on deep, personal and complex relationships between artists, gallerists and collectors, then in the secondary market, artworks circulate through looser, more diverse and contingent networks

---

[8] The one thing likely to destroy these fluid relationships – often unstructured by legal contracts – is if the artist decides to sell an artwork directly from the studio. That's bad.

[9] 'A tournament of value' is a phrase used by Jean Baudrillard (1996) in *The System of Objects* to describe auctions.

outside the manipulation and monopolization of the primary market. While the primary market is reproduced within established communities of taste, the secondary market has to continually perform itself.

In theory, an auction is close to the ideal of a 'free' market. Anyone can participate, and everyone has equal access to the market, all the information regarding the market is readily available, and artworks are distributed on the ability to pay the 'spot' price. Except again, this is an ideological fantasy. Auctions are secretive and information is guarded, auctions are very sensitive to hype, excitement, gossip and rumour. And very, very susceptible to the arbitrary competitive clash of two determined bidders[10]. When two or more collectors are determined to acquire the same artwork, or, when a particular individual wants to make a statement, a sensational or 'sacrificial price' can be achieved. A 'sacrificial price' inscribes a mark in the market 'I can afford this' or 'I want this, this much' or 'Look at the scale of my desire' or simply 'Look at me'!

There could also be a financial logic in the desire to establish a 'sacrificial price'; other comparable artworks already in the collector's collection will (notionally) have a similar evaluation. Simply, a sensational price recalibrates the market.

Anyone can attend an auction, in England no tickets are issued and no booking is required. Like legal trials, auctions are truly public judgements. And, anyone can purchase an artwork offered for sale, as long as they have the access to the appropriate sum of money, or credit-line. In the secondary market, there are only the 'right' reasons to transact. The auction does not care where the money comes from or where the artwork goes, as long as international laws are not seen to be broken. In the secondary market, the only taboo is around stagnation. Artworks must always circulate, and their extruded prices escalate. A stalled lot – an artwork offered for auction which does not reach its reserve price – fails to sell. It's 'passed'. This can damage the artwork, the artist's reputation, and all the other artists artworks currently in circulation or exhibited in private collections. Worse, a stalled artwork could trigger a collapse of the current auction, and confidence can simply

---

[10] Auctions are prone to 'rigging' and price-fixing. Rumours circulate of auctioneers 'taking' fictional – usually telephone – bids to stimulate a sleepy saleroom, or leverage the bid-price over the lots reserve.

evaporate from the saleroom; in an instant. And even more catastrophically, a failed lot can puncture a bubble and trigger a systemic market collapse. So, artworks that fail to reach their reserve price at auction are literally 'passed', they are passed over with a stifled incantation by the auctioneer of words barely audible on the saleroom floor 'pass'.

'Passes' can be contagious. Perfectly healthy auctions can stutter, stop and die[11]. If the secondary market thrives on constant circulation, record-prices and buoyant confidence, on the management of a 'virtuous circle' of evaluation, 'passes' expose the sensitive underbelly of market confidence. If you only want what other people like you want, and they no longer want the goods on offer; it's over. Circulation ceases[12]. 'Passes' are the inverse of the 'sacrificial price'.

One of the instruments for managing circulation of artworks in the secondary market is the reserve price. The reserve is a financial boundary, agreed by the seller/collector advised by the auction house specialist. At auction, if the lot does not reach its reserve it returns to the seller/collector unsold. If bidders drive the price of the artwork above, it's transacted from one collector or dealer to another. Reserves are private financial agreements, usually somewhere towards the lower margin of the published estimates. To encourage collectors to circulate important artworks in the secondary market – and not with a rival auction house – financial guarantees may be offered. The guarantee is a fee, which is probably close to the reserve price, paid to the seller/collector up-front. It's in the auction house's interest to pressure the edge of the previous market evaluation, to tease-up prices. If the lot is 'passed' the auction house loses the financial guarantee, as well as the confidence of the saleroom. To recoup some of their losses, after the sale,

---

[11] At a Sotheby's sale in New York on the 7th of November 2007, almost half the lots failed to sell – the 'passing' of Vincent van Gogh's *Wheat Fields* (1890) is credited as triggering the collapse. The auction house lost $14.6 million in guarantees, and as a consequence 36% was wiped from the share value of the company; overnight (http://www.artnet.com/magazineus/news/waltzer/waltzer11-8-07.asp).

[12] Auction houses financially profit by adding a percentage to the hammer price, through the buyers' premium. The buyers' premium is anything between 25% and 12%.

quietly and behind the scenes, the auction house will try and broker a private sale.

The auction house 'expert', or collector or dealer active in the secondary market needs to be aware of which collector owns what artworks, how the collection is being developed and through which gallerists, and what artwork is about to be 'offered' to the market[13]. A prominent artwork is located, prised from a collection, offered for sale and achieves a record evaluation. It passes from one collector to another, and a window of opportunity opens. An opportunity for other collectors with similar holdings of artworks to 'realise' their value, a chance to 'refresh, or 're-focus' their collection. Or, for the 'experts' and dealers to encourage collectors to buy into this fleeting market opportunity. This is the moment for dealers to 'flip' artworks or 'churn' the market. 'Churn' the secondary market, because it thrives on difference within repetition. There are endless Andy Warhol prints and each one can be narrated into difference.

The traditional slow steady circulation of artworks – with concomitant checks and balances; like a solid record of prestigious exhibitions, a range of critical reviews, citation in refereed articles and scholarly books, representation in respected private collections, museum acquisition, etc. – is being replaced by the shriek of record prices, achieved in the secondary market with artworks straight from artists' studios! If markets mark the *things* that circulate within them, then recently, the slower processes of evaluation of artworks has been overwritten by the swaggering confidence of a competitive market asset bubble. Gallerists, so powerful in the primary, despise the secondary market. It's an aggressive, volatile and parasitic environment. And yet they participate in auctions, either brazenly in person or discretely by proxy. They bid-up or buy back artworks that have temporarily spun outside their sphere of influence, to 'protect' the artists they represent.

ACT 4. Scene 1

A cold evening in London, it is November 2011. News spools from the radio, Spain has elected a centre-right government, Italy is governed by un-elected

---

13 The *'three D's'* – *debt, divorce and death* – are often cited as the main motives for selling.

financial technocrats, Greece, too, and anonymous traders in sovereign debt markets are driving European public policy. As John Ruskin suggests in his Art Treasures lectures, organisational, financial and exhibitionary practices are not imposed on spontaneous modes of creativity. Rather, organisational, financial and exhibitionary practices produce forms of creativity, and a political economy for their management.

By enabling competitive markets to dominate the political economy of creativity, the kind of creativities produced and distributed is limited, severely limited. We know *Its Price in the Market* but have obscured the *Joy Forever*.

3

Notes on Speculation as a Mode of Production in Art and Capital

Marina Vishmidt

General Introduction

The focus of this text is the elision between art and labour from the standpoint of the value-form. What I am trying to do is draw a link between the expansion of the category of art and the expansion of the value-form in the dynamics of social production and reproduction in recent times. Such an expansion, I will argue, is an index of the crisis in the relations of production that have kept art and labour separate, a separation that can no longer hold once that crisis is considered not just a general malfunctioning of a secular logic of valorisation called 'finance', but a crisis in the capital-labour relation more generally, which derives from the terminal logic (for capital) of finance as abstraction. In an unprecedented way, art not only reflects but revises the productive forces, shading into forces of extraction, enclosure and de-valorisation in the era of debt-financed austerity that we are now seeing.

Financialisation: Form Follows Finance

Among the relationships that bind artworks to the political economy of their times, one of the foremost is that identified by Theodor W. Adorno, who conceives of 'aesthetic forces of production' that inescapably imprint the artwork: 'The artist works as social agent, indifferent to society's own consciousness. He embodies the social forces of production without necessarily being bound by the censorship dictated by the relations of production' (Adorno, 2007: 55). Those relations are legible in art, but encrypted in such a way as to underline their contingency. Jean-Joseph Goux relates Marx's schema of the development of a general equivalent to the invention of forms of representation; of art, literature and language (Goux, 1990). This system presents modes of signification and modes of exchange as imbricated. Goux describes capitalist exchange's tendency towards abstraction and the tendency to 'dematerialisation' in art as two sides of a general crisis of representation punctuated by historically locatable crises in the value form (1919, 1929 and 1971). Each crisis marks a limit to the existing system's ability to represent real world goods through money, and in each case resolution of the crisis is by way of an expansion, or further abstraction, of the money-form. Put crudely, the drives towards abstraction in art and money are entwined.

I should mention here T.J. Clark's analysis of the early Soviet currency crisis (re-fashioned into measures taken to abolish exchange-value) and the Soviet revolutionary avant-garde's evacuation of the sign. This analysis occurs in the chapter 'God is not cast down' of *Farewell to an Idea*:

> ... the implication that there is a deep connection between the representational order called capitalism and the belief (which we could call, for short, Saussurean) that all representational orders are at heart systems of difference, of pure exchange-values generated out of the relations between elements of a signifying system. Marxists would say that the insight here – and certainly there is an insight – occludes the further problem of the sign-systems' materiality, and thus their belonging to patterns of material production and reproduction which we call social practice. [...] It takes a very special (and no doubt terrible) moment for these structures to be thinkable at all as socially determined. 1920 was one such. (Clark, 2001: 259-260)

Art is both an innovator of the forms of representation – extending the limit of what can be represented – and, at times, their antagonist – eschewing equivalence and disrupting orders of measure. Art as a special commodity rebels against its commodity status, proposing different orders of value: 'Great 20th-century avant-garde art – and poetry in particular – from Celan to Brecht and Montale, has demonstrated the crisis of experiential units of measure... This emphasis on immoderation, disproportion [...] is where [avant-garde art] edges up to communism' (Virno, 2009).

Arguably in the movement towards financialisation art has tracked capital's proclivity to escape from engagement with labour and into the self-reflexive abstraction of value. As gold became paper and then electronic, money increasingly became autonomous from productive labour. The movement of self-expanding value, appearing as money making money on financial markets, dissolves all prior values and relationships into abstract wealth. Similarly in art, the expansion of its claims upon material previously alien to it tends towards the hollowing out of this material's substance. One notable aspect of 'dematerialisation' in art is its temporal coincidence with deindustrialisation in the late 1960s and early 1970s. This period saw a re-engagement with industrial materials and (vacant) industrial spaces by artists. Another was the move towards information systems and new technologies. This could also be associated to the 'spatial fix' discussed by David Harvey, a regime of accumulation centred on exploiting differentials in land values – and cultural tourism's primary role in this – and the irrevocable changes wrought in financial markets by information technologies, such as the nano-speed trading which makes thousands of transactions on one commodity or quantity possible in a second.

We can likewise examine instances of conceptualism which approached art as a 'fiduciary' object, using speculation as its material. One of these can be seen as the precursor to Robert Morris' *Money*: Abraham Lubelski's *Sculptural Daydream* (1968). The work itself was a pile of paper consisting of 250,000 one-dollar bills borrowed at interest from the Chelsea National Bank. The sculpture, exhibited for five days, ran up a bill of three hundred dollars in interest. Perhaps intending a pun on the 'disinterested' status of the artwork in Kantian aesthetics, Lubelski here posed the same question as Morris' later and better-known piece: is the artwork the sculpture (the physical money) or the interest it accrues? Morris, however, in common with other examples of 'investment art' and more broadly in the current of early conceptualism, showed a lack of interest in the form of the work. With *Money* (1969), the interest (the transactions) is definitely what constitutes the work.[1]

Morris had of course by then developed a vector in his oeuvre that sought to conjugate both linguistic and financial abstraction as conditions for the 'dematerialisation' of the art object. An earlier piece responded to a collector's

---

[1]   Mike Sperlinger has written incisively on this and related works.

non-payment for a work with the production of a certificate withdrawing 'aesthetic value' from the unpaid-for work; the *Statement of Esthetic Withdrawal*, 1963. Naturally this certificate was also collected and displayed, next to the de-aestheticized work (although possibly not by the same collector).

Concluding this very brisk survey on an ironizing note, we can refer to Carl Andre, who wrote:

> The most farcical claim of the conceptualizing inkpissers is that their works are somehow antibourgeois because they do away with objects. In fact, doing away with objects and replacing them with such reifications of abstract relations to production as stockshares, contracts and paper money itself (which is nothing but the fetishization of the idea of exchange value severed from even the dream of production) is exactly the final triumph of the bourgeois revolution. (Andre, 1976; quoted in Shell, 1995: 115)

In this sense, the conditions set by the movements of finance provide the material and conceptual parameters for art. Art operates in these conditions but also upon them to transform their terms. Both are speculative commodities; art is backed by the credibility of the artist and money by the credibility of the state. Yet art is engaged in an endless testing of its own conditions which anticipates negations of the determinations of the value form from inside, rather than beyond, its tensions.

To bring the discussion briefly up to date and into recent and current practice; a little précis of recent art which positions itself in the allegorical mode with relation to finance. There is Maria Eichhorn's well-known *Aktiengesellschaft* (2002), for one, which freezes capital, or Zachary Formwalt, who works on the relation between circulation and visibility of capital. Images of crisis in the media show us capital at a standstill, whereas its movements are normally invisible and intangible (and bound to be even more so with the nanosecond-speed forms of electronic trading recently made possible by the discovery in particle physics of new forms of temporality not covered by the law of relativity) (Foresight, 2011). Here the making public of crisis exacerbates the crisis. Crisis makes circulation visible; when circulation freezes, it becomes visible, like Benjamin's 'dialectics at a standstill' in the dialectical image. With his project on the 1847 Henry Fox Talbot photo of the Royal Exchange in London – almost the exact site of the 2011-2012 Occupy London Stock Exchange assembly at St Paul's – in which the long exposures necessary for the state of photographic technology at the time meant that no people were visible in the streets around the building. It is as though these missing multitudes were represented, through the monumentality of the financial edifice, in absentia. This also links to how finance embodies a crisis of representation, even as representation augurs a crisis in finance. 'Credit instruments, financial innovation – how to represent relations with no correlate in the object world? Financial innovation is basically the production of new saleable objects without ever entering into an external sphere of production. They cannot be represented because they are themselves terms of representation' (Formwalt, 2010).

If this complicity between money and art has led to unseemly games with both, the strain of this relationship has also ushered in forms of critical reflection.[2] Throughout art's development in the face of advanced capitalism, tension with commodification gravitates towards uselessness and negation when it comes to representing or emulating productive labour, and speculation when it comes to representing or emulating the characteristic processes of accumulation.

Speculation and Contingency

> "Modernity" means contingency. It points to a social order which has turned from the worship of ancestors and past authorities to the pursuit of a projected future – of goods, pleasures, freedoms, forms of control over nature, or infinities of information. (Clark, 2001: 7)

The 'disjunctive synthesis' between art and finance in terms of abstraction, indeterminacy and speculation can also be addressed through the hermetic quality common to works of art and innovative financial instruments. This quality stands in for an excess of an otherwise utterly heteronomous or overdetermined reality, but both of course depend on the subjugation and expropriation of labour in order to realize their value in the market. This subjugation and expropriation also has to, perhaps most importantly, happen symbolically; the invisibility of labour which is deemed profane and 'unproductive' of this freedom that only money can guarantee in its

---

2   This specific relationship between financialisation and art is explored in detail in Melanie Gilligan, *Notes on Art, Finance and the Un-Productive Forces*, Glasgow: Transmission Gallery, 2008.

frictionless self-valorisation, is a result of the emergence of speculation as the template for economic, but also personal and social valorisation. Speculation thus pre-eminently arises in the division between mental and manual labour, in the attribution of innovative thought and praxis to a class of people who are not constrained by material need: the 'symbolic analysts' and creatives of art and of finance. The connection to the undetermined, to the future, to the unknown and to the possible is removed from labour and becomes the property of this class, whose dependency on labour is henceforth mediated as the access to universality lent by independence from material constraint, an autonomy from interest. The genesis of such a class division and social division of labour in the concomitant emergence of Enlightenment rationality and industrial capitalism will have to be passed over here, though we can cite the early 18th century, when the rise of the social logic of speculation, as evidenced in the South Sea Bubble and chronicled by the likes of Daniel Defoe and Jonathan Swift, gave rise to the modern antinomies of bourgeois consciousness wherein speculation is linked to new forms of freedom, but also to an anxiety about measure, reduction and degradation of time-tested and dense forms of social exchange based on hierarchy and feudal moral economies. The historical autonomy of art, then, can be sited in the split between mental and manual labour which presupposed the generalisation of alienated labour as the hallmark of social relations in capitalism.

The social existence of art as a distinct sphere of human endeavour enjoys a strong correspondence with the value-form insofar as the basis of both is, in a way, indeterminacy. The value-form is a way of organising and extracting surplus, and art is a materialisation or socialisation of that surplus as open-ended speculation – in the sense of speculative praxis. This speculation is suffused with the ideological freight of open-endedness; the utopian moment that is also corollary to capital – the relationship between the 'unconditioned' that is art, and the pure abstraction that is the core of capital, the pure algebra of value – which is not to downplay the more strictly ideological role of art as affirmation of freedom from capitalist social relations. As cited earlier, the services rendered by autonomy, however provisional and fragile that autonomy is understood to be by now, nonetheless tie in with the paltry individuations offered by the 'creative industries' and the massification of speculation on the 'self' through e.g. social networking platforms. It should be noted that 'speculation' has another purchase as well: it is not simply indeterminate/utopian, or amenable to characteristically financial mediations, such as gambling or the production of subjectivity as a commodity. Speculation is also a type of political thought which departs from the parameters of the actual and draws on them for its sense of possibility when envisioning or constructing change. This implied speculation can also operate in a dystopian or prefigurative mode, both of which are more determined by the present and by history than the exhilarating vacuum of the utopian. Frederic Jameson, writing on Bertolt Brecht's notion of the scientific in aesthetic praxis as the 'experimental attitude' which secures aesthetic praxis as non-alienated labour, discusses speculation in these terms:

> Brecht's particular vision of science was for him the means of annulling the separation between physical and mental activity and the fundamental division of labour (not least that between worker and intellectual) that resulted from it: it puts knowing the world back together with changing the world, and at the same time unites an ideal of praxis with a conception of production. [...] In the Brechtian aesthetic, indeed, the idea of realism is not a purely aesthetic and formal category, but rather governs the relationship of the work of art to reality itself, characterising a particular stance towards it. The spirit of realism designates an active, curious, experimental, subversive – in a word scientific – attitude towards social institutions and the material world... (Jameson, 2007: 204).

Setting aside for a moment the impact of this kind of aesthetic praxis on the division of labour and social change, we can attend to speculation's hegemonic function in the current period. The shift of speculation from being an elite activity to a normative parameter for all labour marks the erosion and eclipse of understanding of class interests as real, divergent and institutionally mediated. The loss of the external referent that labour posed to capital, or use-value to exchange-value, has resulted in the situation of capitalist recursivity that the social logic of speculation needs in order to flourish. This self-referentiality, the harmonious self-regulation that neoclassical economics has propounded for decades, if not centuries, as the regulative ideal of social relations and market transaction alike, produces a kind of loss of measuring capacity which has in certain quarters been called the obsolescence of the law of value. But perhaps such an erosion of measure speaks simply of the great expansion, diffusion, and refinement of that law; it has nothing to measure any longer but its own effects. It is a law founded on abstraction, reduction, and on the proliferation of instruments of abstraction, rather than the institution of abstract equivalence between labour-time and the wage through money that anchored a time when the law of value did apply in some well-defined sense. Thus, the proximity between art thought of as abstract labour and abstract labour thought of as human capital is exemplified by the loss of measure in both under the sign of finance, by the indeterminacy and expansion of art and the indeterminacy and expansion of work. A note on human capital: if we look at the idea of it, both in its original ideological formulation by Gary Becker and as analysed by Foucault, and its unproblematic embrace as a neutral terminology by all manner of policy discourses, it might be helpful to see it as another way of describing what Marx called 'real subsumption', that is, the integration and transmutation of labour into capital in the production process, but which, as in the writings of the Italian autonomists and other more recent trends in political theory, we now see extended into the whole range of social relations, subjectivity and biological existence. Furthermore, human capital can also be seen as the figure of the shift in the guiding logic of capital from the equivalence of exchange (the worker) to the asymmetry of competition (the entrepreneur), and its internalisation by, or endo-colonisation of, the subject.

In terms of updating the topology of heteronomy and autonomy for the present relations of aesthetic production, with an emphasis on labour, art seems to provide a way of reconciling the extension of the value-form — expropriation, privatisation, imposition of work — with the erosion of the law of value that seemed to make some sense out of work before. The social expansion of finance, and the expansion of art, should be seen in strict analogy with the contraction of labour; both are processes of 'real' (?) abstraction, so to speak — they render the processes of social domination ever more abstract in daily life, in reproduction, while locating that reproduction more and more intimately within the sphere of finance. Why this should be the case — why art should play the legitimating role it does for the rule of finance — can perhaps be found in art's privileged relation to contingency, that is, contingency understood as novelty, unpredictability, and the creation of as yet untested and potentially infinite value. Art has the capacity to socialise what, on the face of it, are rather financial imperatives such as these, since art is the name for innovative praxis in a capitalist society, positioned as beyond economic or other deterministic interests, or as 'unconditioned'; a social 'research and development' site even after decades of intensified proximity to market behaviour and government policy. Thus contingency seems to belong to both art and finance insofar as both are speculative practices. It could also be said that contingency is a kind of negativity as well; an 'antithesis to that which is the case'. But to go a little more deeply into this link of contingency between art and finance, what exactly is the structural role of contingency in finance?

The market trader-turned-speculative realist Elie Ayache, in his published lecture 'In The Middle of The Event' (Ayache, 2011), contends that the risk formulas used in derivatives trading, such as the well-known Black-Scholes equation, are ultimately nonsensical since in order to accurately assess the probability of various risk factors of the asset in question, they would end up in an endless recursion of trying to evaluate the volatility of each factor based on its relation to the volatility of all the other factors, which itself relates back to the risk assessment that influences the trading of the assets. His simple counter-argument to such formulas is that if assets traded at the price which risk-assessment value algorithms allocated to them, the trade in these assets would be a priori impossible. The trade depends on the recursivity of the implied rather than assessed risk of the assets; at a basic level, it is the recursive volatility of the market itself which drives trade. Hence he proposes that probability should be dispensed with when predicting, describing or regulating what takes place in financial markets in favour of what he calls 'contingent claims'. The 'absolute contingency' of asset prices in the market retroactively creates its own conditions, which then serve as the basis of the asset prices in the next cycle, and so on. He links this to Henri Bergson's concept of creative evolution, Alain Badiou's theory of the event, and Gilles Deleuze's conceptual dyad of the virtual and the actual. All these are concepts which operate outside the shadow of probability; the radical unforeseeability of the event means that its causes are only discernible in retrospect – the event is an effect that creates its own causes: 'Absolute contingency of the final world gets reflected or translated, ahead of time, by the exchange. The market, or the exchange, is how absolute contingency projects itself ahead of time. This may even act as a definition of exchange' (Ayache, 2011: 35).

Here we can see that financial speculation is formulated as the exemplary instance of absolute contingency, since transactions are powered by the contingency of value-claims: the market is constantly re-setting itself in line with those encounters between claims to value and the contingency of those claims, and this is what keeps the market going – absolute contingency is the market's metastability. It is interesting to juxtapose Ayache's account of the paradoxical aspects of probabilistic risk assessment in a milieu of absolute contingency with Marxist political economist David McNally's description of the Value at Risk formulas as a cancellation of contingency (McNally, 2009: 70)[3]. A contrast emerges between their two visions of the relation between finance, contingency and the emancipatory. Ayache is concerned with ascribing an emancipatory agency to contingency in markets, and not only tries to articulate it using philosophical concepts usually associated with transformative and counter-hegemonic programmes, but to situate it in relation to art – his lecture was delivered in the context of an exhibition at a London gallery. McNally, on the other hand, while agreeing with Ayache's critique of existing models of quantification of risk, frames the critique in a rather different way. For him, market speculation cannot be extracted from its reliance on, or description by, those models, since the speculative agency of finance needs to assume the continuity of the market, e.g. of capitalism, and thus can only operate in the foreclosure of a different future. Consequently, financial speculation is ultimately anti-speculative, if

---

[3] Both Ayache and McNally's critiques of measure in financial markets can be usefully read alongside Christian Marazzi's account of 'endogenous' risk in markets: 'In fact, there is a particular ontological weakness in the models of probability calculation used to evaluate risks due to the endogenous nature of the interactions between the financial operators [...] This explains the "evaluation errors" of risk not so much, or not only, as mistakes attributable to the conflict of interests scandalously typical of rating agencies, but as the expression of an (ontological) impossibility of making rules or meta-rules able to discipline markets in accordance with so-called rational principles. All the more so when, according to the methods used to establish the value of financial assets, like the ones based on the new accounting norms (International Financial Reporting Standards, IFRS, secured by Basel II), the fair value of assets is calculated on the basis of the conflict between their market value and the value at which the asset is being negotiated, that is, its historical value (the method used to establish this valuation is called 'mark to market'). The problem posed by these methods of valuation is that, since fair values act as a reference to calculate the value of a patrimonial asset – in the same way as a private citizen who calculates his real assets, including the current market value of his real estate – there is a strong urge to increase asset value by increasing debt...' (Marazzi, 2010b: 80-81).

'speculation' is taken chiefly in its experimental or creative-innovative sense, since the kind of speculation that happens in markets is concerned to minimise systemic change, or at least, to subsume all change into the logic of profit.

McNally stresses that 'value-forms have been extended at the same time as value-measures (and predictions) have become more volatile' (McNally, 2009: 57). This volatility means that capitalist measure, in the shape of money, is problematised, as the value of money itself is one of the quantities to be measured, or traded. This creates a situation of systemic risk, as the very preconditions of trade (weather, agriculture, governance structures) themselves became tradeable entities and financial commodities. This emergence of systemic risk necessitated the design and deployment of all kinds of risk-hedging instruments, whose trade was conditional on the volatility these instruments themselves put into play, as in the trade of derivatives contracts, CDSs and CDOs, and other and more recondite forms of risk insurance. As the markets for risk-assessment and risk-managing devices expanded, this in its turn led to an escalated level of volatility, a 'positive feedback' loop (or chaos), as most recently witnessed in the speculative attacks on the Euro, or the 1990s attack on the Pound by George Soros. Bets on debts going bad are profitable when those debts stand a greater likelihood of going bad due to the inimical market conditions created for those debts by those bets. The geopolitically decisive, if not absolute, power of ratings agencies in both determining the policy options of sovereign nation-states and feeding speculative markets in sovereign debt is something we are witnessing now in the most explicit ways in the consequences of the brutal austerity programmes imposed at the behest of those agencies and markets in Greece and other Mediterranean countries. While generating geopolitical turmoil, such speculation tends towards enhancing the stability and accumulative capacities of the financial markets, as the political fallout of currency attacks have demonstrated time and again – social turbulence is an easily hedged risk in the global financial architecture, provided it doesn't impinge on the dominance of that architecture as well. In distinction from the apocryphal derivative trade on 'the end of capitalism' reported in the early days of the crash, the stability of this architecture is the basis of the burgeoning levels of speculation; the law of value itself cannot enter as a risk factor into the 'absolute contingency' of speculative markets. Not only this, but the assumption that the law of value will continue to hold fuels what is the hallmark of financialisation; that is, the trade in fictitious capital,[4] or claims to future surplus-value not yet produced. Variants of this have been mentioned in the foregoing account, which produces temporal closure, or rather 'securitisation' – the indefinite extension of the present, a present quantified by instruments such as the Black-Scholes equation or the Value at Risk (VaR) formula.[5] While McNally sees such instruments as clear instances of the 'single metric' tendency of capitalist measure which needs to establish common bases for commodity exchange (money as the general equivalent, abstract labour as the common substance of value), he links the financial crisis to the dysfunctionality of these instruments, and takes this dysfunctionality to be a symptom of the inability to measure risk in an economic climate of constant currency fluctuation (instability of the general equivalent) and where calculations of risk are increasingly recursive and

---

4   Sander gives the following *precis* of Marx's concept of fictitious capital: 'In one sense, all financial capital is fictitious since its value, its power to represent real commodities, ultimately depends on fiction, on "faith in money-value as the immanent spirit of commodities" (Marx). But money is also "only a different form of the commodity" and must therefore expand together with the value of the commodities it represents. To the extent that financial capital's expansion is disconnected from the expansion of value of the commodities it represents, it is fictitious. More specifically: fictitious capital is capital neither invested in the physical means of production, infrastructure, or the wages of workers, but rather in assets (stocks, bonds, securities) that are expected to yield profits at some future time. It constitutes claims to future production and the profits that this may generate – paper claims to wealth. While the existence of fictitious capital is inherent in the development of a capitalist banking and credit system, its actual development in present-day capitalism in the form of both public and private *debt* necessary to sustain economic activity constitutes a huge and unsustainable burden on future earnings that may never be repaid or which creates credit bubbles the bursting of which constitutes a formidable threat to the very stability of the capitalist system' (Sander, 2011).

5   The concept of Value at Risk or VaR is glossed by McNally (2009: 70): 'First developed in the early 1990s, VaR has become the fundamental basis upon which financial institutions and investors assess the riskiness of their investment-portfolios. Indeed, over the past decade, it has also been the basis upon which banks establish their own capital-requirements.'

unmoored from any of the value they claim to measure: 'Using a set of models that share a common mathematical framework, VaR is supposed to measure literally any asset under any and all conditions. Crucial to the operation of VaR assessments is the assumption that all points in time are essentially the same and, therefore, that tomorrow will be just like yesterday and today' (McNally, 2009: 70-71).

Thus

> time is reified, treated as a purely quantitative variable, and qualitative breaks or ruptures in a temporal continuum are ruled out. [...] The process of abstraction these models undertake involves treating space and time as mathematical, as nothing more than different points on a grid. This homogenisation of space and time assumes that what applied at any one spatio-temporal moment applies in principle at any other. But crises destroy any basis for such assumptions... (McNally, as above)

Another view on temporality and finance comes from Randy Martin, when he writes 'Derivatives have a temporal aspect, making a future possibility actionable in the present, and a spatial dimension where certain features of what is local take on global salience and the far becomes near' and

> [D]erivatives work through the agency of arbitrage, of small interventions that make significant difference, of a generative risk in the face of generalised failure but on behalf of desired ends that treat the future not simply as contingent, uncertain, or indeterminate but also as actionable in the present, as a tangible wager on what is to come. (Martin, 2011: 156)

This discussion of the time of finance disrupted by crisis recalls the role of time as a social form which is a corollary of the relations of production, as the collective Endnotes writes: 'Communism is thus understood not in terms of a new distribution of the same sort of wealth based in labour time, but as founded on a new form of wealth measured in disposable time. Communism is about nothing less than a new relation to time, or even a different kind of time' (Endnotes, 2010: 79).

It may be added here, parenthetically, that 'a new relation to time, or even a different kind of time' is a modality that would seem equally if not more at home in aesthetic practice or thought, or, perhaps more broadly, a speculative praxis oriented towards transformation of experience, as well as but not limited to the relations of production. While the 'absolute contingency' of the market formulated by Ayache has explanatory power and is conceptually suggestive, it seems hard to discount McNally's analysis of Value at Risk as a repudiation of the actual contingency operating in markets; a contingency which is recursive but not in any sense social, nor truly contingent as in an event that disrupts calculations, as Ayache would like it to be, since in the end there have to be conditions for a financial market, whatever anomalous events transpire within it. A truly anomalous event, following McNally, could not be internal to markets and the type of contingency which animates them. This suggests that despite certain provocative analogies, speculation as a mode of production is not consistent between financialised capital and art from the standpoint of horizon, since financial speculation has to exclude the suspension of the law of value, and is thus only speculative within the defined parameters of chronologically attenuated and homogeneous risk.

Hence financial speculation, the speculation confined to the value-form, lacks the key element of negativity which would enable it to be actually speculative in the philosophical or aesthetic sense that Ayache intends for it. This means that financial speculation and the indeterminacy of the aesthetic do not really share a common ground, despite earlier appearances. In comparison to the deceptive normality of labour's 'use value', the pure form of value as seen in finance does indeed give us an insight into the level of abstraction and contingency proper to labour performed under capital's value relations. But this contingency of exchange value and value, or, negativity with regard to use, runs up in the positivity of its own drive to expand. This requires a homogeneity of time and stagnation of the social which seem to vitiate the speculative drive of the value-form as we have witnessed it in the expansion of finance over the social terrain over the last several decades. The political theorist Robert Meister has spoken of the 'options-form' replacing the 'commodity-form' as the central form in which value is manufactured and traded, making temporality itself the typical commodity for an era in which risk is the main driver of social reproduction. His account starts in 1973, when derivatives or options theory developed as a way for capitalism to re-think itself once the gold standard was jettisoned – so the future orientation is also a shift to a kind of reflexivity. He also sees this shift as a way of putting the struggle with socialism in the past – first conceptually and eventually politically. Class struggle became a factor of individualised risk management, juggled among economic variables, e.g. human capital theory. Then financialisation as a hedge against uncertainty in an ever-more economically volatile and unequal society/economy starts to become the dominant logic. Human capital investment e.g. tuition, is a hedge against the uncertainty that the rule of finance itself has established. If it can be priced, it can be commoditised – this is the outcome of turning social contradictions into risks that could be hedged. 'What you know long-term simply raises the price of uncertainty about what you know will happen next'.

Contingency only has value because it is part of an overarching narrative wherein which nothing is forever. All past history is accumulated in the current price in the option-form mode of capital, the speculative mode of production or, here, finance, just as all past suffering (dead labour) is accumulated in the current accumulation of wealth according to the labour theory of value. The options-form is also interesting within relation to forms of immaterial property such as IP (intellectual property). Here rent supplants final sale; no sale is ever complete, and rent ensures the sale can happen again and again, under different conditions. Here the shift from the commodity-form to the options-form opens up the commodity to time in a radical way, leaving behind the closed loop of self-expanding value in the usual sense. The art market remains relatively traditional in its transactional forms and property contracts by comparison, though it is a truism that, particularly in the last decade, the market has been driven, or inflated, by fortunes made via dealings in 'innovative' financial commodities which operate with the kind of risk temporality described above, that is: derivatives and hedges.

Art of course is also a space where reflexivity and recursivity are the main engines of production of meaning since at least the conceptual art era, but tendentially before, since the 'game of reference' became an operative rule for artworks and art per se, i.e. the readymade. On the other hand, art derives its 'speculative value' from not just the parameters and value-games of art, whether significatory or financial, but also from the suspension or dissolution of art itself, and the social relations that underlie the existence of art as a discrete institution with its own laws. As Rancière writes, the contemporary 'aesthetic regime' of art is precisely predicated on exacerbating the confusion about what art is or where it belongs, and its boundaries with other regimes of meaning, practice or validation. Crucially, though not emphasised by Rancière, the speculation of art (or, the speculation that is art), measures and dramatizes its speculative capabilities through its relation to labour, be that a relation of proximity or negation. In this sense, art cannot be considered in relation to politics without first being considered in relation to labour – and this is even more the case when artistic subjectivity and modes of production become a supplement to the restructuring of the labour-capital relation away from the wage and its equivalences to the precarious and 'infinite' demands of creativity. Art as a model of emancipated labour both figures unalienated activity which is not measured in money and the infinite, unwaged exploitation that capital is imposing on all of us in the drive to find new sources of accumulation. It can be seen as a relic of the past, of feudal relations, produced in an artisanal rather than industrialised way for the most part (the domestic regime, as Luc Boltanski describes it). Or it can be a prototype for the future, whether that will be a bad infinity of the present, or operating in radically transformed condition; in which case art's relationship to 'free labour' in its current sense, exacerbated in its post- or trans-object period (both liberated and dependent on selling itself or its products to survive) will itself no longer be a reliable category when art and labour cease to exist in their current forms.

PART TWO:
THE LABOUR OF CREATIVITY

4

The Value of Painting. Notes on Unspecificity, Indexicality and Highly Valuable Quasi-Persons

Isabelle Graw

Introduction

In the following, I will first try to develop a medium-*un*specific notion of painting that is nevertheless able to capture its residual specificity under conditions that led to its despecification. These conditions – often referred to as a 'post-medium condition' (as described in Krauss, 2000) – will be addressed in view of their implications for painting. If painting has expanded and tends to be everywhere, as I will argue, then it seems to make little sense to delimit its realm. Yet this is what numerous painting-exhibitions keep doing: they treat painting as if it was a clearly circumscribed entity. The only thing is, however – painting has long since left its ancestral home, that is, the picture on the canvas, and is now omnipresent, as it were, and at work in other art forms as well. We therefore can't be sure to what we are referring, when we talk 'about painting'. Do we mean painting in the sense of a medium, a technique, a genre, a procedure or an institution? As a way out of these semantic quandaries I will propose a less substantialist notion of painting that conceives it *as a form of production of signs that is experienced as highly personalised.*

This understanding of painting as a highly personalised *semiotic* activity has several advantages: it is less restrictive, allowing us to see how painting is at work in other art forms as well *and* it is able to capture what is specific about its codes, gestures and materiality. In addition to this, the focus on painting's indexicality enables us to grasp the particularly strong bond between the person and the product that we encounter here. I will therefore investigate the highly personalised nature of this particular sign production and relate it to the way in which value gets attributed to it. There are many indications of painting's lasting popularity: it keeps fetching the highest prices on the art market *and* it survived the manifold historical attempts to declare it finished, dead, obsolete etc. I will conclude by offering one way of explaining its tenacity: as an art form it seems particularly disposed to support the expectation – widespread in the art world – that by acquiring a work of art, you get a hold on the artist's labour capacity and therefore own a slice of her life. Buying artworks indeed comes close to buying people – and this is especially true for painting.

1. For an Expanded Notion of Painting

I have already hinted towards the problems of defining painting: when most artistic practices, not only painterly ones, have undergone massive differentiation and expansion, it becomes rather difficult to pin down painting. How to determinate an 'unresolved category', to quote a press release accompanying a recent exhibition on this subject in Bergen[1]? I would like to suggest that we work with an *expanded* notion of painting that breaks with the modernist understanding of it as a clearly delineated practice, characterised by given norms and conventions. Since the borders between the different art forms have become permeable at least since the 1960s, we have found ourselves in a situation where different media relate to, re-fashion and re-model each other. This process has been termed 're-mediation' (Becker, 2009). Such re-mediation occurs when the features that have been ascribed to one medium – say flatness or representational strategies in painting – are addressed by another medium – say large-scale photography[2]. And sure enough, artists from Jeff Wall to Wolfgang Tillmans have tirelessly demonstrated that photography can take up the representational and narrative

---

[1]   See Press release of the exhibition *Gambaroff, Krebber, Quaytman, Rayne*, Kunsthall Bergen, November 2010, available at www.Kunsthall.no.

[2]   Michael Fried (2008: 1-4) has written a whole book about how earlier themes which he detected in 18th century painting – absorption, theatricality – are now taken up by contemporary photographers.

strategies of painting; that it can aim at creating surfaces that suggest the materiality of abstract painting. The crucial point remains here that the modernist idea of an art that is defined by the 'essence of its medium' (Heidegger, 2008) has clearly lost its relevance. Once the medium can no longer be delimited, then no qualities can be inherent to it either. Its character, rather, depends on how the artist will proceed with it.

2. Good-Bye to Medium-Specificity?

Clement Greenberg was the leading champion of the idea that modernist painting in particular is not only characterised by 'essential norms and conventions' such as the flatness of its surface (Greenberg, 1993: 89), but that each painting has to ideally criticise these limitations 'from the inside' (*ibid.*: 85). It is interesting to note how the descriptive and the normative level merged in his notion of the medium. Not only did he essentialise painting, ignoring the fact that it actually shares its supposedly 'essential' condition – the flat surface – with writing. He moreover expected the artist to defend the imaginary purity of her medium by criticising it from within.

Now, this privilege that Greenberg had accorded to the medium became historically untenable once painting lost its purity and expanded into life, as in the Combine Paintings of Robert Rauschenberg.

Greenberg's position became even more questionable when those conceptual art practices emerged in the late 1960s that strongly relied on different technologies, such as film photography or diagrams.

This was an art that was more generic than medium specific, as André Rottmann has rightly pointed out (2011). One might add to this that the rejection of the privileged status of painting has a much longer history, and regularly occurred in painterly practices as well. As an example of a painting that says goodbye to the tradition of 'pure painting', I would refer to Picabia's *Nature Morte* (1920) – a painting that contaminates the alleged purity of its medium by drawing on different formats: 1) the readymade (in the form of the stuffed animal that is attached to the surface and 'stubbornly clings to the domain of painting', as George Baker (2007: 101) put it so adequately); and 2) text (the written names of 'great' male artists like Cézanne, Rembrandt and Renoir, whose portraits we are meant to see and who turn out to be nothing but a dead animal, *natures mortes*). Cézanne for one, whose work was always considered to be the epitome of pure painting, is declared to be as dead as the stuffed ape. The status of painting as a higher art form and the correlating belief in its purity and essence are doubly threatened here: not only by the incorporation of a readymade that enforces the external logic of the commodity and of productive labour into the painting, but also by the textual elements, which equally threaten to bury painting's alleged essence.

Are we then obliged to deduce from this that there is nothing medium-specific about painting anymore? I believe that we have to concede at this point that some artists, and painters in particular, do indeed encounter problems in their practice that they ascribe to the specificity of their respective medium. But it is one thing to acknowledge a certain degree of medium-specificity at this level of artistic production, and another to derive a highly questionable general norm of medium-specificity from it.

3. Painting and Indexicality

So, how to define painting once it has merged with other procedures – from the readymade and linguistic propositions to the insights of institutional critique? How to determine a practice that renders the rigorous distinction between what is intrinsic and what is extrinsic to it impossible? I want to propose that we conceive of painting not as a medium, but *as a production of signs that is experienced as highly personalised.* By focusing on painting's specific indexicality, we will be able to grasp one of its main characteristics: that it is able to suggest a strong bond between the product and the (absent) person of its maker. This is due to the way indexical signs actually operate: according to Peirce, an index shows something about a thing because of its *physical connection* to it (Peirce, 2000: 193). Since he mentioned photography as an example for this 'class of signs', art historians tend to mainly treat photography as the indexical art form *par excellence* (see Krauss, 1977). But I would argue that it is painting that suggests such a physical connection even more strongly. Someone has left her marks. Frank Stella's observation that painting is a sort of handwriting was actually quite to the point (Glaser, 1995: 157). Its signs are indexical insofar as they can be read as traces of the producing person. Now even if we opt for a deconstructivist approach to the trace thereby insisting on how the trace equally addresses 'the formal conditions of separation, division and deferral' (Derrida, quoted in Krauss,

1993: 260), we are still dealing with the ghost of a presence. This is also true for those paintings that avoid handwriting by using a technical device, as in Gerhard Richter's abstract paintings produced with a squeegee. The more negation there is of handwriting, the more this negation will be considered to be the handwriting of the artist[3]. In other words: attempts to eliminate the subjectivity of the artist from the painting usually lead to a re-entering of subjectivity into painting (Graw, 2012).

Yet linking indexicality to painting does not imply that we ignore the split that occurs between the artwork and the authentic self. What we encounter in painting is not so much the authentically revealed self of the painter, but much rather signs that insinuate that this absent self is somewhat present in it. As a highly mediated idiom, painting provides a number of techniques, methods, and artifices that allow for the fabrication of the impression of the author's quasi-presence *as an effect*.

For this indexical effect to occur the artist does not need to have literally set her hand to the picture, or to have brandished a brush, or to have thrown paint on it. A mechanically produced silkscreen, say by Andy Warhol, who often delegated his work to his assistants, or a printed black painting by Wade Guyton, is no less capable of conveying the sense of a latent presence of the artist – by virtue, for instance, of imperfections deliberately left uncorrected, selected combinations of colours, or subsequent improvements. Painting, then, would have to be understood as the art form that is particularly favourable to the belief – widespread in the visual arts more generally – that by approaching or purchasing a work of art, it is possible to get a more immediate access to what is assumed to be the person of the artist and her life.

4. Painting as a Highly Valuable Quasi-Person

There is one feature of the indexical sign that I haven't yet mentioned: according to Peirce, the indexical sign is able to capture our attention because

---

[3] 'Noch ein Medium, das Handschriftlichkeit ausdrücklich negiert kann Ausdruck der Handschrift eines Künstlers sein.' (Lüthy and Menke, 2005: 9).

it is affected by the power of its object [4]. Now, in the case of painting's indexicality, this object is a subject – the person of the artist. This is why painting can be potentially experienced as being as intriguing in a way that only an intriguing person could be. Now you might object to this that sculpture is able to do exactly the same thing. Isn't sculpture marked by a similar kind of indexicality and doesn't it therefore also suggest that it is a quasi-person?

Yes it does, but to a lesser degree. It is only painting for which many historical arguments have been raised which point to its subject-like power – arguments I believe do reach into our present. The very first systematic treatise on painting produced in the modern era, Leon Battista Alberti's *Della Pittura* (1453), for instance, already aimed to raise the reputation of painters in order to advance their emancipation from the larger class of craftsmen. Indicatively enough, Alberti based his preference for the painter over the sculptor on his view that the former worked 'with more difficult things' (Alberti, 1966: 66), making painting an intrinsically intellectually demanding activity. Once painting was declared to be intellectually challenging, it was only a matter of time that the intellectual powers of a subject would be claimed for it. It was Hegel who defined painting as a mode of artistic representation into which the principle of 'finite and internally infinite subjectivity' has forced its way (Hegel, 1970: 17). Everything that is fundamentally part of a subject accordingly urges toward painting's surface. Subjectivity, however, designates here not that of the artist but a universal faculty – 'the principle of our own being and life' (*ibid.*). According to Hegel, we see in the artifacts of painting what is 'at work and operative within ourselves' (*ibid.*). And it is precisely because we believe we recognise in it a familiar potential that we at once feel 'at home' in it. In other words, painting, in Hegel's view, moves us also because it stages principles that strike us as familiar and that constitute us. The decisive point of this argument is that Hegel aligns painting with the subject by ascribing a capacity for it – the capacity of subjectivity – that is properly speaking the exclusive privilege of subjects. Only subjects possess the ability to evolve an independent mental

---

4   'Ein Index ist ein Ding – von einer Kraft seines Objekts affiziert – mit seiner Kraft seinen Interpretanten beeinflusst und ihn veranlasst, seinerseits von der Kraft des Objekts affiziert zu sein.' (Peirce, 2000: 428)

life. By according a subject-like power to painting, Hegel laid the ground for what I would describe as the central trope around painting in the 20th century, namely the assumption that there is a thinking of painting, that painting itself is able to think. French painting theorists like Louis Marin or Hubert Damisch in particular have put forward this argument – that painting is a sort of discourse producer that arrives at its own insights. Once it is declared to be able to think it becomes subject-like.

But how does painting's capacity to evoke the sense of a subject-like force, how does its power to suggest that it actually operates like a person relate to the value that is attributed to it?[5]

For an artwork to be considered valuable, it first of all has to be attributable to an author. One could say that it thereby gets loaded with intentionality. This process gets intensified in the case of the indexical signs of paintings. Here someone has left her traces (even if mechanically produced, this suggestion of a handwriting persists) and this enhances the impression of an intentional artwork, of an artwork that itself has agency. While all artworks have to function as an index of the one who brought them into existence in order for value to be attributed to them, painting seems to go further by suggesting that it is a quasi-person. Or to put this slightly differently: painting is particularly well equipped to satisfy the longing for substance in value. It indeed seems to demonstrate how value is founded in something concrete – the living labour of the artist. Let's recall how Marx conceptualised value. While it is certainly true that his reflections on value were bound to the commodity and not to the artwork as a commodity of a special kind, his notion of value has two undeniable advantages: 1) it doesn't confound value and price and thereby prepares the ground for a notion of symbolic value that is crucial for artworks; and 2) it insists on the relational, metonymic quality of value thereby reminding us that value has no substance and is always elsewhere. Indeed: Marx on the one hand emphasised that no

---

5   I'm not distinguishing between symbolic and economic value here on purpose. I am referring to value in the sense of the place where social relevance is attributed to an artwork. All the claims that have been made for painting constitute its symbolic value. While symbolic value doesn't get automatically translated into economic value, it is never the precondition for economic value to occur.

commodity is valuable in itself, that value is a 'purely social' phenomenon[6]. This is also true for artworks: no artwork is valuable *per se*, its value is the result of an ongoing and never ending social negotiation. On the other hand, he pointed to how value represents 'the overspending of human labour in general'[7]. This would mean that value eclipses concrete labour and turns it into its opposite – abstract human labour[8]. Now, painting seems to be one of the last places where the desire for a concrete foundation of value *seemingly* gets fulfilled. Not only does it generate the illusionary impression that it is possible to grasp a fibre of the living labour that was mobilised for it. But it moreover promises the existence of an imaginary place where labour actually remains private and concrete, detectable in the concrete materiality of its surface and the gestures that it displays. The process of labour is not hidden but seemingly exposed as if the living labour of its author was something we could hold on to, as if it hadn't been transformed into 'objectified labour' (*vergegenständlichte Arbeit*) (*ibid.*) during the process of exchange. It is painting's capacity to appear particularly saturated with the lifetime of its author that makes it the ideal candidate for value production.

It is important to note that this search for value within living labour gets even more pronounced in the current context of ongoing devalorisation. It is one of the effects of the financial crisis from 2008 that more and more desperate searches for value take place. The belief in the 'personality' of the artwork and painting in particular is of course not a solution to the crisis; it is a way of both delaying and extending it.

---

[6]   'We may twist and turn a single commodity as we wish; it remains impossible to grasp it as a thing possessing value. However, let us remember that commodities possess an objective character as values only in so far as they are all expressions of an identical social substance, human labour, that their objective character as values is therefore purely social. From this it follows self-evidently that it can only appear in the social relation between commodity and commodity' (Marx, 1976: 138-139).

[7]   'But the value of a commodity represents human labour pure and simple, the expenditure of human labour in general.' (Marx, 1976: 135).

[8]   'The equivalent form therefore possesses a second peculiarity: in it, concrete labour becomes the form of manifestation of its opposite, abstract human labour.' (Marx, 1976: 150).

Let me conclude by saying that the *topos* of painting as a quasi-person has historically turned up in many different guises – starting from painters themselves, like those who have all either seriously (Bacon, von Heyl) or ironically (Oehlen) referred to the idea that painting tells them what to do. The belief in the self-activity of painting is one of its central myths, a myth that is of course closely interwoven with the experience of production. I have mentioned already how several French art historians like Louis Marin or Hubert Damisch have made a slightly different claim for a metapictorial 'thinking' of painting, demonstrating how it is able to produce its own discourse[9]. While I would not deny the possibility that a painting can occasionally deliver its own interpretation, I find it nevertheless important that we realise that by claiming agency for painting (or for artworks in general), by treating them as quasi-persons, as I have aimed to show here that we tend to do, we become somewhat implicated in the process of value attribution, a process that has in any case already been fired up by our propositions regarding the nature of the artwork.

---

[9] On Poussin's *Et in Arcadia Ego*: 'Dieses Gemälde interpretiert sich selbst, denn es stellt den Repräsentationsprozess der Geschichte dar.' (Marin, 2003: 30).

5

What kind of Petrified Human Lifetime are You Buying when You are Buying Art – And How Do You Want to Reliquify It?

Diedrich Diederichsen

I am doing two things in this paper: firstly to ask how it has happened that the consensus of all European governments that the investment in culture, especially in contemporary art, is economically reasonable, has been shaken, and even reversed by many. Don't tell me it's 'the crisis'. Secondly, I would like to look at the economic side of art production in general, not to offer something completely new, but to propose a slightly different, but of course related, angle to the one I use in my book *On (Surplus) Value in Art* (Diederichsen, 2008).

It is perhaps not so surprising to talk about the topic of this conference in relation to works of art, given the relation to the art world, or one of the art worlds, in the professional histories and biographies of many of the participants and organisers. But artworks are normally not considered to be produced by the multitude; they are not even considered to be interesting from the perspective of labour. They are debated aesthetically or economically as objects; objects which carry values, messages, aesthetic decisions, ideology and other immaterial items, but, particularly since conceptualism and neo-conceptualism, they seem not to be made and produced by human physical labour, and even the mental labour is often delegated to social processes and a willing participating audience, which loves to produce content for free. That, of course, is a mistake. Even though the labour in works of art so often disappears in the shadows – assistants are invisible and, unlike every driver, gaffer and intern in Hollywood, receives no credit – it is a crucial factor in relation to value. However, in this case I am not so much interested in the exploitation of the labour of others, but will look at the labour of the artist her- or himself, and the time he or she spends while making art in one way or another. In the contemporary economic set up all time spent by humans with anything is a form of production and an economic factor, including browsing the internet, reading a newspaper, staring into the setting sun over Poland from a train from Berlin. All these moments generate possible decisions in my brain; consumerist decisions or productive decisions. They lead to consequences, which would not have been if this time had been spent otherwise, or not at all.

Nearly everything in our world is at some level about objectifying human time. Every human-made object can be seen as a petrification of the time spent producing it. There are seemingly at least two types of time that you can buy from human beings. There is mechanical and rational time; the kind of time, when we directly become an instrument of an intention, a telos. On the other hand, there is affective, receptive, mental and even irrational time. In both cases I refer to humans who spend time in that way. Humans plus machines or tools equals human time of the first kind; humans plus institutions, education, informal learning, art reception, processing of cultural data et cetera equals human time of the second kind. Of course, they are not as easily separable in the practical reality of a profession or a job. Rational tool using of the first kind needs informal and institutional education of the second kind as well. But one can talk about this distinction in terms of tendencies: one type of labour is more dependent on the first or the second kind of time-spending.

Artworks are at first glance a kind of objectification of the second kind of time; of course, they are not the only type. But they are a specific type; so specific that one needs to put them into an extra category. So we can divide objects into three types, in relation to the time spent making them. First: Objects which mechanically consumed the time it took to make them, by humans and machines, like the famous box by Robert Morris (*Box with the Sound of Its Own Making*, 1961; see also Berger, 1989). To make an object there is a need for a certain number of labour hours. These are largely only the human plus machine hours that have been invested in the making of the object. The factor of the machine and the making of the machine, or the extra surplus value necessary to buy the machine, can be neglected since they are clearly less than 10% of the hours spent by men and women just producing a specific object with the machine.

The second type is the object in which it is not the actual time spent on making it that dominates, but time spent on the education of the person making it; time spent on the building and rebuilding of the institution providing that education, and also the informal time to develop the necessary emotional and behavioural framework. Even divided by the number of goods produced in a given time, and divided again by the number of people educated in the same university, or informally educated in the same leisure hours, is still much higher than the time spent on the work. This is the case for many services, for lawyers' and doctors' work, and of course for so called knowledge products.

But the proportion of the formal education invested in these products is much higher than that of informal knowledge; the chaotic and irrationally produced knowledge and the type of education which is the basis for the production of art. In artworks, much as in type 2 products, the human time necessary to produce them is to a far larger degree time spent with education, preparation and symbol processing of all kinds than with working with a tool on the actual product. But, in contrast to type 2 products, the majority of time necessary for the production of artworks is not spent on formal but on informal education. State sponsored art academies organise the informal, with the formal largely on an institutional level in connection with other institutions. At the same time there is another milieu around them, which takes care of the informal or the extra-institutional informal part of education: bars, alternative lifestyles, projects, communes etc. So the human time necessary to produce artworks is to a very high degree informally spent time; time spent outside the rules that apply for workers, employees and students of other kinds. We call this the exceptionalism of art, which is an element of the function of art in bourgeois history, but also in many versions of bourgeois ideology.

Now I would like to briefly introduce – albeit unnecessarily, given the high degree of Marxological knowledge evident in all of your contributions here – the notion of socially necessary labour time. This Marxian category means the average amount of a type of a labour time or human work hours necessary to produce a product. One can say that art pieces are so many different things that it does not make sense to construct such an average. But if you include in the calculation the sheer number of hours which all artists have spent at the same institutional and extra-institutional, informal and exceptional places seemingly doing nothing but enjoying their life while in reality learning how to be an artist, you come to such a high number that the average starts to make sense. You will then look at the originally large difference between projects and products in the art market and the large variety of prices with different eyes. You will realize that they are as different as car prices in relation to a factory producing different models, or the prices of different dental care procedures or operations in relation to the education of dentists and the decades they spent in universities and colleges. There is, however, a big difference between cars and dental care, and even old paintings on the one hand, and contemporary art on the other. Of course I am talking here less about visual arts of the conventional type, like painting, but rather about genres like performance art, technology based media art, conceptual and project based art. This difference is that the hours spent learning that went into car production were hours of being taught to do something, and be someone else at the same time, just as later in the factory: do something, use your craft, but dream of your leisure time. Live expertly in other people's teeth, but write a poem at home later. Dream of the other side of town while drilling in that rotten mouth! Whereas artists were not learning to do something and think of something else, but learning to be someone – and the product would come automatically from their being what they were. The crucial element – the existential factor, the sensitivity, the sensuality, the criticality – were not crafts or skills but elements of their personality which they acquired while living the exceptional life, learning informally at Cedar Tavern[1] and Max's Kansas City[2]. So the classical worker or doctor learned to

---

[1]   The Cedar Tavern (or Cedar Street Tavern) was a bar and restaurant in New York opened in 1866 on Cedar Street. Art historians consider it an important incubator of the Abstract Expressionist movement. It was famous as a former hangout of many prominent Abstract Expressionist painters: Jackson Pollock, Willem de Kooning, Mark Rothko, Franz Kline and beat writers including Allen Ginsberg, Jack Kerouac, Gregory Corso and Frank O'Hara (see Lieber, 2000: 127).

be semi-attentive, being here to a degree, but only as much as is necessary to do the job, but the artist learned to be just where he or she was, but there fully – and the production would come magically just out of this concentration of the self.

But their patrons were people who worked their way to the top. They were a bourgeoisie that was still mainly shaped by old Protestant or even puritan values. Even if it was old money, put into a collection, which in the case of the Sculls, Ludwigs and many others, it was not, this money was built from accumulated chunks of surplus value which had been generated by exploiting people who would not live an exceptional life. Their masters and exploiters had themselves to adopt the ideology necessary for this, at least in some spheres of their lives. So this bourgeoisie which collected art in the long 20th century was buying and collecting in order to reliquify petrifications of a very special kind: petrifications of a good life, a meaningful life; sometimes an excessive life, sometimes a heroic life, sometimes an erotic life; a scandalous life, a drugged life, a psychedelic life, a homosexual life, a critical life, a radical life, a drunken life – all these lives they could not have lived.

Their specific reliquifying activity was not an attempt to get this other life after they had missed it. They knew they could not have it, they might not even have wanted it, but they wanted the trophy; they wanted these other products, indexes, traces of those good lives. They could have them too, without having produced them, paid for by the surplus value they generated from discipline and exploitation. This bourgeoisie also laid the foundation for the idea that it is good to build institutions around contemporary art. After their death, or even before, collectors gave to institutions – in the USA – or they contributed by philanthropic and not-so-philanthropic acts and deeds to

---

2   Max's Kansas City was a nightclub and restaurant opened by Mickey Ruskin in December 1965 at 213 Park Avenue South, New York, which became a gathering spot for musicians, poets, artists and politicians in the 1960s and 1970s. It quickly became a hangout for artists and sculptors of the New York School, such as John Chamberlain, Robert Rauschenberg, as well as Carle Andre, Dan Graham, Lawrence Weiner, Robert Smithson, Joseph Kosuth, Donald Judd, Richard Serra, Lee Lozano, Philip Glass, William S. Burroughs, Barnett Newman, art critics Lucy Lippard, Clement Greenberg and art dealer Leo Castelli. It was also a favourite hangout of Andy Warhol and his entourage (see Kasher, 2010).

the general desire to build and nurture museums and academies in the hands of the state in Europe. It is the Protestant backbone of the EU – Scandinavia, Holland, parts of Belgium, Germany and Switzerland, but of course northern and Catholic countries as well, who contributed to that consensus - a consensus which made a compromise with sin, with the good life on earth, firmly placing in art as petrified index of its existence to edify us all, and from time to time allow some of us to even live it.

It is important that the notion of compensatory culture, which is a key idea of critical theory, is not limited to its traditional area of explanation, namely those cases where it was meant to keep the masses quiet; in order to keep them from rebellion they were pacified by spectacles and colourful candy experiences. It also kept the bourgeois actors quiet by giving them the opportunity to acquire the trophies which witnessed the life they had missed when busy exploiting, or representing father's exploitations.

This is why it was such a shock when, of all countries, the Netherlands announced the terrible cuts of their national spending on the arts; when museums and institutions in the USA were closed after the Lehman Brothers crisis, and when other European governments decided to cut state spending on the arts and art education – because we all took this compromise for granted, not as ideal, but as a basis of our daily negotiations with governments and institutions. Of course, there are many reasons, and some of them are not structural but short term. But a few are new, and they are structural. For example, for the first time in a long period the new right wing governments announced the cultural cuts without apologies, but enjoyed them as long overdue revenge against the cultural left. Moreover, it is also the first time that an open fascist became the director of a state funded theatre in Europe, as now in Budapest.

But back to the Dutch situation: right wingers would normally not have the chutzpah to behave in such a triumphalist manner and dwell in the enjoyment of humiliating an opponent who is rhetorically their superior. They must be quite confident. They behave in such a way because the very bourgeoisie which had an investment in the state sponsoring of artists' good times does not believe in them anymore. It does not believe in them because, among other reasons, they now finally want the good life for themselves. They are no longer protestant or quasi-protestant entrepreneurs; they have made their money from money, not from immediate production. The concept of simple surplus value is alien to them, and the combination of long term, state-like investments in infrastructure, in even an informal infrastructure or an infrastructure of the informal, with all its complexities and mechanisms of delay, which used to be the system of state- or funding-sponsored art, is far too complex for their desire to immediately show off. This post-bourgeoisie does not collect cakes or indexes of their being baked, they want to eat them.

To avoid misunderstandings: I am not simply arguing for a classical productive Protestant bourgeoisie and against a post-bourgeoisie of finance-jugglers and speculation-criminals. This is a vulgar-Marxist cliché, at best social-democratic, at worst anti-Semitic. The old construction could not survive the new capitalism anyway, not only because the people who have replaced the ruling class have no sense of culture, which means a sense of its slowness; the slowness of cultivation in the most literary sense: of investment and the postponement of gratifications. I am only offering an argument for why the bad conscience of the old ruling class, which has been one of the economic cornerstones of the old art world, is slowly crumbling away.

Another is of course that the specific informal education of artists, an education that does not teach them a skill, but to become something or someone – and that production will immediately follow from their personality – is now a concept which has taken over regular business anyway. Regular people who work in presentation and service jobs, in performance- and presence-oriented immaterial production, function in this way anyway, and they have never been educated in such a way in specific institutions; they have learned it in the streets. So the specific immaterial object of the 'fascinating personality' and its related by-products can be owned without any infra-structure in a far more unconventional manner. It can be bought rough and ready in the favelas and streets, it can be picked up on the high streets and malls, secondary schools and clubs of the global precarious hedonism; it does not need to be nurtured. This basically means that in the long run we cannot rely on any ruling class coming back to sense in their cultural politics in the near future. The ruling class is no longer a bourgeoisie, and it will no longer sponsor or support the type of state a bourgeoisie used to need not only for its self-understanding but also to guarantee its business. They don't need such a state and they buy their culture elsewhere, if it is culture at all.

6

Notes on the Exploitation of Poor Artists

Hans Abbing

In this text[1] I argue that presently the exploitation of poor artists differs structurally from that of other knowledge workers and that this difference has consequences for actions aimed at the reduction of exploitation. The exploitation of poor artists is largely an affair internal to the art world: it is foremost an art elite that profits from low incomes in the arts.[2,3]

1. Believing that the Arts Play a Pioneering Role in the Critique of Capitalism is Attractive

Generally, artists are poor and their socio-economic situation is uncertain. One month they may have some income and the next none at all. Their situation is precarious. The term precarity in connection to labour has been brought to the foreground by social scientists who emphasise that, since the late twentieth century, an economic and social transformation towards post-Fordism has resulted in the increased precarity of workers. The powerful

---

[1]　Some arguments pitched in the current paper I elaborate more thoroughly in my upcoming book. Draft versions of some chapters are available at www.hansabbing.nl.

[2]　I would like to thank Kuba Szreder and Georgios Papadopoulos for their comments on earlier versions of this text.

[3]　The concept of economic exploitation used in this text refers to a structural use of people's labour without adequate compensation. This is not necessarily the same as the Marxist concept of exploitation; in the latter an entire segment or class in society is exploited by another.

notion of post-Fordism as a contemporary form of capitalism, favouring flexibility, precarity and affective engagement in performed labour, emerges as a result. It is telling that, over the last years, the use of the terms precarity and post-Fordism has become popular in art circles, whereas a decade ago the terms were almost unknown; today they appear to be on everybody's lips. Several explanations for this are likely to apply. First, the terms are illuminating. They contribute to a renewed attention to the bad economic position of artists in our society. Second, over the last two centuries, in spite of occasional alliances with deprived people, the position of artists in society has been predominantly one of relative isolation. Therefore, for critical artists, it is attractive to show that the socio-economic position of artists is not special anymore, and that making a common front with others makes sense. Third, in a time in which the negative effects of capitalism increasingly exceed its positive effects, it is tempting to blame capitalism for all of the artists' problems and not look at causes which are not directly related to capitalism, like possible exploitation internal to the art world itself. (For me capitalism is an immoral system, which nevertheless brought prosperity to many people, but probably not anymore.)

Fourth, artists and people in the art establishments like to see and present the arts as a forerunner in society, as a continuous avant-garde. This notion increases their self-esteem and the esteem coming from others. They believe that artists in the '60s and '70s of the previous century were pioneers in the criticism of capitalism. It is true that there were many artists among those who criticised capitalism for its stultifying and inhuman (Fordist) modes of production; nevertheless, it were foremost students who expressed this criticism most vehemently. In line with this belief, it is now attractive to think that the arts – with working conditions that have been precarious already for a long time – are presently the first to criticize the increasing precarity in capitalism and carry this load.

Some art world people even think that after the war the arts served as a kind of laboratory for the new, more human modes of production which emerged, but which gradually also increased precarity. That Boltanski and Chiapello called the 1960s critique an 'artistic critique' has added to this idea. But they clearly did not want to say that the critique stemmed from artists or even that those artists played an important role in it (Boltanski and Chiapello (2005 prim. ed. in French 1999). However, even without assuming that the arts served as a kind of a laboratory for the new modes of production, it is probably correct to say that the arts, as the field of creative self-realization, served as a point of reference for the formulation of the artistic critique of capitalism.

As a side note, it is useful to note that although it is true that the artistic critique of the rigid post war society and capitalism at large preceded the post-Fordist rhetoric and may have contributed to the latter, it certainly did not *cause* the emergence of the rhetoric and even less *caused* the new modes of production to come into being.[4] Chronological succession does not imply causality. It is far more likely that both artistic critique and new modes of production are the result of long-term developments in technology, production and administration.[5] Moreover, I think that the belief that the arts hold an avant-garde position, both as a laboratory of production and with respect to criticism, rests on a vast overrating of the importance of the arts in society. If there has been and is a laboratory, it is located more generally in the culture industry, which includes the popular arts.[6]

Fifth, I think that the eagerness with which members of the art establishment who earn normal to high incomes now use the term precarity can also be explained by the fact that this enables them to exhibit their progressive stance. It brings them prestige in many social circles in which they participate – including circles that are not necessarily leftwing. And finally, it enables the establishment to victimise the arts again, while emphasising the exceptionally high symbolic value of the arts. This way, their own privileged position is accentuated and maintained – see below. (This is not to say that there are no people within the art establishment who honestly believe in these notions and adhere to progressive ideas.)

---

4   Though a superficial reading of their text may suggest the opposite, Boltanski and Chiapello (2005 [1999]) as well clearly do not think in terms of a causal relationship.

5   They are part of what Norbert Elias (1994 [1939]) has called a civilization process, which in the second half of the twentieth century led to, amongst others things, de-hierarchization and informalization – see Wouters (2007).

6   I distinguish, on the one hand, art and artists and, on the other, popular artists and popular art. Generally, people, including popular artists, do not consider the latter as 'real' art.

Before continuing, it may be useful to ask who belongs to the art establishment and who does not. Whereas many readers may have a rather clear idea of people they know or have heard of who may belong to it, it is difficult to draw a line. It seems reasonable to say that those in the art world who are poor do not belong to the establishment. This applies to the large majority of people in the art world, foremost artists themselves, but also to support personnel, volunteers and interns.[7] In the case of the establishment I am thinking of, first of all, successful artists who are not only successful but also earn a more than decent income. The latter form a vey small percentage of all artists. Secondly, there are the people who administer art institutions, especially those with steady and better paid jobs, as well as many curators and mediators. The latter include a relatively large number of people who mediate between art institutions and artists on the one hand and, on the other, local and central government bodies and foundations. Third, quite a few people within governments and foundations as well as private donors and collectors can be said to be part of the art elite. Finally, the same applies to politicians and an elite of art lovers, from collectors to regular visitors of art performances, like classical concerts and opera, who associate themselves with the arts.

2. How Similar or Different are Artists and other Knowledge Workers?

An inventory of similarities and differences between the positions of the typical artist and the typical knowledge worker with a comparable level of professional schooling can help answer the question if the exploitation of artists is of the same nature as that of other knowledge workers, who share similarly precarious working conditions.

At first glance, the correspondences are striking. (1) Performance is immaterial and often tied to the body of the worker (as is clear in the live production of music, theatre and dance, while visual artists as well produce a product with foremost symbolic value). (2) There is little routine in the labor involved – de-routinization being a characteristic of post-Fordism *par excellence*. (3) Working hours are flexible. The majority of workers have

---

[7] Support personnel, a term used by Howard Becker (1982), helps in the realization of artworks without being in charge, like for instance technicians. Often support personnel consists of former artists or artists who do this work as second job.

temporary contracts or are self-employed. (4) There is no clear distinction between work and the private sphere. (5) So-called multiple jobholding is a widespread phenomenon. (6) Informality (as generally characteristic of a bohemian attitude) is important and there is little respect for hierarchical differences (at least visible or ostentatious). (7) Communication and discourse are important. (Most contemporary artists are indeed good with words.) (8) Emphasis is on creativity. Creativity is a measure of success. There is a desire to explore new creative possibilities. Continuous development and innovation are important. 9) Individual autonomy is much appreciated. (10) Self-realization and authenticity are significant goals. (11) Finally, work stress, existential doubts and frustration, burnouts and depressions caused by professional failure or the inability to realize one's own creative potential are common.

But there are also telling differences. (1) The typical artist is very poor. In most Western countries the total income (i.e. including second jobs) of 40% to 60% of artists is small enough to put them below the poverty line.[8] Evidently, artists are willing to work for very low incomes. At present, the typical knowledge worker with an equal level of professional training is not poor and often relatively well-to-do. In those cases in which their income becomes very low, they will re-train and attempt to find work in a different direction or profession. (2) Unlike comparable knowledge workers, artists have already been poor for a very long time, while working conditions were precarious. (3) Artists have a stronger work-preference. Often when more money comes in, part or all of it is used not for consumption and comfort but for working fewer hours in second jobs and more hours as artists, or for investments in their work as artists.

Moreover, none of the economic logic that prevails in non-art fields of cultural production exists in the arts, as the following differences demonstrate. (4) In the dominant social imagery, in and outside the arts, there is a tension between a strong dedication to art and commercial success.[9] The

---

[8]   For more data on poverty in the arts, their proper interpretation, and on the criteria of defining artists as a professional category, see Abbing (2002) and various articles I have written since, which are available at www.hansabbing.nl.

[9]   It is true that presently a small but growing number of foremost successful artists openly show commercial behavior. This particularly applies to artists who already

intention of the artist is to be altogether dedicated to art and to be as autonomous as possible. For other knowledge workers, positions in which they are less autonomous are often more satisfying, also because they bring more money. Other knowledge workers can be dedicated to their work and they as well like some degree of autonomy, but they also have goals other than 'work for the sake of work' and they will not negate the underlying economic purpose of their activities. This particular artist-intention is celebrated and propagated by artists, but it is also what is expected from artists. This celebration is absent or far less important in the case of other knowledge workers.

(5) When people, including knowledge workers, are poor, they are ashamed of their poverty and they are looked down on. In our society being poor is bad. This apparently does not apply to artists. Unlike other poor people, artists do not have to be ashamed of being poor. (They may be ashamed, but they will not show it, nor will others openly look down on them for being poor.) (6) A comfortable life is not a widely shared goal in the arts. There is distrust of the pursuit of comfort and a solid career. (7) Public and private support is regarded as good and righteous. For the typical knowledge worker, it is a sign of failure. (8) Authorship and signatures matter far more than in the case of other knowledge workers. (9) Unlike pop and sport stars, very successful artists are (still) seen as geniuses rather than heroes. (10) The need for contemporary artists to be altogether innovative goes much further than in the case of most other knowledge workers. For the latter, creative variations on an existing theme are allowed and often demanded, while presently for artists this is taboo. Often the art world puts down artists who are not innovative enough or start to 'repeat themselves'. (11) Finally, and

---

become successful shortly after graduating. This phenomenon draws much public attention, but one should keep in mind that the relative number of artists involved is very small, that part of the showing-off is provocative, if not an artistic act, and that it therefore indirectly proves that the image is still one of opposition between dedication to art and commercial success and suspicion of the latter. In this context, it is worth noting that almost all very successful artists who fall in this category do not behave like pop and sport stars, for whom commercial success is altogether okay, and unlike them do not mingle with the jet set. For different opinions, see Graw (2009) and Stallabras (2004).

very importantly, respect for art, and artists, is (still) much higher than that for other creative workers.

Therefore, along with many correspondences, there are also important differences between artists and knowledge workers. Specifically, the combination of precarity and low incomes in the arts, which has already existed for a long time, poses many questions. Given the differences, is it possible that the exploitation of poor artists is, at least partly, of a different nature than that of other knowledge workers? In order to see if this is true a detour is necessary.

3. Rationalization and Bureaucratization Contributed to the High Symbolic Value of Art

A relationship between the low incomes of artists and the high symbolic value of their work exists, which does not exist in related professions. At first glance, low incomes in the arts seem to contradict art's high value: in spite of the high value of art, the majority of artists are poor. But maybe another logic applies: because the symbolic value of art is high, artists are poor. (This would imply that, if the symbolic value of art drops, in due time artists will start to earn more and will be less poor.)

I am talking about symbolic value. Nevertheless, a high financial value both depends on it and contributes to it. The financial value of artwork and art-related objects can be very high. Some artwork costs millions of dollars, while governments and foundations spend huge amounts of money on prestigious new museums and concert halls – think, for instance, of the Louvre museum in Abu Dhabi and the Elbphilharmonie concert hall in Hamburg. Moreover, large sums of money are involved in public and private support. Support signifies the high symbolic value of art. But the typical artist is poor.

High respect for art is related to what has been identified as the 'romantic ethic at the origins of consumerism'.[10] The rationalization, bureaucratization and disenchantment in modernity, which was emphasized by Max Weber, has

---

[10] *The romantic ethic and the spirit of modern consumerism* is the title of a book by Campbell (1987).

been accompanied by the equally significant process of re-enchantment.[11] Already in the 19th century, this romantic ethic went hand in hand with an emphasis on creativity, self-expression and self-discovery. There is a romantic longing and search for individuality and authenticity. However, for 'normal' members of the bourgeoisie, the latter was beyond reach. Artists were the exception. Hence the high respect for art and artists.[12]

Since the middle of the 20th century, this situation has somewhat changed. In people's *perceptions*, not only for artists but also for other knowledge workers and increasingly for everybody, some degree of authenticity and self-realization is attainable. Authenticity has become both a possibility and a necessity. In this context, authenticity refers to that what people *claim* to be authenticity. Therefore, more authenticity does not necessarily imply less alienation. Moreover, in contemporary capitalism, the attainment of such authenticity is only a temporary situation. To remain authentic, there is a need to consume ever-new products which can give people the feeling of being authentic.

But for the time being, artists remain exceptional, in the sense that they are still seen as more authentic in both their work and life. They can better realize themselves. Indeed, when it comes to work, any knowledge worker, even the CEO of a large company, is replaceable. Within a week after his departure, another has taken his place. The newcomer may have a slightly different approach, but the nature of production and the product does not change. However, when an artist dies, no further works will appear in his typical style or with his sometimes very valuable signature. For instance, the death of Karel Appel implied that no more new and genuine 'Appels' were produced.

The postwar democratization of authenticity and of education is not without consequences for the art world. The arts have become more accessible and attractive. When anybody can be authentic, anybody can become an artist, and becoming an artist can be a realistic goal. One can be a successful artist without having to be a genius or an extremely gifted craftsman. Since artists can still realize the goal of self-realization better than

---

[11] Only this can explain the consumer revolution in 18th century England. There can be no capitalism without high consumption – see Campbell (1987).

[12] Cf. the text by Diederichsen in this book.

others, while it is highly appreciated, the arts profession is very attractive. Hence the number of students entering art schools has increased. Presently, in a country like the Netherlands, the number of students admitted to the autonomous departments of art schools is five times higher than it was 40 years ago. [13]

4. Exploitation of Poor Artists is Foremost an Inner Art World Affair

Reasoning like an economist, one could argue that artists have chosen to be poor. They chose to be 'poor and happy'. When deciding to become artists, they imagined that they would be compensated for their low incomes by non-monetary forms of remuneration, like work enjoyment and status. Implicitly, such an opinion follows from thinking in terms of exchange: artists are willingly exchanging money for other rewards. But this is not the way people act. At best, they may somewhat weigh short-term costs and benefits.[14] The assumptions of neo-classical human capital theory are incorrect - artists (and others) certainly do not estimate and weigh lifelong financial income and non-monetary income while taking into account overall costs of, among other things, training. Nevertheless, when we forget about rational choice and look at artists from outside, the notion of compensation or lack of compensation makes sense. I would argue that artists are not compensated for low income. The hardship of artists appears to be real and considerable. In the case of excited young artists, the low income may be somewhat compensated, but only a few years after leaving art school, compensation starts to diminish. Whereas an average lawyer is neither poor nor unsuccessful, the large majority of artists are poor, regard themselves as unsuccessful and are regarded by others as unsuccessful as well. This does not worry starting artists

---

[13] It is true that prosperity has increased at the same time, as perhaps did the demand for some art products. However, since the number of artists was already large and increased even more, this demand did not bring work and income for the large majority of artists.

[14] My thoughts have developed in this direction since I wrote my book *Why are artists poor?* (2002), which was still too much informed by the neo-classical economic perspective.

but, over time, many artists start to consider themselves as failures, even though they will not easily admit this openly.[15]

At the same time, hardship and failure in the arts are essential for the existence and maintenance of the high symbolic value of art, that is, the exceptional prestige of art in society. If artists are so dedicated that they are willing to be poor and possibly fail, something very precious must be at stake. After all, artists appear to sacrifice themselves for this sacred object called art. In the common romantic imagery surrounding the arts people sacrificing their time and money for art and rejecting commerce (still) plays an important role. (And given their low incomes the overall donation artists make to art far exceeds overall private and public support.) The high symbolic value of art is not solely founded on poverty in the arts and the generosity of artists, but poverty certainly is one of its foundations. Without poverty among artists the symbolic value of art would be less high and the association with art would bring less distinction.[16]

Because within this system the labour of artists is structurally used without adequate compensation we can speak of systemic economic exploitation. But this does not imply that a single group can be held responsible for this state of affairs. A system like this, which partly rests on the poverty of many of its participants, is reproduced by everybody involved, including the exploited. In one way or another every group has some interest in its reproduction or at least it believes it has an interest. The 'distinction' the association with art brings does not only go to a well-to-do art establishment or to art lovers in general, it also goes to poor artists. Moreover, given their low income, their rejection of commerce is sometimes more credible than that of other

---

[15] In Abbing (forthcoming) I say more about this and discuss several other forms of hardship. As far as I know, no empirical research on hardship in the arts exists, though it could well be done and should be done. Instead there is much research on success in the arts and on successful artists – a small minority of artists. Evidently researchers are more inclined to do research on the bright side of the arts than on its dark side.

[16] The distinction which the association with art can bring is the main topic of Bourdieu (1984 [1979]).

participants.[17] Usually poor artist as well are aware and proud of their special position. But in the case of poor artists, most of all those who have been poor for quite some time, the symbolic benefits do not take away hardship. At the same time, the costs for people in the establishment or for art lovers are low or absent. Seen from outside, it is the latter who benefit most from the low incomes in the arts.

In any profession similar relations exist and the difference is always a matter of degree. (Priesthood used to be a profession in which the incomes of some were very low, while the net benefits of a few were high.) But compared with most present day professions of knowledge workers requiring a similar level of previous training the difference is very significant. In the latter professions, the symbolic value of the core activity is much lower and thus is the interest in low income. Moreover, seen from the outside, persistently low incomes in such professions are not in the interest of neither professional elites nor capitalists. Flexibility is profitable, but persistently low incomes and poverty are not, at least not in highly industrialized countries.

5. A Wild West Economy Exists in the Arts

Before looking into the mechanisms that sustain the overall system of exploitation in the arts, it is useful to mention some forms of day-to-day exploitation that are enabled by the extreme willingness of passionate artists to work for very low incomes, which can easily be overlooked. This willingness enables a Wild West economy in the arts. There is extreme and unrestrained competition. However, since this goes against the belief in the goodness of art, it remains hidden or is denied and, likewise, artists themselves do not want to see it.

Due to the high value of art, a belief exists in the arts, among artists as well as art institutions, that everything which serves art is good. The slogan is: 'everything for art'. However, the consequence is also an 'anything goes'. Typical artists are ready to give up income and sacrifice a lot to get their works across, also when this way they harm their colleagues who demand

---

[17] Bourdieu (1983) points to the phenomenon that anti-commercial behavior can bring symbolic benefits and in the case of a few participant, it can, in the long run, also bring financial rewards.

proper payment. On the other side, institutional functionaries believe that if their institutions serve art they are justified to offer artists low or no payments at all.

It is telling that this phenomenon does not only exist in commercial art sectors but that non-profit art institutions are also involved. Especially at the level of transactions with poor and unsuccessful artists, the 'everything for art' in the non-profit art sector often leads to severe exploitation of artists. For instance, it is common for non-profits to not pay artists' fees, while for-profit organizations do, although not much. Or non-profit organizations pay ridiculously low fees; but they, *de facto*, let artists pay for being able to perform or show their work by letting them pay for transport, frames, stage-props and so forth; all for art's sake.

Usually poor and unsuccessful (or not yet successful) artists go along with this attitude. When it comes to serving art, they trust that non-profits behave better than for-profit organizations. They also believe in an 'everything-for-art' while, at the same time, they desperately attempt to become noticed; for future income or recognition, but even more for art. Therefore, it is understandable that artists and non-profit organizations often cooperate in keeping costs and income down by paying no, or very low, fees; the initiative for this can come from either side. For instance, a small theater company may approach the director of a non-profit telling him that they understand that he has a limited budget and that therefore they are, of course, willing to play for free if (in exchange) he will include them in his program. Or the director takes the initiative. He really wants the group in his festival. Therefore he explains to them that he has, of course, a very limited budget, but that he is willing to have them on his program and pay part of the transport costs, as long as (in exchange) they do not expect payment. [18, 19]

---

[18] Another explanation for this behavior could be that, in working for low incomes, artists invest in a future in which they will be properly remunerated. Some artists probably believe this is the case or they are made to believe so, and this can partly explain their behavior, but because their chances are so small it is not at all a realistic investment.

[19] It is common that interns get paid less in the arts than elsewhere. Therefore, a similar but less extreme mechanism exists in their case. Because interns have a small but nevertheless much larger chance than artists to become successful and

All such behaviour leads to what can be called unfair competition. For instance, fringe festivals that often behave badly harm non-profit festivals that (try to) behave more decently. Likewise, artists who deliberately take less money than would have been possible harm artists who refuse to do so. In either case, the decent party may be forced to become more indecent or otherwise stop its activities. Another telling but less shocking example are the numerous competitions with no compensation for participating artists, with prizes which only come in the form of some recognition and publicity. Another example is the common practice of inviting artists to offer work or services for free for charity auctions or events. And poor artists are willing to do so. These behaviours also demonstrate the taking advantage of a group (artists) that is already in a weak position.

All this is not to say that the exploitation in the for-profit art sector is less severe. Moreover, there as well it is often somewhat covered up by an 'everything for art' logic. Especially in the relations of for-profits with somewhat successful artists, exploitation can be ruthless. Nevertheless, in day-to-day operations, often standards of proper business behaviour exist which do not exist in the non-profit sector. For instance, in most countries, publishers pay no less than 10% of their whole sale price in royalties. If fiction writers are prepared to accept lower or no royalties, or are willing to pay in order to have their work published, publishing houses generally refuse these arrangements. As always, exceptions do exist, but if they become known, the publisher will be shamed. Another example is that of dealers participating in art fairs. Artists are often prepared to pay part of the cost of the stall if the dealer will exhibit their work at the fair. Going along dealers could pass part of the risk on to the artist. But in most fairs and countries this is not done. And again, violators are shamed.

Art consumers certainly profit from the willingness of passionate artists to work for low incomes. If artists would only work for decent incomes, ticket prices would be higher as would be the average price for visual art. In addition, firms that operate outside the arts take advantage of artists' weak bargaining position. For instance, when the services of both an artist and a graphic designer are required for a project in the cultural industries, generally

---

find comfortable jobs in the arts sector, the investment aspect in their willingness to work for low or no income is larger.

the artist gets paid far less than the graphic designer.[20] However, the weak bargaining position of the artist is not caused by these industries but by the ethos of artists and art institutions, which is reproduced within the art world.

6. An Art Ethos Enables Inner Art World Exploitation

In the arts, commerce is denounced and, if necessary, denied or covered up. An art for art's sake is incompatible with commerce. But it is unlikely that the strong denunciation of commerce in the arts only follows from this. The wish to separate art and entertainment is just as important. In order to derive distinction from one's association with art, a strong boundary between art and entertainment must exist. Since entertainment (including popular art) is commercial, art cannot be commercial. Therefore, an opposite relation exists as well: there is a struggle for autonomy to maintain a boundary between art and entertainment. In the course of the 19th century, in the US, simultaneous processes of classification, isolation and framing vested this boundary. People were taught what was art and what was not; art increasingly was to be consumed in special venues; and people learned the 'civilized conducts' required for art consumption. In post-aristocratic times in Europe, the previously existing boundary was reproduced, modified and strengthened. The belief that art is not entertainment, and must not be entertainment, remains strong .[21]

Art is not entertainment and therefore commerce in the arts is denounced, while a strong dedication to art and a striving for a maximum of autonomy is promoted or even required of artists. Beliefs and moral convictions – for example: that art is not entertainment, commerce in the arts is bad and autonomy and dedication to art are good – are all part of a more encompassing art ethos that is produced and reproduced throughout society. For instance, almost anybody will agree that artists must not compromise, that success may come late and that poverty in the arts is okay (even though it may not be okay in the case of individual older artists). Meanwhile, at the

---

[20] Habenundbrauchen (2012) presents other examples of exploitation of poor artists by for-profits.

[21] In fact in their critique of the 'culture industry', left wing people like Adorno and Horkheimer (2002) de facto reinforced this demand.

level of art education, additional moral convictions are installed and reproduced. As professional logics they become part of the mindset of artists. At this level, the conviction that dedicated artists must try to make work that is as autonomous as possible is particularly important. In addition, the notion that, if necessary, artists must be willing to work for very low incomes, for the sake of art, is part of the ethos. Depending on art form or style, other examples can be that artists must connect to existing traditions in their work, that art is complex, that people do not appreciate good art, and so forth.

Nowadays, there is a small but growing number of artists who try to operate differently by striving for various goals at the same time like serving a larger audience, local communities or political goals, and so forth. Heteronomy replaces autonomy. But these more entrepreneurial and market oriented artists who, after a brief period of investment, are no longer willing to work for very low incomes and who care less about the boundary between art and entertainment, are regarded with suspicion and put down as commercial not only by artists making art for the art's sake but also by critical artists. Nevertheless, the increase in the number of these kinds of artists may well signify an increasing uneasiness with the 'everything for art' mentality in the arts. These artists do not see themselves as an avant-garde in the resistance against the existing system of exploitation in the arts, nor are they regarded as such by critical artists, but, seen from outside, they do represent a real threat to the system. However, instead of being acknowledged for this, critical artists with their anti-commercial stance tend to criticise them.

7. Strategies of Resistance

Important differences in the causes of the exploitation of poor artists and of other knowledge workers and in the ways they are exploited exist. This has consequences for strategies of resistance. For instance, the promotion of a new art ethos, which allows or even encourages the pursuit of non-artistic goals as well, like reaching a larger audience, striving for political change and making a profit, and more generally a more entrepreneurial attitude among artists, could well represent an important form of resistance against exploitation in the arts while, in other sectors of knowledge production, this could be a giving way to neo-liberalism, which only serves the interests of capitalists.

I think that, in any case, it is essential that critical artists and art theorists who want to fight against exploitation in the arts should revise their negative attitude towards moderate forms of entrepreneurship and a pursuit of profit in the arts, certainly if it concerns artist, since they anyway run small enterprises. Although there is no capitalism without a market economy and commerce, the opposite does not apply.[22] Moreover, the pursuit of non-artistic goals including the making of profit, and thus operating actively in markets, does not have to go together with an uncritical embrace of the notion of private property. Specifically, the fight against the increasing privatization of public space, in which artists often play a role today, probably strikes at a cornerstone of capitalism (see Habenundbrauchen, 2012).

In this context, it is useful to assume that various constraints which come with so much feared heteronymous influences on the process of art making, can stimulate rather then hinder genuine creativity. For instance, the self-imposed constraint of getting one's art across to an audience wider than only a small group of primarily peers and people within an art world elite can well enhance creativity and innovation. In this respect, artists can learn from popular artists. The former could also make an effort to work within the popular arts more often. It could prove more rewarding and challenging than participating in Documenta and alike, even if the exhibitions feature critical art. The curators of such events *de facto* misuse critical art to celebrate art in general and to safeguard the existing privileged positions.

What matters in the struggle against exploitation in the arts is not a noncommittal adherence to social criticism, but concrete action. A good example of the latter is the certification of art institutions that pay proper fees to artists. If they don't, they run the risk of being shamed and, as a consequence, their reputation is tarnished. Presently in New York, the artist's coalition W.A.G.E. actively and successfully pursues a gratification scheme of visual art non-profit organizations.[23] Gradually, certification could be

---

[22] Moreover, one has to keep in mind that capitalism alternatively promotes and opposes a free market economy. A succession of periods with large-scale free trade and with large-scale monopolization and the restriction of trade by legal power is characteristic of capitalism.

[23] See http://www.wageforwork.com. Art Leaks (http://art-leaks.org/) is a somewhat comparable initiative that aims at exposing bad practices in the arts

extended to for-profit organizations, from galleries to commercial festivals. These and other concrete actions may well contribute to the gradual installment of standards of proper business behaviour, also among non-profit organizations who presently appear to believe that, for art, 'anything goes'.[24]

Most importantly, it would be useful for artists to develop a professional ethos and a mindset that prohibits working for ridiculously low incomes. They should increasingly refuse to do so and make clear to their customers and intermediaries, including art institutions, galleries and impresarios, that if they underpay artists, they can no longer count on their services. Since this often goes against the short-term interest of individual artists, it would, indeed, require a different mind set and practices and new forms of solidarity.

However, the main causes of the artist's continually precarious and exploited condition rest in art education. Here, the detrimental 'everything for art' mentality of artists is (re)produced. In order to change this situation, the mindset of teachers has to change fundamentally. Less emphasis on autonomy and an art for the sake of art and more on the possibility and attractiveness of having multiple goals is essential. (So far, the new curricula for instruction in cultural entrepreneurship primarily enable other teachers – the majority – to carry on in the old way.)

As far as public cultural policies are concerned, we would need less emphasis on '*excellence*' in the arts. There is sufficient interest in art that is supposed to be of very high quality. Government policies (and government money) promoting excellence among a small group of usually already successful artists primarily serve international cultural competition. Because it puts art for which there is little public demand on a footstall, it encourages artists to make also such art, and this is not in the interest of the average artist.

More importantly, public support for institutions and initiatives which guide artists in their attempts to broaden their field of activities is called for.

---

and at shaming of the institutions involved. The London based Precarious Workers Brigade (www.precariousworkersbrigade.tumblr.com) is also active in this area.

24 Certification works better than formal government regulation, because regulation is experienced as just another legal obligation, while both parties willingly and actively take part in certification.

In this context, it is important that the status of activities in the sphere of community art, activities with amateurs, in prisons, in public space, in therapy and so forth becomes higher and comparable with art as it is traditionally provided. There are not necessarily too many artists, when the definition of art and artwork becomes wider and artists are prepared to offer their labour in markets that were traditionally not regarded as art markets.[25]

I think that at the moment professionalization and the development of more entrepreneurial attitudes among poor artists (i.e. the majority) is a good thing; and government supported institutions as already exist in some countries can help artists in this. Being down to earth and developing an entrepreneurial and even somewhat commercial attitude can well be regarded as an act of resistance against the existing art-regime. Artists should not always be altogether dedicated to art and attempt to be as autonomous as possible. They should allow themselves to have non-artistic goals as well, including the making of some profit. However, this certainly does not imply that I propose a maximum of commercialization or privatization in the arts sector. On the contrary, striving for the continuation or establishment of public spaces where there is room for relatively autonomous art (including popular art!) is also a form of resistance; not only resistance against the exploitation within the art world itself, but also against the excrescences of capitalism.

---

[25] Nevertheless, at present a temporary decrease in the number of students of art academies and conservatories may be needed to improve the bad situation of artists.

7

Labour, Emancipation and the Critique of Craft-Skill

John Roberts

The relationship between labour practices and craft-skill has once again become a topic of considerable importance, in the light of recent reflections on the growth of immaterial labour within certain sectors of the global economy (immaterial labour here being defined as labour that produces the creative informational content of a commodity, or labour that involves the routine processing and distribution of information within primary production or the service economy) insofar as both kinds of immaterial labour, creative and routine, have 'intellectualized' various aspects of manual and non-manual labour processes. Indeed, for Maurizio Lazzarato (1996), Toni Negri (Hardt and Negri, 2000), and Luc Boltanski and Eve Chiapello (2005) – to name the most prominent contributors to the debate – under these new conditions there has been a demonstrable increase in the cognitive and affective content of various sectors of the labour process across the productive and non-productive labour divide. This is partly to do with the vast extension of computers into the workplace, but also the reorganization of labour-management relations horizontally in response to the need for prompt, effective and creative solutions to problems at the point of production and distribution. Thus, in the 'new creative' sectors of the economy – which in many ways have been driving technological change at the point of production since the early 1990s – some aspects of the new workplace appear closer to the freedoms of artistic production than they do to customary forms of bureaucratic and top-down exchange between management and workers.

Among these transformations, particularly significant are the shared, processual involvement in autonomous activities, and the open engagement and dialogue with others in order to initiate a project or resolve a given problem. As Lazzarato argues, these new conditions require that workers combine 'the results of various different types of work skill: intellectual skills, as regards the cultural-informational content; manual skills for the ability to combine creativity, imagination, and technical and manual labour; and entrepreneurial skills in the management of social relations and the structuring of that social cooperation of which they are a part' (Lazzarato, 1996: 137). Similarly, according to Negri, in retail and sales, and the new public services, the expansion of the affective aspects of non-productive labour – the qualitative increase in customer, client or patient care or attention – make the older bureaucratic forms of provision crude and inelastic. Negri makes two interrelated political points on the basis of these would-be changes. With the rise in processual skills and affective skills immaterial workers are able to *share* a skill base across the sectional divisions between productive and non-productive labour. However limited this sharing may be, the 'computer' as a facilitator of social exchange comes to operate in an unprecedented way as a universal tool within the labour process, allowing workers to establish greater and more flexible forms of interaction and support across sectional divisions than was hitherto possible. Indeed, Negri goes as far as saying that the nascent democracy provided by the incorporation of sections of the labour process into the new digital network culture possess an immanent proto-communist content (Hardt and Negri, 2000).

This debate on immaterial labour clearly revives, admittedly in a highly provocative fashion, the classical debate on the alienation of labour. In a tendentious rejection of the Marxist (and even social democratic) tradition, Lazzarato, Negri and Boltanski and Chiapello argue that these changes in the labour process weaken the usual picture of the worker as subject to the dissolution or fragmentation of his or her skills as a result of the refinement and increased specialization of the technical division of labour. On the contrary, workers in the new creative industries, retail industries and public services, provide what in fact is another picture of the industrial worker: the immaterially *re-skilled* worker. In this respect it is Negri who pushes the 'transformatory' potential of the new labour processes the furthest, claiming that given that many of the immaterial skills operative in the workplace are extendable and adaptable outside of the workplace, new forms of worker autonomy and resistance are emerging within a new work/life continuum (Hardt and Negri, 2004).

Now, Negri's wholly sanguine account of the immaterial worker has rightly come in for a great deal of criticism. The number of workers that fall under this category globally is relatively low, meaning that his political optimism is highly skewed in relation to the overall dynamic of the world economy. In addition, the idea that immaterial workers are not subject to the same forms of routinization and surveillance as traditional industrial workers is a fantasy, borne of a familiar ideological over-investment in emerging forms of technology. The new horizontal forms of network management only stretch so far, so to speak, and only under highly specialized, 'blue-skies' conditions. Yet in reply to his critics, Negri defends his views from an orthodox Marxist position: the rise of the immaterial worker is only a *tendency*, based on an analysis of the most advanced sectors of the economy globally, precisely the method adopted by Marx in the *Grundrisse* and *Capital*. As Marx asserts: 'In all forms of society there is one specific form of production which predominates over the rest, whose relations assign rank and influence to the others' (Marx, 1973: 106-107).

When Marx was writing *Capital* there were more workers engaged in service in Britain than there were in the emerging factory system, but this didn't mean that Marx was therefore best advised to focus on service workers. The emerging tendency was the rapid growth of wage labour within the big factories: it was this that reflected the deeper dynamic of the system. Similarly, the transition from feudalism to capitalism is best understood by focusing on the emergence of wage labour in the fledgling urban guild system (specifically Florence and Genoa) rather than on the majority of workers, who were landless serfs and tenants still working on the land. These new forms of wage-labour were eventually to have a profoundly transformative effect on class relations (in particular the movement of labourers from one job, one city, to the next)[1], and on technological development in the

---

[1] There was, of course, a comparable movement in the countryside in the 14th and beginning of the 15th century in England, as free tenants moved from their place of birth and took up available plots of land, made increasingly available after the

fourteenth century. The guilds, as Steven A. Epstein (1991: 230) puts it, 'incubated' technological development, insofar as they offered a basic institutional framework for generating and sustaining innovation. 'Masters were able to enforce work rules and methods in their shops, and so they could make their employees adopt new techniques' (*ibid.*: 247). Thus wages paid in the city had a qualitatively different set of expectations and outcomes than wages paid in the countryside. Wages in the city encouraged the division of labour, and with it the development and transmission of technical and artisanal knowledge.[2] With the increased movement from the countryside to the cities in the fourteenth century there is, accordingly, no evidence that the compulsory labour practices of feudal manorial estates found any footholds in the handicrafts or trades.

So Negri's defence is admittedly not without certain orthodox credentials, and as such possesses a certain conviction. But at the same time, he drops from view what has remained crucial to labour process theory from Marx to Harry Braverman: in what ways is the improvement or amelioration of the conditions under which workers labour representative of substantive changes in the conditions of workers as such? In what ways do such transformations – here, immaterial and affective changes – contribute to, or allow us to re-think, the emancipation of labour generally? Now, historically this question of labour's emancipation has been tied to a normative, or at least an ideal, evaluation of labour under various modes of production: classical slave labour, feudal villeinage, and capitalist free market labour. How might the labourer best labour, with what tools and materials and under what terms and conditions? And, accordingly, what elements of these three modes of production are best able to contribute to these possibilities?

The debate within the Marxist and Romantic anti-capitalist traditions has tended to focus, therefore, on what has been lost or devalued in the transition from the classical mode of production and feudalism to capitalism. In what

---

plague, by lapsed tenancies, in response to the demand for labour for the market in rural areas close to towns or cities, such as East Anglia with its strong connections to London (Hilton, 1969).

2   One of the great examples of this transmission process handed down to us is Cennino d'Andrea Cennini's (c1370-c1440) *The Craftsman's Handbook*, written in Florence, most likely in the early 15th century (Cennini, 1960).

ways does capitalism destroy the craft-integrity of certain kinds of productive labour? For Marx, this loss of craft-integrity in the transition from feudalism to capitalism may reveal the limitations of industrialized labour in the struggle for the emancipation of labour, but it cannot in itself answer the broader question attached to the emancipation of labour itself: what forms might the freely determined content of non-alienated labour actually take? For Marx the question of what is lost in the transition from feudalism to capitalism, is not, therefore, the whole story. This is because – contrary to Romantic anti-capitalism – craft-integrity is only one aspect of non-alienated labour. Let us look in more detail then at the status of the medieval craftsman, because it will offer us greater clarification around the issue of the alienation of labour today.

Craft-Integrity

To reiterate: reflections on the medieval craftsman in the Marxist and Romantic anti-capitalist tradition largely begin from the same premise. Although the classical mode of production and feudal villeinage share a reliance on various forms of coerced labour, the craftworker and artisan under feudalism are held to exhibit an extraordinary and admirable convergence between their skills and their social role. As Marx and Engels argue in *The German Ideology* [1846], in the medieval period:

> The limited intercourse and the weak ties between the individual towns, the lack of population and the narrow needs did not allow of a more advanced division of labour, and therefore every man who wished to become a master had to be proficient in the whole of his craft. Medieval craftsmen therefore had an interest in their special work and in proficiency in it, which was capable of rising to a limited artistic sense. For this very reason, however, every medieval craftsman was completely absorbed in his work, to which he had a complacent servile relationship, and in which he was involved to a far greater extent than the modern worker, whose work is a matter of indifference to him. (Marx and Engels, 1976: 66)

In other words, because the medieval craftsman is assumed to identify his craft skills fully with a given task, his labour is held to be fundamentally unalienated. In the same way, the Romantic anti-capitalism of John Ruskin and the Romantic Marxism of William Morris both offer a highly garlanded interpretation of this medieval worker, as the fount of integrated creativity.

As Ruskin declares in *The Stones of Venice* (1854b), the Christian medieval craftsmen who built and ornamented the great Gothic cathedrals possessed a rough skill that was in harmony with their capacities.

> The Greek gave to the lower workman no subject which he could not perfectly execute. The Assyrian gave him subjects which he could only execute imperfectly, but fixed a legal standard for his imperfection. The workman was, in both systems, a slave. But in the medieval, or especially Christian, system of ornament, this slavery is done away with altogether; Christianity having recognized, in small things as well as great, the individual value of every soul [...] And it is, perhaps, the principal admirableness of Gothic schools of architecture, that they thus receive the results of the labour of inferior minds; and out of the fragments full of imperfection, and betraying that imperfection in every touch, indulgently raise up a stately and unaccusable whole. (Ruskin 1854a: 6-7)

And as Morris explains in *Signs of Change* [1888]:

> the medieval craftsman was free in his work, therefore he made it as amusing to himself as he could; and it was his pleasure and not his pain that made all things beautiful that were made, and lavished treasures of human hope and thought on everything that man made, from cathedral to a porridge-pot. (Morris, 2007)

Admittedly, Morris did not believe such freedom was undetermined by the violence of medieval society: the Church and State 'repressed art in certain directions' (Morris, 2007). Yet even so, for Morris, the medieval craftsman took direct and unalloyed pleasure from his work.

It is no surprise therefore, that the notion of the medieval craftsman determining the quality of his labour at the point of production becomes one of the key determinants of the debate on the emancipation of labour in the second half of the nineteenth century, as wage labour becomes massively concentrated in a narrow range of routinized, dangerous and oppressive occupations in the new factories and extractive industries. Marx, Ruskin, and Morris all deferred to some version of this vision of 'integrated labour', in order to open up an imaginative gap between would be bourgeois progress and other modes of production. But if all three shared a view of the medieval craftsman as 'unalienated', for Marx this 'unalienated' status is highly *delimited* in its freedoms, something that Morris and the Romantic anti-capitalists overlook or dismiss. Indeed, in an interesting Hegelian transcription of the problem of craft-integrity, in *The German Ideology* Marx and Engels invert the would-be unfreedom of the industrial wage-labourer into something quite different to its image in Romantic anti-capitalism. The medieval craftsman may provide evidence of craft-integrity and he may take pleasure from his endeavours, but this is because he is unable to imagine alternatives to his present condition, or if he is able to do so, to freely act on them (Marx and Engels, 1976). The 'admirable convergence', therefore, between the craftsman's skills and his social role is evidence, in fact, of a conspicuous lack: the ability of the worker to reflect on the outcomes of his labour as the result of his freedom as free economic agent. Hence Marx finds a hidden freedom in the formal freedom of the alienated, industrial worker under capitalism: that is, his or her capacity to *disidentify* with his role as worker, and therefore imagine his labour and creativity as distinct from the coercions of wage-labour. This is a kind of freedom *in* alienation, because although the worker is separated from the integral skills that the medieval craftsman takes for granted – losing as a result his secure place in the collectivity of labour – at the same time he or she is able to envisage themselves as freely determined individual. Consequently, from the fourteenth-century guilds to the nineteenth-century factory system, the coercions of wage-labour provide the wider conditions of labour's emancipation: in short, the eventual release and development of intellectual self-determination and creative singularity. Thus, if under capitalism the emergence of individuality progresses through the conditions of self-alienation, under communism or post-capitalism, individuality is secured through the subject's free and fulfilled engagement in his or her daily labours. But this classical reading of the development of free labour of course raises more questions than answers. Indeed it raises a number of questions that Marx himself in his later writings was unable to answer, or found far more troubling than he first imagined, when he argued in *The German Ideology* that under communism, the freely determined labourer would hunt in the morning, fish in the afternoon, rear cattle in the evening, and criticize after dinner.

Firstly, how do we square the massive and systematic tendency within capitalism to create forms of unsatisfying work with the creative possibilities of 'freedom in alienation'? As Harry Braverman argued in *Labor and Monopoly Capital* [1974]: 'The capitalist mode of production systematically destroys all-round skills where they exist, and brings into being skills and occupations that correspond to its needs. Technical capacities are henceforth distributed on a strict "need to know" basis' (Braverman, 1998: 57). As a result, how does the vast landscape of alienated, deskilled labour under capitalism prepare a transition to actual forms of self-directed, unalienated labour? What conditions, resources and relations are currently in place in the labour process that would make this transition a realistic possibility, or not? In other words, how might the transition to a new mode of production *support* unalienated labour for all, given the fact that under capitalism labour is alienated mostly for all?

Necessary Labour and Craft-Integrity

This is a question that is rarely addressed these days, although it has a rich, if fragmented history, in anti-technicist thinking within the Marxist tradition in the 20th century (Rosa Luxemburg, Walter Benjamin, the Soviet Productivists Alexsei Gan and Boris Arvatov, Raniero Panzieri, Theodor Adorno, André Gorz). For this tradition a new mode of production has above all else to qualitatively transform the forces and relations of production, not just enhance productivity, efficiency and technical expertise. That is, the decisions, operational plans and targets, have to incorporate processes and outcomes that are creatively self-directed, individually and collectively. The *poiesis* of artistic production remains, as in Romantic anti-capitalism, as much as in early Marx and Negri, the key to this vision. In the absence of market discipline and production-for-profit, the vicissitudes of necessary labour are dissolved through democratic and non-instrumentally achieved ends. As Gan and Arvatov argued in the 1920s, the worker becomes an artist, and the artist becomes a worker. Hence in this model of unalienated labour artistic labour doesn't just converge with productive labour; it *redirects* it (Gan, 1988).

The actuality of this redirection, however, remains highly attenuated. The Productivists in their artist-in-factory experiments in the 1920s soon realised that the collaborative initiatives of artists in factories and, as such, the possibility of workers becoming artists – even under a fledgling revolutionary regime – were subject to the instrumental demands of the productive process itself. The call that the Productivists made to artists to train as engineers became precisely that, dissolving the aleatory aspects of artistic production into the disciplinary requirements of necessary labour. From an opposite perspective Morris' development of a model of unalienated labour based on

the craft-integrity of the medieval period, could only be truly operational –
that is generalisable – *outside* of mass production in a modern economy. Inside
the economy it would be technically retarded and thus wholly impractical.
Unalienated labour on this basis is something the worker possesses and
develops in his or her own, leisure time. Similarly, Adorno's model of
liberated labour is confined in the abstract – as a kind of ideal horizon – to
the labour of the artwork itself. There is no actual process of mediation
between this autonomous labour and the vicissitudes of productive labour
(Adorno, 2007). And again, Gorz offers a liberated model of labour
independent from, and indeed in opposition to, the realities of the labour
process: under conditions of structural unemployment, extended part-time
work, and the increased routinizations of productive and non-productive
labour, the liberation of labour is best conceived outside of labour itself
(Gorz, 1985). In this light, Negri is actually quite right to describe himself as a
classical Marxist, insofar as he retains the possibility that the emancipation of
labour will come about *through* the immanent transformation of labour itself.
(Thus, the integration of network culture into the labour process is a
continuing indication of how capitalism produces and reproduces the
conditions of 'freedom in alienation' and as such produces new forms of
alienated singularity; from inside the routinizations of the new digital culture
new and creative skills are born). But how 'classical', in fact, is Marx himself
in this respect? That is, Marx may in *The German Ideology* talk about the
'freedom in alienation' of waged labour under capitalism, as a precursor to the
emancipation of labour under communism, but in his later writing he is less
sanguine about 'artistic labour' shifting or unburdening the strictures of
necessary labour. In volume 3 of *Capital*, the ontology of necessary labour
asserts itself:

> … the realm of freedom actually begins only where labour which is
> determined by necessity and mundane considerations ceases; thus in the very
> nature of things it lies beyond the sphere of actual material production. Just as
> the savage must wrestle with nature to satisfy his wants, to maintain and
> reproduce life, so must civilized man and he must do so in all social
> formations and under all possible modes of production. With his
> development this realm of physical necessity expands as a result of his wants;
> but at the same time, the forces of production, which satisfy these wants also
> increase. Freedom in this field can only consist in socialized man, the
> associated producers, rationally regulating their interchange with Nature,
> bringing it under their common control, instead of being ruled by it as by the

blind forces of Nature; and achieving this with the least expenditure of energy and under conditions most favourable to, and worthy of, their human nature. *But it nonetheless still remains a realm of necessity* (Marx, 1972: 820, emphasis added).

Now this is a less than optimistic view of the transformative or corrective powers of artistic process – or craft-integrity – on the labour process. Indeed, as the last line makes clear, because all economic systems are ultimately reliant on necessary labour, none can support unalienated labour for all, all the time, particularly in the light of having to meet the daily needs of hundreds of millions of people. Rather, unalienated labour is, in the end, that which is supplemental to productive labour, what is, in short, pursued through independent leisure.

This, however, is not evidence of a political retreat secreted at the end of Marx's labours on the capitalist system. There is nothing to suggest in *Capital* that anything short of the ending of private property and the dissolution of the value-form will release humanity from the burdens of capitalism's recurring and chronic crises. But these late reflections do represent a shift away from Marx's early Schillerian Romanticism that he shares with his Romantic anti-capitalist peers, insofar as he appears here to be stressing that not all forms of labour will be subject to aesthetic redemption – nor, more importantly, should they be. How might artistic process redirect street cleaning, animal slaughter, garbage disposal and sewage maintenance, the care of the elderly and a hundred other difficult, demanding or unpalatable activities? Thus, in the above passage, collective control over nature and the productive process is quite separate from the control and reduction of necessary labour, which is irreducible. The irreducibility of necessary labour then blocks the full entry of unalienated labour into the labour process, in as much as certain kinds of labour are instrumentally determined by pre-given outcomes and fixed processes, and as such are non-aestheticizable. Marx doesn't discuss the implications of this blockage. In fact, it appears that he does not consider such implications at all, leaving the early Romantic model in political and philosophical abeyance (this is why when the subject of emancipation and labour comes up, the famous quote about hunting and fishing from *The German Ideology* tends to be revived, and not the quote from *Capital* vol. 3).

Yet the consequences of this later passage are clear enough – underwritten by suggestive comments on the emancipation of labour elsewhere in Marx's writing. In a system freed of the hierarchical and competitive demands of the value-form the universalization of unalienated labour will, nonetheless, experience its own limitations and constraints. That is, there will remain forms of labour that will be impervious to the de-alienation of labour, and remain so. Now, this is not to say that certain tasks and processes in certain sectors of the productive economy will not be opened up to 'artistic' skills and decisions, or that previously unaestheticizable activities will become aestheticized, but many tasks inside and outside the productive base will not. This will set up a very different temporalization of labour than under the unilinear directives of the value-form. Firstly, access to unalienated labour, as primary labour, will be displaced from traditional patterns of career structure allowing those engaged in forms of necessary labour to share in this work, after relevant training. Indeed, the switch over from necessary labour to unalienated labour, and back again, will constitute the re-temporalization of labour generally. And secondly, this re-temporalization means that by requiring that all contribute at some level to the demands of necessary labour, necessary labour is removed from its inherited subordinate position within the system of unalienated labour as a whole.

Under a system of use-values divorced from productivity for profit, necessary labour may provide something like 'alienation *in* freedom'. That is, workers may actually take pleasure from the disproportionate exertions of necessary labour, knowing that their labours are contributing to the primary reproduction of the new society, and the generation of new use values. This is not as utopian as it may first seem. For, as Marx recognised, not all alienated labour can be dissociated from pleasure. Indeed, if there was not pleasure to be had from all kinds of freely alienated labour under capitalism, capitalism would not be able to secure the continuing adherence that it does. A post-capitalist system will need to draw such adherence to the pleasures of alienation, as an important source of transformative energy for those workers involved in maintaining the forward movement of the new system.

On this basis, therefore, the emancipation of labour is only tangentially related to the reconstitution of craft processes within the labour process. Certainly, the exercise of traditional craft processes implies a very different kind of work rhythm and control over material, of hand to machine, than the discipline of the factory and office. As such, for many the reconstitution of craft-integrity requires a reconstitution of the non-linear temporal order of the early and late medieval period. Henri Lefebvre's (2000) critique of capitalist time certainly draws on this connection, as does the pre-modern pastoralism of the potter Bernard Leach (1940), who placed a high value on handwork in his reflections on the emancipation of labour. But it is not the distended labour of the crafts that is able to drive the wider dynamic of labour emancipation. What is of greater importance is the *control and disposal of time as such*, and it is this in the end that has the greater efficacy in Marx's writing. The emancipation of labour is not about winning back for the labour process the 'unalienated' labour of the medieval craftsman, but about winning control over the labour process itself, in order to reorganize production in the interests of securing the benefits of autonomous labour, where possible inside the labour process, and correspondingly, in the interests of expanding freely determined leisure time.

In these terms, the re-temporalization of labour expands the quality of, and reduces the length of, the working day. Moreover, this produces a further qualitative change in the relations between the labour process/necessary labour and freely directed activities. The boundaries between work and life are recalibrated – which clearly has echoes of Negri's reflections on the recent expansion of immaterial labour: skills developed freely outside of the labour process find a place of value in the labour process, just as skills developed in the labour process find a new home or value outside of the labour process. Yet, if this generates a liberated continuum between labour and freely determined activities, freely determined activities are precisely that: they are not the liberated home *of* labour, but the space where intellectual and artisanal activities are advanced without preconceptions. Thus, the realm of freely determined activities may, in fact, be the space where all images of productivity, intellectual, immaterial, or creative, are laid to rest. There is nothing to presuppose that the autonomous labours of the industrious artist will be the only model of emancipated labour developed outside of the 'unalienated labour' and necessary labour of the labour process. Outside of the labour process human activities may have no charge and ambition other than the cultivation of laziness or one's garden or the development of life skills: of caring for others, of talking and listening, of noting and taking pleasure from nature.

So where exactly does the ideal of craft-integrity sit within an emancipatory model of labour? For a hundred and fifty years this ideal has taken the form of an alternative or counter productivity to the one embedded in capitalist rationality. In the artisanal labour of the craftsman or craftswomen the elemental attributes of human creativity are supposedly laid bare. This is because, it is argued, the craftsperson exhibits a kind of perfected, or at least highly developed, expressive control over his or her materials. Accordingly, capitalism is held to be the very antithesis of the image of this self-discipline; or rather, very few people engaged in wage labour under capitalism achieve, or are in position to achieve, the requisite levels of concentration, repetitive discipline, and patience to master a craft. As Richard Sennett puts it, the ideal of craft-integrity is best defined as a 'temporary suspension of the desire for closure' (Sennett, 2008: 221). This is why capitalism is so time-poor. It expands the realm of labour (of wage-labour) yet reduces the capacity of the majority *to* labour – that is freely labour – hence the centrality, historically, of the time-rich craftsman to the critique of this sense of closure. Yet, as I have argued, seeing the reconstitution of craft-integrity in material or immaterial forms as the primary answer to this temporal-poverty is misconceived, because to focus on the loss of craft-skill under capitalism is to reduce the re-temporalisation of the capitalist labour process simply to a matter of reconstituted craft-skill, as if craft-skill itself will heal the vicissitudes of alienated labour. Whereas, in fact, the emancipation of labour needs to be seen as the outcome of a more fundamental shift: *a control over time (of productive time) as such.* Sennett, then, in the manner of much Romantic anti-capitalism, enforces a split between craft-time – what he calls 'slow craft time' (Sennett, 2008: 295) – and the control over productive labour and necessary labour; craft-skills and the labour process do not connect in any transformative sense. The point is not that the development of craft-skill is unable to secure us some freely determined time and, as such, some respite from the alienations of capitalist time, but that there is no truly freely determined time without control over productive time as a whole.

In conclusion, then, the Romantic anti-capitalist defenders of artisanal craft-skills have tended to lose sight of this distinction, fetishizing artisanal skills as the corner stone of the emancipation of labour and the critique of alienation. Similarly, Negri's model of immaterial labour tends to fetishize 'intellectual craft' at the expense of the worker's alienation and the temporal discipline of the value process. This is why there are losses and gains from his adaptation of Marx's model of 'freedom in alienation'. By arguing that new skills emerge through the new forms of intellectual and immaterial labour, he rejects the notion that capitalism destroys all forms of craft integrity. The qualitative expansion of the immaterial content of labour, for Negri, actually reconceptualises and redefines the notion of craft skill, in keeping with the changes in the relations of production since the 1960s: the increased scientific and technical inputs into the labour process. But this model is delimited because of the *over*-valorisation of these new forms of labour. Given that immaterial labour is not a separate part of the labour process and therefore is indivisible from material labour (from the wider constraints of the value-form), it is subject to the same pressures of routinization as factory work and the service industries. Consequently, claims about the broader devaluation of workers' skills across the system as a whole, and the alienation of both the new knowledge worker *and* manual worker, lose their critical leverage. And without these claims there is no sense of a temporality beyond the reach of capital. Accordingly, the development of new creative inputs into labour is not the answer to the systematic alienation of labour, even if a privileged minority of knowledge workers – the 'creative class' – have benefited from this shift, and at some level do match Negri's and others' view of the post-Fordist labour process as an enhanced model of communication and organization for workers at the point of production. But only a minority of knowledge-workers benefit from these new processes of creative self-valorization. There are two interrelated issues at stake therefore: firstly, there is no integral model of craft to be won back from the labour process; and secondly, whether immaterial labour is tendential or systemic, its creative expansion cannot fundamentally alter the downward pressures of capitalist time and the value-form.

PART THREE:
THE CONTEMPORARY FORMS OF EXPLOITATION

8

Slavery, Contemporary Forms of Exploitation and Their Temporalities

Massimiliano Tomba

If there is a way to comprehend the phenomenon which today goes under the name of globalisation, it certainly involves the assumption that the distinction between the first, second and third worlds has been overcome. The inadequacy of a whole way of reasoning in terms of tendency and residue is now so obvious that one cannot disagree with the severe judgement of Chakrabarty when he affirms that to speak of a 'survival of an earlier mode of production' means to reason with 'stagist and elitist conceptions of history'. Disagreeing with theories of 'uneven development', he maintains that it is historicist to consider 'Marx's distinction between "formal" and "real" subsumption of labour [...] as a question of historical transition' (Chakrabarty, 2000: 12-14, 261, footnote 37). But the same critique is also valid for many Marxisms, including one of the most intelligent theoretical and political traditions of European Marxism: *l'operaismo* (workerism). This tradition, which started from the perspective of the political centrality of the mass worker (*operaio massa*), went on to consider industrial labour as secondary and residual in that, according to Negri's recent writings, we live 'in a society characterised ever more strongly by the hegemony of immaterial labour' (Negri, 1998: 8). Rejecting the law of value, Negri worked on an extension of the notion of productive labour, which comes tendentially to coincide with wage labour. In order to overcome the law of value, Negri pushed Marx beyond Marx: the *Grundrisse*'s greatest insight, according to Negri, is in the analysis of the 'Fragment on machines' in which he expressed the 'necessary tendency of capital' towards the subsumption of the entire society (*ibid.*: 170; Bellofiore and Tomba, 2009: 407-431). At this point, Negri affirms, 'the capitalist appropriation of society is complete' (1998: 173). Negri follows Marx enthusiastically when Marx writes that 'production based on exchange-value falls'; for Negri, it is a case of the 'impossibility of the measure of exploitation', of the 'emptying out of the theory of value' (*ibid.*: 178). The evacuation of the 'theory of value' – a term which is not Marx's – from every element of comparison transforms it into 'pure and simple command, a pure and simple form of politics' (*ibid.*). Because value would no longer be measurable, 'the theory of surplus-value, in its centrality, eliminates any scientific claim to centralization and of domination conceived from inside the theory of value' (*ibid.*: 30).

That interpretation overrated some parts of the *Grundrisse* that become an 'extraordinary theoretical anticipation of mature capitalist society', where Marx tells us that 'capitalist development leads to a society in which industrial workers' labour (insofar as immediate labour) is now only a secondary element in the organisation of capitalism'. When capitalism has subsumed the society, 'productive labour becomes intellectual, cooperative, immaterial labour' (*ibid.*: 7). The consequence that Negri draws is clear: 'we live today in a society evermore characterised by the hegemony of immaterial labour' (*ibid.*: 7–8). If, on the one hand, according to Negri, 'all forms of labor are today socially productive [...] there is [nevertheless] always one figure of labor that exerts hegemony over the others' (Hardt and Negri, 2004: 106-107). Thus the industrial labour of the nineteenth and twentieth century has lost its hegemony and, in the last decades of the twentieth century, 'immaterial labour' has emerged in its place (*ibid.*: 108). The general intellect becomes 'hegemonic in capitalist production', 'immaterial and cognitive labour become immediately productive' and the 'cognitariat' becomes the 'fundamental productive force that makes the system work': the new hegemonic figure (Negri, 2006: 167, 183-184).

I wanted to sketch out this interpretation, because it is representative of a historicist and Eurocentric perspective on global capitalism. In order to avoid surrendering to these historicist equations, according to which the industrial working-class today stands in the same relation to immaterial labour as the peasantry did to the industrial working-class in the nineteenth century, it is necessary to follow the chains of valorisation that, with delocalisation, not only exit the factory but cross national frontiers, and thus the salary differentials from which capital profits. But a mapping of delocalisation would be only a faded photograph in black and white, without the vivid colours of living labour; of the migrant workers who, affirming their freedom of movement, clash with the capitalist interest to construct and preserve salary differentials within and outside Europe.

From the *Grundrisse* to *Capital*

As is well known the incipit of the *Grundrisse* – 'II. Money' – refers to a first chapter, still unwritten, on value. It is therefore false to maintain that the 'Fragment' celebrates the downfall of the law of value, if Marx's reflection on value was still not yet mature at that stage. This theoretical work occurs in the manuscripts of the 1860s. It is important, however, for the question posed by the 'Fragment', that in the *Grundrisse* Marx had not yet defined his own notion of socially necessary labour as labour that, in a determinate quantity, is objectified in exchange-value. When he speaks of necessary labour, his reasoning remains blocked by difficulties that he continues to attribute to Ricardo, whose theory of value, still sometimes considered legitimate in 1858[1], would be definitively presented as confused between values and cost prices in the middle of the writing of the economic manuscripts of 1861-3 (Marx, 1986: 394). *Grundrisse* mostly looked at capital in general, but in the 1860s Marx's thorough analysis of the world market led him to investigate the competition of capitals, the history of non-capitalistic societies and their 'early integration into the world market'. He concentrated on anticolonial revolts, and brought the unilinear models of historical explanation into question (Anderson, 2002: 93; 2010). Up to the end of the 1850s, Marx held a positive view of the 'propagandistic (civilising) tendency' (Marx, 1986: 466) of capital and believed in the thoroughness with which British industrial capital would destroy non-capitalist societies in the process of its worldwide expansion[2]. In

---

[1] Marx continued to work on value also during the different editions of *Capital* (Hecker, 1987).

[2] According to Mohri: 'In the 1840s and 1850s Marx emphasized the "revolutionary" role of British free trade, basing himself upon a general expectation that it would destroy the framework of the old society which was an obstacle to the growth of productive forces, and would generate in its place the

the 1850s Marx's pronouncements on colonialism were often more ambivalent. He wrote that English colonialism in India would have a 'double mission [...]: one destructive, the other regenerating – the annihilation of old Asiatic society, and the laying the material foundations of Western society in Asia' (Marx, 1979c: 217-218). This historicism fascinated many Marxisms, as it indicated the development of the productive forces as the tendency that must be followed by all other forms which are defined as backward or residual. The supposed 'regenerating' aspect disappears from his writing of the 1860s, and the destruction of the native industry of India or Ireland by the British capital is no longer regarded as 'revolutionary'[3].

By the end of 1858, seeing the ability of capital to metabolise the crisis, Marx was led to reconsider his analysis. In a letter to Engels dated 8th October 1858 he writes:

> There is no denying that bourgeois society has for the second time experienced its 16th century, a 16th century which, I hope, will sound its death knell just as the first ushered it into the world. The proper task of bourgeois society is the creation of the world market, at least in outline, and of the production based on that market. Since the world is round, the colonisation of California and Australia and the opening up of China and Japan would seem to have completed this process. For us, the difficult question is this: on the Continent revolution is imminent and will, moreover, instantly assume a socialist character. Will it not necessarily be crushed in this little corner of the earth, since the movement of bourgeois society is still, in the ascendant over a far greater area? (Marx and Engels, 1983: 347-348)

In this letter one can find the coordinates of Marx's theoretical and political work in the 1860s. One can already observe the difference with the *Grundrisse*. There are three important issues in this letter. First of all, the bourgeois society, Marx writes, 'has for the second time experienced its 16th century'.

---

kind of development that would lay the basis for a new society. However, this view was discarded by Marx himself from the 1860s onward, as he became well aware that the destruction of the old society would not necessarily give rise to the material conditions for a new society' (Mohri, 1979: 40).

[3] Mohri remarks that 'On the contrary, the destruction of native Irish industry is now looked upon as the first step toward demolition of the base for the Irish revolution itself, or, we may dare to say, it is obviously taken as "counter-revolutionary" rather than as "revolutionary"' (1979: 38).

This second 16th century of capitalism leads Marx to conceive of an enduring primitive accumulation, which one cannot confine to the beginning of capitalistic production (Bonefeld, 2001; Glassman, 2006; Wainwright, 2008). Secondly, both theoretical and political analysis must be done at the level of the world market. 'The world is round', writes Marx, and capitalism puts into relation different geographical areas and different forms of exploitation. One cannot analyse capitalism only by considering the countries where it is more developed. That being so, the third consideration is that Marx poses the 'difficult question': whether a socialist revolution in Europe could be successful while the movement of capitalistic society is still 'ascendant over a far greater area'. From this moment a eurocentric point of view on capitalism and working class movements is directly reactionary, as were all attempts to construct socialism in one country.

Still, in the celebrated 'Preface' of 1859 Marx delineates the progressive process of universal history according to definite stages. The Asiatic, classical, feudal and bourgeois modes of production are qualified as 'progressive epochs', with respect to which the bourgeois is 'the last antagonistic form of the process of production' (Marx, 1987: 263-264). Marx liberated himself from this historical-philosophical (*geschichtsphilosophisch*) legacy with difficulty, perhaps only during the maturation of the conceptual structure of *Capital*[4]. Directly confronting the Asiatic modes of production and the Russian populists, he understood that there are not predetermined stages of capitalist development. In a letter at the end of 1877 to the Editor of 'Otecestvennye Zapiski', he wrote that his sketch of the genesis of capitalism in Western Europe could not be transformed 'into a historical-philosophical theory of universal development, predetermined by fate, for all peoples, regardless of the historical circumstances in which they find themselves'. He had learnt that one could never understand historical phenomena 'with the passe-partout of a philosophy of history whose supreme virtue is to be suprahistorical' (Marx and Michajlovskij, 1989: 201). Marx arrived at this understanding by refining an idea of the development of the forces of production in the light of the concrete replies of history; that is to say, the histories of the struggles that, interacting with the atemporal historicity of capital, co-determine its history.

---

4 Marx overcomes his own eurocentrism towards the end of the 60s, opening himself to the problematic of 'peripheral' Russia. See Dussel (1990a, 1990b).

It was an error to read the development of capital in evolutionist terms: politically, this view has coincided with that of progress. Thus not only is any society denied the possibility of leaping over the 'natural phases' of its development, but forms of exploitation are laid out diachronically, when they are instead completely complementary. This can be seen in the case of absolute and relative surplus-value, that is, of the extortion of surplus-value by means of a lengthening of the working day and the intensification of labour through the introduction of machines. The passage from formal subsumption to real subsumption, from the extortion of absolute surplus-value to relative surplus-value, does not take place according to a paradigm of stages in which the first gives way to the second. The passage from the third part ('The production of absolute surplus-value') to the fourth ('The production of relative surplus-value') is marked by the final lines of chapter ten, where the workers, 'as a class', succeeded in establishing legal restrictions on the duration of the working day. If in fact 'the creation of a normal working-day is [...] the product of a protracted civil war, more or less dissembled, between the capitalist class and the working-class' (Marx, 1996: 305), capital responds to the war with an augmentation of the productive force of labour by means of machines. 'Progress' is measured by this intensification of exploitation. For this reason, it is unrealistic, even when not acting in bad faith, to prophesise the liberation of labour by means of machines within capitalist relations of production, when the use-value of labour remains intrinsically capitalist. Innovation is a response to the insurgency of living labour. That means that capital introduces new machinery because it is compelled to, both by the unruliness of the workers and the physiological limit reached in the exploitation of labour power.

On the Differentials of Surplus-Value

It is important to understand exchange-value, beyond some logical-conceptual shifts present even in the writings of the mature Marx, not as the objectification of labour immediately spent in the production of a determinate commodity, but as an expression of the quantity of social labour objectified in the commodity: 'that which determines the magnitude of the value of any article is the amount of labour socially necessary, or the labour time socially necessary for its production' (Marx, 1996: 48). It is in Capital that we find the highest level of conceptual determination of social labour, and it is this determination that needs to be assumed in order to test Marx's entire theoretical edifice. What needs to be clear, and what also contains a moment of real difficulty, is that the labour objectified in the exchange-value of a commodity does not correspond to the quantity of labour immediately spent in its production. Instead, it is the fruit of mediation with socially allocated labour. In this sense, the expression 'individual value' (*individueller Wert*) is a contradiction in itself: not only because, as Marx emphases in the 'Marginal notes on Wagner' in 1881-82 – the dates are important in this case – 'exchange-value in the singular does not exist' (Marx, 1989: 531-562), but because it presupposes a value determined quantitatively by labour individually employed in the production of this commodity, and not by social labour. This value, on the other hand, does not have a definite size. Rather, it is variable, and its variability retroacts on the determination of the quantity of social labour contained in a commodity. If the general conditions in which a certain quantity of commodities are produced change, Marx affirms, a reverse effect (*Rückwirkung*) takes place on them (Marx, 1990: 75). It is possible that a determinate quantity of labour time already objectified in a commodity changes due to a change in the social productivity of labour, which reacts on the exchange-value of the commodity itself.

The notion of retroaction allows Marx to explain a change in value that has its origins outside the process of production, and specifically following a change of the cost of raw materials or the introduction of a 'new invention' (Marx, 1996: 318). This important Marxian understanding is possible only within a constellation that is clear on the social character of the labour that valorises value: 'The value of a commodity is certainly determined by the quantity of labour contained in it, but this quantity is itself socially determined. If the amount of labour-time socially necessary for the production of any commodity alters... this reacts back on all the old commodities of the same type, because [...] their value at any given time is measured by the labour socially necessary to produce them, i.e., by the labour necessary under the social conditions existing at the time' (*ibid.*). In other words: the changes in the intensity and power of social labour react back on the commodities already produced, causing a change in the labour time objectified in them (De Angelis, 2005).

If *Capital* represents the high point of categorical elaboration, it is here that we must find the most mature consequences of this way of understanding social labour and exchange-value. As we have already seen, according to Marx 'the real value of a commodity is, however, not its individual value, but its social value; that is to say, the real value is not measured by the labour-time that the article in each individual case costs the producer, but by the labour-time socially required for its production' (1996: 324). If therefore the value of a commodity depends upon the labour time objectified in it, it should be kept in mind that this labour time is not that which is effectively employed for the production of a given use-object, but can be either greater or smaller than that. The generic human labour time objectified in the substance of value must be adjusted to the time that social labour would need to carry out that same job. Surplus value is not a quantifiable amount within the accounting of a single firm.

The idea, recurring in numerous places in Marx's analysis, according to which surplus-value would be determined by the labour time that exceeds that which would be necessary for the worker employed by an individual capital to produce his own wages, is a simplification. This is an abstract representation of capital in general, that does not take into consideration the competition between capitals. The value is an objectification of socially necessary labour and it is not deductible from the labour actually expended in a single productive process. If the productive force of the latter is below the productivity of social labour, it is possible that, despite the depression of wages and the increase in labour time in this particular sector, the production of surplus labour remains very low. In such cases an hour of work of high productivity corresponds to two hours of social labour, in the places where the society as a whole still does not make use of a technological innovation. This exchange, where one is equal to two, violates only the intellectual principles of grade-school mathematics; the value of commodities in general, and therefore also of those produced with new technology, is its social value, that is, the quantity of social labour objectified in it. This phenomenon imposes itself violently in the world market, where an increase in the productive power of labour through the introduction of a new machine counts as an increase in the intensity of labour if the capitalist can sell the commodities at a higher price, equivalent to the labour necessary to produce the same commodity for other capitalists who still lack that machine. The fact that the labour time effectively expanded is inferior to that which is socially necessary changes nothing in the relationship, except that the capitalist, selling the commodity at its value, appropriates social surplus value, and therefore exchanges one hour of labour for two. 'If therefore, the capitalist who applies the new method, sells his commodity at its social value of one shilling, he sells it for three pence above its individual value, and thus realises an extra surplus-value (*Extramehrwert*) of three pence' (Marx, 1996: 324). Beyond numbers, the *Extramehrwert* that is appropriated by the capitalist corresponds to the quantity of social surplus value that he can withdraw from the society; he is an extractor of relative surplus value.

In this way a greater number of hours of work physically performed pass through the hands of the capitalist, who utilises a greater productive power of work without violating the law of equivalence. The difference between capitalists who exploit work of differing productivity is therefore necessary so that it will be possible to extract relative surplus value from the advantage that springs from the technological innovation. This can be seen not only on a worldwide scale, where capital is continually in search of masses of absolute surplus value, but also within the western metropolises and even within the same corporation, broken up into apparently independent productive segments and in competition with each other: capital is in any case searching for the maximum gap possible between the intensity of labour in phases that, even if they are part of the same cycle, are recomposed through circulation.

The differential quota between a given productivity of labour and social labour is realised through a transfer of value from production spheres in which the intensity of labour is low relative to those in which capital exploits labour at an intensity that is higher than the social average. The immediate repercussion of a technological innovation is a prolongation of labour time wherever the innovation is not yet employed: 'One of the first consequences of the introduction of new machinery, before it has become dominant in its branch of production, is the prolongation of the labour-time of the labourers who continue to work with the old and unimproved means of production' (Marx, 1990: 323). The introduction of a new machine generates an increase in relative surplus value, an increase that, in order to be realised, must be sustained by a proportional increase in the extraction of absolute surplus value where the innovation has not yet been employed. It is in this sense that relative surplus value is relative, because, to be real, it must be placed in relation to absolute surplus value. To the extent to which the capitalist that takes advantage of a technological innovation realises at least a part of the relative surplus value that is potentially his, this surplus value takes form through a social transfer of value from productive areas of high absolute surplus value to those of high relative surplus value. The relative increase in the labour productivity and of the surplus value in some sectors of production leads to a de-valorisation of labour-power that could also manifest itself as growth of the exploitation of reproduction work whether waged or unwaged. Indeed, we should always keep in consideration the quantity of labour that is indirectly commanded by capital through a wage.

Only when Marx clarified further the nature of exchange-value was he able to show that the machine not only does not create value, but that it also does not produce surplus value: 'As machinery comes into general use in a particular branch of production, the social value of the machine's product sinks down to its individual value, and the following law asserts itself: surplus value does not arise from the labour-power that has been replaced by the machinery, but from the labour-power actually employed in working with the machinery' (Marx, 1996: 530). When a technological innovation becomes widespread, the growing intensity of labour obtained through its employment becomes socially dominant and there is less chance of extracting quotas of social surplus value from the means of production of relative surplus value.

The production of surplus value make use of machines in at least two ways: indirectly, through the devalorisation of labour-power following the expulsion of workers replaced by machines; and in relative surplus value *sensu stricto*, exploiting the sporadic introduction of machines. The latter circumstance is that which allows the exploitation of labour of a greater productivity than the social average, such that the individual labour objectified in this commodity is less than the quantity of socially average labour (*ibid.*). We know by now that only the latter determines exchange-value. When the productivity of labour obtained by a technical innovation becomes socially dominant, it unleashes 'the most ruthless and excessive prolongation of the working day, in order that he may secure compensation for the decrease in the relative number of workers exploited by increasing not only relative but also absolute surplus labour' (Marx, 1996: 531). The extraction of relative surplus value generates, in those parts of the world where workers' resistance is lower, a great mass of absolute exploitation. This means that the introduction of new machinery is not a pre-determined route in the history of all countries, but on the contrary different capitals in head-to-head competition with each other in the world market must seek out or create geographic areas where different labour powers have different wages and productive powers (Marini, 1991: 8-10). If the reciprocal implication of the various forms of surplus value are grasped, then it is only out of faith in some progressive and Eurocentric philosophy of history that it is possible to consider some forms of production as backward, and wage labour, extended to the whole world, as residual.

Historical Multiversum: High Tech Production and Slavery

Formal subsumption is the basis of capitalist production as the creation of surplus value in a process whose end is the production of commodities for the market; real subsumption presents itself instead as a specifically capitalist form because it doesn't allow the previously existing social relations to remain, but revolutionises the technical processes of production and the formation of social groups (Marx, 1996: 645). To these two forms should also be added a third, rarely studied: that of the hybrid or intermediate forms (*Zwitterformen*) of subsumption (Murray, 2000; 2004). Marx speaks of them for the first time in *Capital*. They are forms in which surplus labour is extracted by means of direct coercion (*direkter Zwang*), without formal subsumption of labour to capital. Marx observes how they can indeed be understood as transitional, but can also be reproduced in the background of large-scale industry. The hybrids, though they are not formally subsumed to capital and though labour is not given as wage labour, fall under the command of capital. That allows us to comprehend the contemporaneity of apparent anachronisms like slavery, which are not mere residues of past epochs, but forms that, though with an altered physiognomy, are produced and reproduced in the background of the current capitalist mode of production.

The exploitation of child labour in Asian countries, and working hours of up to eighteen a day[5], are not cases of capitalist underdevelopment, but express the current levels of production of social surplus value[6]. If we

---

[5] On the conditions of labour in China, see Chan and Xiaoyang (2003).

[6] Globalization makes political command capitalistically productive that asserts itself along the borders to conserve the valorising potential of wage differentials. See Gambino (2003), Sacchetto (2004).

consistently assume the reciprocal co-penetration between absolute and relative surplus value, the distinctions between North and South of the world, between first, second and third world, or if one prefers, between core, semi-periphery and periphery with 'advanced' and 'backward' capitalisms, lose a great part of their significance. It is no longer possible to reason in terms of tendencies and residues: the various forms of exploitation are to be understood in a historical-temporal multiversum, in which they interact within the contemporaneity of the present. This interlinking should be followed materially along the lines of the differences between national salaries. Analysis and practical intervention here should fuse together.

Absolute and relative surplus-value are not to be thought in a diachronic succession, but synchronically in a historical-temporal multiversum. Relative surplus-value is such only in relation to absolute surplus-value: relative surplus-value not only does not replace absolute surplus-value, but necessitates, for its own realisation, an increase in the quantity of socially produced absolute surplus-value. As we will see, the production of absolute surplus-value, far from being an archaic form of capitalist exploitation or a residue of the nineteenth century, is a form of extortion of surplus-value absolutely adequate to our times. The existence of conditions of labour where the working day is much longer than eight hours and the wages are below the level necessary for survival – that is, high absolute surplus-value – is not to be attributed to past capitalist forms that live on only in economically depressed zones. Rather, it is a case of the result and the presupposition of the 'progress' of capital. The more capital uses technology, and thus machines, and therefore the more elevated the mass of surplus-values that is produced, so much more must the direct extortion of absolute surplus-value increase. The question doesn't in fact examine the co-presence of diverse forms of exploitation, but rather how the production of relative surplus-value gives way to the production of enormous masses of absolute surplus-value. The different forms of exploitation aren't set beside one another in a sort of postmodern universal exhibition. Rather, capital must continually produce, through the use of extra-economic violence, differentiations of wages and of productivity of labour.

Capitalistic modernity was born globalised in the entanglement of colonialism and slavery. As the case of the American colonies shows, workers' escape or exit constituted the principal problem of capitalistic accumulation between 1500 and 1800 (Moulier-Boutang, 2002: 26). The purpose of English legislation during the 16th and the 17th centuries was the immobilisation and discipline of the labour-force, even through slavery. This wasn't an anomalous case in the colonies but was a common authoritarian answer, to the question of how to control the mobility of European and North-American living labour on the market (*ibid.*: 158). According to Moulier-Boutang, it is not trade that produced slavery but rather bonding wage labour which produced its modern forms (*ibid.*: 232). Modern slavery is a disciplined variant of 'free' wage labour. Slavery is not a dark moment confined to the protohistory of capital but is continually reproduced from the capitalistic mode of production[7].

The colonial system supported the development of the industrial system. Marx' editing of historical materials shows different counter-histories and the dark side of a 'progress' whose focus was 'a vast, Herod-like slaughter of the innocents' (1996: 745). Capital asserts itself on world-history, showing its deadly face at once. This violence was extreme in 'plantation colonies destined for export trade only, such as the West Indies, and in rich and well-populated countries, such as Mexico and India, that were given over to plunder' (*ibid.*: 741). Through this violence capital was able to pull out a labour-force to be employed on plantations, and the intensity of labour was set to the clock of the world stock exchange. For this reason 'the negro labour in the Southern States of the American Union preserved something of a patriarchal character, so long as production was chiefly directed to immediate local consumption. But in proportion, as the export of cotton became of vital interest to these states, the overworking of the negro and sometimes the using up of his life in 7 years of labour became a factor in a calculated and calculating system (ibid.: 244).

To be understood, the world market requires a historiographical paradigm which is able to comprehend the combination of a plurality of temporal strata

---

7   The overall number of human beings forced to leave the African coast amounts to about 11 million. The slaves actually introduced in the Americas between 1519 and 1867 would be 9.599.000 (Pétré-Grenouilleau, 2004). There was a progression in the slave population of the Americas, which reached 33.000 in 1700, nearly three million in 1800 and peaked at over six million in 1850 (van der Linden, 2007).

in the violent synchronising dimension of modernity. The post-modern juxtaposition of a plurality of historical times, where slavery is contiguous with high tech production in the overcoming of the dualism of centre and periphery, doesn't explain anything, and is even concealing. The post-modern mosaic of temporalities and forms of exploitation, even though it represents them as interconnected, poses the different times in a state of indifference to each other, when the very problem is their combination through the mechanisms of synchronisation in the world market. The nexus of value and socially necessary labour is now the most adequate category to comprehend the mechanism in which the labour-time of computer-based production requires and is combined with compulsory labour in several parts of the world. From this point of view, George Caffentzis does not exaggerate when he argues that 'the computer requires the sweatshop, and the cyborg's existence is premised on the slave' (Caffentzis, 1999).

Slavery becomes something new when it is subsumed to the world market, as with its development all people are entangled in its net (Marx, 1996: 750). The net of the world market holds together not only different forms of exploitation while combining them synchronically, but – and this is the other history – it bridges over different working classes. The very important issue that Marx posed at end of the 1860s concerns the synchronic combination of different forms of exploitation, their entwinement starting from the relation between absolute and relative surplus value (Tomba, 2013). Capital needs to create geographical areas or productive sectors where it can produce an enormous quantity of absolute surplus value to support the production of extraordinary surplus-value; relative surplus-value produced through mechanical innovations.

Globalisation renders the political command that it exercises along the borders capitalistically productive in order to conserve the valorising potential of differential wages. This command is manifested over migrant workers without any niceties. Sovereignty, rights of citizenship and control of the borders operate economically in order to delineate different wage areas that can be preserved only by reducing to a minimum the movements of labour power from one area to the other. The chains of valorisation cross a multiplicity of wage areas, national and intranational, using those differentials of profitably. Delocalisation makes the difference of the productivity of labour and of wage levels capitalistically productive: that would not be possible without political command over migrant flows. These migrant flows therefore justly rank highly among the forms of workers' resistance to control and the forms of self-determination of the wage against capital. The migrant workers are not bare life (Colatrella, 2011) but forces of labour that, violating the borders, tend to disrupt the division of labour and national differentials of wages. The policies of regulation of the migrant flows, on the other hand, are economic policies of segmentation of the labour market and of the demarcation of wage differentials. As if the assembly lines had left the factory in order to undertake a long world tour, the chains of valorisation cross the borders of states, profiting from the national differentials of wages. In this context, political command over the borders and capitalist command over labour power are fused. Contemporary forms of the removal of wage differentials should thus be investigated together with subjective insurgencies in different part of the world.

9

A Brief History of Labour: From Subsumption to Multitude

Alexander Neumann

We are living in a time of global crisis, in the middle of a theoretical paradox. European governments say they are trying to save their key industries, to avoid systemic collapse of a so-called post-industrial society, yet the state intervention in Europe and the United States has recently focused on the rescue of the automobile sector and other industries. Mass protests respond to mass unemployment and precarious living conditions, while 'cognitive' capitalism presents itself as a post-material or immaterial entity. These paradoxes point to a major theoretical gap in the social sciences since 1980, between the concept of wage labour and the concept of political action. This kind of debate reminds us of the philosophical oppositions from before the French Revolution, or Stalinist *doxa*: materialism versus idealism. Over the last thirty years, all intellectual efforts have focused on the conceptual opposition between labour and politics (or wage labour and the public sphere, as in Habermas' theory of communicative action: Habermas, 1981), which artificially separated labour and communication (or culture). Touraine in France, Giddens in Britain and many others have reproduced this basic pattern, exploiting the theoretical potential of the linguistic turn. This movement coincided with the burial of traditional Marxism, which believed that work and politics converge naturally through the collective action of the industrial working class. It is true that nowadays this class exists only as a historical relic in the form of bureaucratic trade unionism or working class parties without a significant proletarian base. Most labour studies and sociological surveys focus on isolated situations of specific companies, or on specific groups like the unemployed. This contributes little or nothing to global social critique. The great defeat of the European working class from 1978 to 1983 was consequently coupled with defeat on the theoretical battlefield, when the critique of wage labour was identified as a variety of the ideological Marxism of the weakening labour parties. However, the critique of labour was always the opposite of traditional Marxism and its positive attitude towards labour value. In fact, this critical approach was expressed at the margins of the great public debates, in journals such as *Futur Antérieur* (see also Brandt, 1990) at the University Paris 8 Vincennes, or in sociological research inspired by the Critical Theory of the Frankfurt School. The main thesis of this intellectual tendency is that no one can envisage his or her life by identifying herself or himself as a variable part of capital, given that wage labour is defined by Marx as variable capital.

There is a school of thought that has built a rich conceptual network of relations between labour, action and global capitalism. This set of ideas, from the first Critical Theory of the Frankfurt School, was carefully avoided by doctrinaire Marxism as well as by the institutional successors of the Frankfurt School, Habermas and Honneth. This lineage, which linked the critique of political economy to Critical Theory, includes such remarkable thinkers as Theodor W. Adorno, Alfred Sohn-Rethel, Gerhardt Brandt, Jean-Marie Vincent, Oskar Negt, and more recently Nancy Fraser and John Holloway (see Neumann, 2010a; 2010b; 2014).

They have all been attacked by mainstream academics as doctrinaire Marxists, and at the same time were denounced as bourgeois idealists by communists. One of the main theoretical concerns of this tendency is to clearly distinguish industrial labour as an empirical object on the one hand, and the theory of wage labour as a critical counterpoint on the other. So this type of Critical Theory is at once with Marx and against Marx. Marx himself believed it impossible for his concepts to account for the possibility of global capitalism, given that he looked forward to the socialist world revolution rather than to neocapitalism. However, his concept of 'real subsumption' ('reale Subsumption' in German) of wage labour to capital sketches a picture of completely commodified societies that consider any kind of labour as a market value. In an additional chapter of *Capital* entitled 'Results of the immediate process of production', published a century after the first version of the book, Marx explains how key industries have to mobilise transportation networks, communication structures, various services, scientific knowledge and financial supports, on a worldwide scale, leading to a global market and capitalist globalisation (Marx, 1976). Within this theoretical framework, the opposition between productive and unproductive labour is no longer important, as there are many services needed in different places and at different moments of global value extraction. At the end of the story, and of this conceptual development, there is no longer any 'mortal contradiction' between productive forces and relations of production, which should lead to world revolution in the mind of Marx. Fully developed capitalism is characterised by the fact that its organisational principles are at work in the whole society and the whole world. In this unpublished chapter, Marx develops his observation on the basis of industrial production, but this is only the starting point of his analysis. The new type of organisation and cooperation, called real subsumption involves all economic sectors, and thus extends over the entire society, by the use of technology, scientific knowledge, stock markets, electrical grid, communiucation systems (telegraph etc.) and modern transportation systems (Marx, 1976: 220). Marx explicitly leaves the field of industrial labour, with a theoretical orientation that directly leads us to today's phenomena of capitalist globalisation as network management and electronic exchanges. Without these exchanges and global flows, no businesses could work today. In a sense, the Marxian concept of subsumption abolishes Marx's own theoretical distinction between productive and unproductive labour. Abstract labour, fully commodified, mobilises both material and immaterial acts at different times, different places and different levels of the world market.

There is an extension of this idea in the third volume of *Capital*, where Marx leaves the theoretical framework of the industrial factory, in order to review the modes of generating value that are not dependent on industrial production. Marx explicitly considers the shareholders, global trade (and the unequal exchange that it maintains), economies of scale and technical innovation, as well as luxury consumption. Similarly, he mentions the effects of government intervention on surplus value production (Marx, 1979b: 247-250, 494). Despite his own convictions, Marx anticipated a situation throughout this argument in which the proletariat would no longer be outside bourgeois society, but would be directly involved and integrated as variable capital, as wage labour socialised by the market, via organisational networks and mass communication. This is probably the reason why the concept of real subsumption is absent from three books of the Capital, and only appears in later manuscripts, published in 1970. As global capitalism became a historical reality, we have to overcome conceptual oppositions that Marx considers central to *Capital*, between productive and unproductive labour, concrete and abstract labour, etc. It also means abandoning the false opposition between an industrial and a post-industrial society, given that, at the analytical level, in a global capitalist market it does not matter if an iPhone is produced in a European or Chinese factory.

Even if Theodor W. Adorno was unfamiliar with Marx's unpublished chapter on real subsumption, he came to the same conclusion in his famous essay on late capitalism in 1968, in which he asserted that the working classes of the western world had been integrated into the capitalist regime, which meant that the theoretical opposition between productive forces and relations of production was no longer relevant. He underlined the fact that the concept of 'industrial society' was not appropriate to describe the global development of capitalism. Adorno and Horkheimer first followed this approach when they examined the Hollywood culture industry, but they did not directly analyse the market and organisational arrangements that are at stake here. This view deserves to be expanded, in my opinion, to take in the current arrangements of globalisation: computerisation of production and distribution, international dispersion of production stages, globalisation of capital and financial markets, marketing, advertising, consumption and credit, state reform, and so on. Adorno understands the global nature of capitalism, but he does not track down the process of incorporation and mediations of living labour; he goes directly into the company's total fetish, without exploring the fields that I have mentioned, which are held in a multiplicity of conflict, resistance and experience.

The main sociological invention of Adorno, at the German Congress of Sociology in 1968, was that sociology must formulate the critique of capitalism, not of 'industrial society', and countered the assertion that any reference to Marx was outdated (Adorno, 1971: 149-166). Key critical concepts from Marx, such as the fetishism of commodities or abstract exchange, are used by Adorno to weaken both the ongoing neoliberal and traditional Marxist schemes. This interpretation of Adorno, that I sketched in my book *Conscience de casse* (*Crash consciousness*), has been systematically followed by Dirk Braunstein, in a book devoted to the critique of the political economy of Adorno, published in 2011. Conceptually, Adorno clearly distinguishes the Marxian concepts of the Marxist tradition, which he underlined in an article on 'Marx and the basic categories of sociology' (Adorno, 1997).

According to Marx, developed capitalism breaks the concrete link between the worker and his employer, creating a situation where objectified labour uses living labour. Capital, as objectification of living labour, subjugates all persons depending on work by reducing them to wage labour. From the perspective of an individual employee, his insertion into a large production process makes him definitely lose track of his relative contribution to the economy as a whole. Market and capital appear as an abstract totality that lie beyond his or her control. In the unpublished chapter of *Capital*, we find arguments that show how capitalism works as a well organised and market driven global network, for instance by using economies of scale, modern transportation and communication systems, worldwide commerce, stock markets, and by making great use of scientific knowledge. To put it in one word: globalisation. All persons working within those processes, at different places, times and levels are part of the real subsumption. As a consequence, cognitive skills and electronic exchange are part of abstract labour, no matter if we call a Notebook an industrial product or not.

Adorno wrote of the unprecedented nature of this social aggregation, which mixes the false representation of reality and the objective existence of the market:

> Although we are able to break through the facade of the company, this does not change the aspect of commodity fetishism: any merchant that calculates business is obliged to behave in a manner consistent with this fetish. If he does not, he will sink. (Adorno, 1997: 509, author translation)

Similarly, if employees want to live, they must agree to be paid, which means that they take part of the abstract representation of capitalism. Any worker, whether employee, self-employed, freelance designer or other precarious networker, is defined as variable capital of capitalism, regardless of the type of employment contract or compensation available to him. Marx explicitly emphasises this fact in the unpublished chapter of *Capital*, where he says that the formal submission of contract workers has historically been supplanted by the commodification of any kind of labour. Jean-Marie Vincent has pointed out the characteristics of this universal constraint:

> to sell himself, to be appreciated as a bearer of measurable labour power, to involve others in commodification, to develop strategic business activities trumping all others (including emotional aspects) (Vincent, 1998: 80, author translation).

Far from being an illusory perception of reality, the abstract representations describe an ultimate form of social reality, by validating the priority of commodified relations. Marx calls them the 'objective ways of thinking' ('objective Gedankenformen', Marx, 1979a: 90), as thinking must take account of the objectivity of the social situation.

From this perspective, the critical analysis of capitalism, led by Marx, is paving the way for a sociological critique of social forms and practices. The enchantment of the suggestive power of the commodity, fetish performances, the mode of consumption and possessive individualism, based on the real submission of wage labour, are trumping other principles of social life. Vincent summarises:

> The lives of individuals are marked by the logic of commodified development of value, and their life forms (daily life) fit forms of value or social things (*ibid.*: 231, author translation).

This is an interpretation of the Marxian concept of commodity fetishism which tries to understand how social experiences get involved in capital development.

The finding of Vincent, that life forms adapt to social objects, updates the analysis of Adorno and Horkheimer, who emphasised that modern individuals no longer have space to harvest 'authentic' experiences under the conditions of abstract representations, mass media and the cultural industry. The sensory experience is influenced by a mode of social exchange that is regulated by things (goods, money, technology), while culture, creation and communication are filtered by commodified standards.

Indeed, Adorno and Horkheimer's thesis on the culture industry directly and explicitly refers to the Marxist concept of commodity fetishism in the original version of the *Dialectic of Enlightenment* of 1942 (Adorno and Horkheimer, 1990: 128). The reference to Marx was then erased for political reasons; namely for fear of anti-communist frenzy. In *Dialectic of Enlightenment*, Adorno and Horkheimer point out the regressive burden of Western civilisation, which is able to return to barbarism.

To Adorno, the social abstractions that form modern reality, identified by concepts such as the real subsumption of wage labour, and the culture industry, form a repressive totality which leaves little room for an autonomous life, despite the liberal discourse of freedom of choice. The General trumps the Particular. Adorno's vision here again finds common ground with Marx, who had insisted that the market value depends on the subjective mobilisation of workers paid for their ability to work, not for the work itself. The degree of effectiveness of the work is, in fact, closely related to the moral, cultural and symbolic motivations of employees. As a consequence, capital depends on subjectivity, and is exposed to resistance and revolts, no matter if they take place within companies or within the system of the culture industry, once the players are projected into the world with their own conflicting interpretations. The 'totality' mentioned by Adorno when he talks about the *Verblendungszusammenhang* is much more fragile than it appears at first glance. Shifts, historical discrepancies and differences between the general movement of society on one side, and individual lives on the other, in my opinion make it possible to think of the individual experience of the loss of sensitive human encounters that are now covered by the real abstractions of modern society.

However, the Frankfurt thinkers neglect the discrepancy between sensory experience and overall socialisation through abstract exchanges. Even if we can follow Jean-Marie Vincent when he shows the persistent connections between 'the logic of capitalist development and the forms of life' (Vincent, 1998: 231), the fact remains that this connection frequently crumbles to pieces, due to the emergence of significant social actors, experiencing the contradictions, inconsistencies and discontinuities of the dominant values.

The question of whether the congruence between market value and forms of social life can be achieved, or whether separations, conflicts and disharmony will prevail, is at the heart of the debates of Critical Theory. At his conference of 1968 on late capitalism, Adorno contradictsed Marx's *Communist Manifesto*, as he found that there was no explosive, mortal contradiction between the productive forces and relations of production (or between the production and distribution of wealth), but rather a dialectical tension that links the two intertwined aspects. Thus, capitalism will not be abolished by its own logic. On the other hand, he highlighted the potential for 'resistance' within capitalism. This was a more fundamental critique of the social forms of 'late capitalism', than the mainstream model of 'industrial capitalism' that later turned into 'post-industrial capitalism'. In other words, Adorno seeks to save the Marxian critique from Marxism, while Honneth tends to remove 'economism' from the concepts of Marx's *Capital* by treating them as Marxist economics.

The limitation of the position Adorno took at the Congress of Sociology in 1968, in my opinion, is a lack of articulation of commodification on the one hand, and the constitution of society as a whole on the other. Soon, Adorno is just drifting through a critical pessimism which interprets society as a blinding connection, and does not highlight the sources of resistance to conformity. The convergence of productive forces and relations of production he observes, is correct in principle, but does not allow for understanding of social conflicts and mediations which constantly recompose profit-driven societies.

It seems possible to extend the conceptual dynamics of Adorno, by using his own concept of 'non-labour' (*Nicht-Arbeit*, which is an intuition seen within his sociological essays). The first opposition of Marx between productive and unproductive labour has to be replaced with a more radical opposition between wage labour and non-labour, as a practical and aesthetic principle of resistance to instrumental and commodified action. This concept of non-work has already been raised rapidly by Pierre Naville in his critical sociology, and recalls the rebellious subjectivity Negt and Kluge talk about in their book *Geschichte und Eigensinn* (Naville, 1953, Negt and Kluge, 1993).

In this approach, the opposition to capitalism is not produced spontaneously by the social forms of capitalism itself, but it may arise from the creative principle of resistance. Herein lies a major difference with the *Communist Manifesto*, in which Marx believed that capitalism had made its own gravedigger in the form of the proletariat, while Adorno noted in 1968 how the proletariat was subsumed under late capitalism. For the same reason, there is an irreducible difference between the Critical Theory of the Frankfurt School and Hardt and Negri. Jean-Marie Vincent, mentioned in the thanks at the beginning of Empire, outlined Negri's position in his *Critique of Labour*, where he sums up Marx's *Grundrisse* and Negri's interpretation of it (Vincent,

1987: ch. 4). While Marx expects a dialectical reversal of deprivation and frustration suffered under capitalism towards working-class solidarity, socialism and world revolution, Negri hopes that the precarious workers of the multitude will spontaneously produce a new revolutionary subjectivity within cognitive capitalism. While Marx finally gave up the idea, giving emphasis to the historical formation of labour movements, Hardt and Negri think they can do without the principle of resistance and democratic debate that is otherwise required, in order to arrive directly at the global shift. The two authors assert that the multitude will turn into a political subject, 'without any form of mediation' (Hardt and Negri, 2000: 393). The complexity of public discussion in recent oppositional movements, from Tunis to New York and Athens, shows that this desire will again be disappointed. Critical Theory has proposed the concept of oppositional public sphere to name the ongoing process of sensitive experiences and public debates that produce a distance to the market players, the State and the mass media.

The global crisis which began in 2008 – comparable to the global crisis of 1929 – calls for a revival of original sociological concepts that are today placed at the margin of European sociology. With the collapse of the self-regulation of financial markets, the theory of systemic self-regulation (from Luhmann to neoclassical economics) has clearly reached its limit. Theoretically, this finding also questions the import of these approaches in the communicative action theory of Habermas.

Applied to phenomena in Europe, the critical shift that I propose could occur, ultimately, as a moment in which sociology refocuses on its own critical legacy, which was originally marked by the global crisis of 1929. Today, the erosion of collective norms, the problems of legitimacy of capitalism and the massive collapse of democratic representation within the State are empowering, or could empower oppositional public spheres.

10

Governing Social Creativity through Benchmarking. From Xerox Management to 'Innovative Europe'

Isabelle Bruno

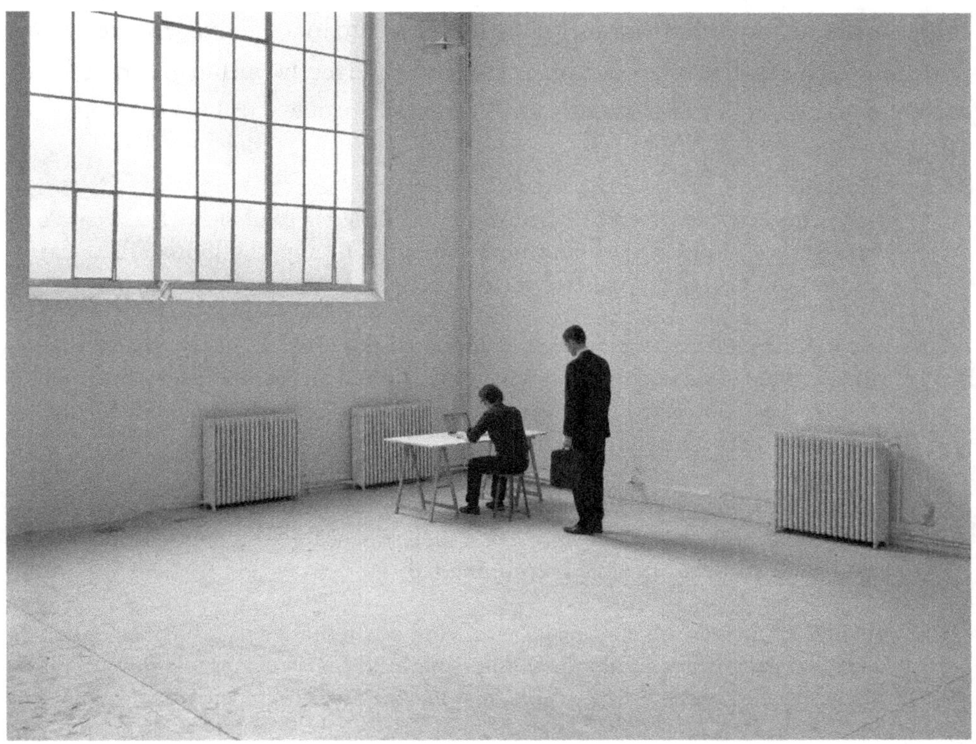

However surprising it may seem, the man at the table on the picture above (Le Chevallier, 2008) is… an artist at work! His name is Martin Le Chevallier.

And the man behind him is a consultant auditing him. This picture is actually artwork. It was part of an exhibition – called 'The Audit' – that simply displays this photo with a voice-over reading the conclusions reached by the consultant's assessment. When listening to the audit report, the visitor of the exhibition was thus invited to follow the dialectic curves of the business mind being applied to artistic activity to the point of absurdity. Thereby, Le Chevallier wanted to pinpoint – not without a sense of humour – both the convergences and the contradictions between business logic and artistic approach nowadays.

In 2008, Martin Le Chevallier indeed appealed to a consulting firm in order to be subjected to an 'artistic performance audit', which would evaluate his approach and design a success strategy, just like for any other company. In doing so, he was of course wilfully ironic. However, the audit process was carried out very professionally and seriously (Le Chevallier, 2008). Therefore, the consultant identified the target in terms of financial value, market rating and fame. The goal was to establish the artist perfectly within the market by means of a business plan. To this end, the audit process followed a four-step approach:

- first, the consultant established what he called a 'Balanced Scorecard', which is a kind of dashboard providing not only traditional financial metrics but also non-financial performance measures and strategic targets;

- second, he assessed the current situation of the artist, his commercial and artistic position in relation to what was offered by competitors. In other words, he conducted a 'competitive analysis' which resulted in the emphasis on a 'competitive gap';

- third, he projected performance goals so as to close the gap between the artist and his competitors. To reach these goals, guidelines and monitoring indicators were recommended;

- finally, all these tools and processes were put together in a business plan, as if the artist was an individual enterprise and his artistic work something likely to be rationally manageable, just like any corporate activities.

For instance, according to the marketing plan, the artist should 'reinvent himself' to be more attractive and so, more marketable. Specifically, he was advised to 'rebrand' himself: Martin Le Chevallier was not catchy enough, so he was advised to change his name, for example. Likewise, according to the strategic plan, if Martin's ambition was to become a key artist, a leader in his market, he should have a vision and be risk-taking like any other entrepreneur. And like any other enterprise, his organization should always be searching for the 'best practices' to be competitive. Management has a saying about all that. It says: 'If you want to better yourself, you have to measure yourself; if you want to be the best, you have to compare yourself'. To this end, a special technology was developed that is called benchmarking.

To some extent, what the consultant advised Martin Le Chevallier was to benchmark himself, that is to compare himself with competitors; to measure the gap between his results and those of the best performers; to set quantified targets for closing this gap; to search for the 'best practices', for *benchmarks* in order to improve his performance. This approach, which is not conceived as a one-shot experience but a relentless discipline, is indeed called benchmarking.

Benchmarking Process Steps

This process seems quite harmless since it merely consists in measuring and comparing oneself – apparently nothing new. It is, in fact, more far-reaching and powerful than it seems. Why? Because it aims at improving any performance in any organization by identifying and applying the best demonstrated practices, which can be found externally or internally, potentially everywhere. Unlike traditional competitive analysis, benchmarking does not limit the comparison to direct competitors in a specific industry or marketplace. In doing so, it opens an unlimited space of commensuration and of competition, integrating all organizations whatever are their activities, their size or their members, be they factory workers, engineers, researchers, teachers, students, doctors, pensioners, volunteers, citizens, or... artists. Everyone is a potential competitor, even where there is no economic competition, strictly speaking, as long as there is an organization that can be broken up into processes.

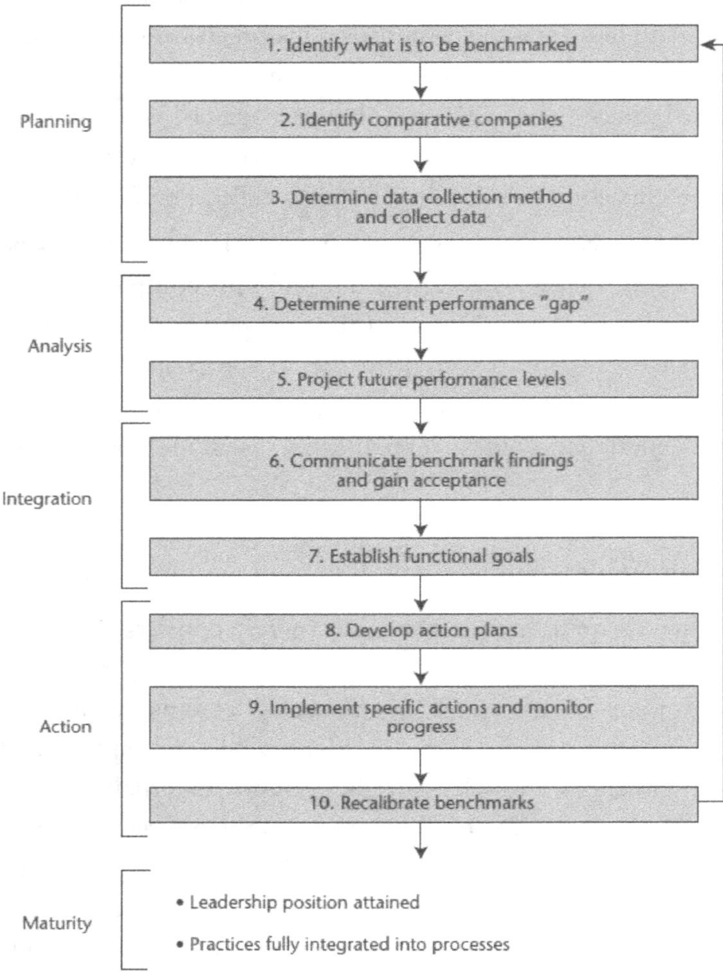

Benchmarking Process Steps (Camp, 1989: 17).

Consequently, benchmarking has been devised and promoted as a universal method, applicable everywhere and useful in every kind of organisation. The goal of benchmarking is simply to find examples of superior results and to understand the processes driving that performance in order to tailor and incorporate these best practices into one's own operations. Not by imitating, but by innovating. Benchmarking thus consists in steering social creativity through the pressure of examples and numbers, of peers and of emulation. It underpins power relations that are evidence-based, depersonalised, mediated by hard facts and so-called 'unquestionable' data. In addition, this kind of power is all the more efficient since it is neither coercive, nor legal. Obedience relies on willingness and incentive, rather than on constraint and punishment. What is at stake is no longer doing things well or improving them, but being the best, always. The strength of benchmarking lies in this competition-oriented rationality, which makes an endless race to the top possible. It is often spoken of as 'a race without a finish line'.

To put it differently, benchmarking is a technology of agency and of involvement, which softly governs behaviour by framing practices of liberty (Haahr, 2004: 209-230). Foucault once spoke of the 'environmental technology'[1] specific to neoliberal governmentality, which consists in equipping actors to enable them to be creative and competitive. Hence the toothless reputation of benchmarking, according to those who failed to understand that neoliberal governmentality produces freedom because it needs to consume it. It feeds on freedom of information, of cooperation, of creation. But we shouldn't delude ourselves; the liberty produced by neoliberal devices like benchmarking is closely channelled and controlled to be market-friendly and profit-oriented. That's why it may be enlightening to take benchmarking seriously.

At first sight, benchmarking is nothing but a buzzword, or a passing fad. Of course, there is no denying that management tools go in and out of fashion, and that they are a business in themselves: they are trademarked and sold by consultants. Benchmarking is no exception. It's even a profitable business. However, it would be misguided to boil down benchmarking to a trivial gizmo, because it has much to say about cognitive capitalism and its new spirit. To quote Foucault, we could say about benchmarking that: 'In

---

[1] 'On the horizon of this analysis [of neoliberal governmentality] we see instead the image, idea, or theme-program of a society in which there is an optimization of systems of difference, in which the field is left open to fluctuating processes, in which minority individuals and practices are tolerated, in which action is brought to bear on the rules of the game rather than on the players, and finally in which there is an environmental type of intervention instead of the internal subjugation of individuals.' (Foucault, 2008: 259-260)

appearance, it is merely the solution of a technical problem; but, through it, a whole type of society emerges.' (Foucault, 1995: 228).

It is worth noting that benchmarking has proliferated for the last thirty years and, far from vanishing, it is now deep-rooted and widespread in all kinds of organizations. According to ten thousand executives surveyed around the world by the business consulting firm Bain & Company since 1993, benchmarking is always among their 'top ten tools', if not the 'number one'.

Top Ten Tools 2009

1	Benchmarking
2	Strategic Planning
3	Mission and Vision Statements
4	Customer Relationship Management
5	Outsourcing
6	Balanced Scorecard
7	Customer Segmentation
8	Business Process Reengineering
9	Core Competencies
10	Mergers & Acquisitions

Top Ten Tools of 2009 (Rigby and Bilodeau 2009: 3).

Since its first experimentations at Xerox Corporation at the turn of the 1980s, benchmarking has proliferated throughout the world and throughout sectors. In this regard, taking a glance at the titles of the review *Benchmarking: An*

International Journal[2] is quite revealing. 'Successful implementation of Six Sigma: benchmarking General Electric Company'; 'Benchmarking the port services: a customer oriented proposal'; 'Airport benchmarking: a review of the current situation'; 'Association-sponsored benchmarking programs'; 'Benchmarking in the non-profit sector in Australia'; 'Benchmarking: achieving best value in public-sector organisations'; 'A system dynamics framework for benchmarking policy analysis for a university system'; 'Benchmarking the best practices of non-corporate R&D organizations'; 'Benchmarking in health services'; etc. Here are some examples displaying the wide scope of benchmarking, which has been implemented both in big firms and SMEs (small and medium enterprises), in manufacturing or services, in associations and non-profit organizations, in the public sector, and especially in universities, R&D organizations and health services.

Moreover, benchmarking has been disseminated worldwide. After the USA and Japan, benchmarking first reached 'the Commonwealth': New Zealand ('Using routine data for benchmarking and performance measurement of public hospitals in New Zealand'), Australia ('The role of benchmarking within the cultural reform journey of an award-winning Australian local authority'), and the United Kingdom ('The burgeoning of benchmarking in British local government'). Then, continental Europe: for example, Germany ('Benchmarking concepts in the UK and Germany'), Italy ('The benchmarking of information systems supporting the university administrative activities. An Italian experience') or Slovenia ('Benchmarking the Slovenian competitiveness by system of indicators'). France, as always, was first reluctant but followed suit ('Perceptions about benchmarking best practices among French managers: an exploratory survey'). And countries outside the OECD – like India ('The propagation of benchmarking concepts in Indian manufacturing industry') or Kenya ('Key performance Indicators in the Kenyan hotel industry') – are not safe either.

Furthermore, benchmarking is not limited to business processes. Everything is a potential object of benchmarking. Some weird titles illustrate the supposed universality of benchmarking: 'Cross-laboratory benchmarking

---

2   First entitled *Benchmarking for Quality Management & Technology* from 1994 to 1999 and published by MCB University Press, *Benchmarking: An International Journal* is now published by Emerald.

in pathology'; 'Benchmarking government's roles to assure the cooperation in collaborative technology innovation'; 'Benchmarking the impacts of US magnet schools in urban schools'. 'Benchmarking organizational commitment across non-profit human services organizations in Pennsylvania' is indeed quite unexpected. Even more unexpected are 'Policy benchmarking: a tool of democracy or a tool of authoritarianism?'; 'Benchmarking the presidential election of Barack Obama'; and 'Benchmarking of thesis research'. Last but not least, 'Benchmarking the benchmarking models'! That's the height of benchmarking.

As one can guess, there is nothing natural and self-evident about the dissemination of benchmarking. Its 'success story' cannot be explained by its great effectiveness and common-sense usefulness. A genealogical investigation would lead us from the U.S. Department of Defence to post-war Japanese employers; from the CEO of Xerox Corporation, David Kearns, who joined the U.S. Department of Education under Bush Sr., to the European Roundtable of Industrialists; from PUMA, the public management service of the OECD, to the European Union. To make a long story short, the spreading of benchmarking was not supported by the weight of evidence, but by powerful institutions, networks and leaders, who endeavoured to promote it as a multi-purpose and policy-neutral method.

For example, this text is extracted from the proceedings of a joint seminar on benchmarking co-organized in Brussels by the European Commission and the European Roundtable of Industrialists (ERT) in order to induce policy-makers to use benchmarking[3]. It dates back to 1996. From then on, benchmarking has been used to compare national performances first in the domain of industrial policies, then in the economic and monetary fields, and finally in all domains where member states need to co-operate in order to establish framework conditions favourable to business and conducive to international competitiveness of both European companies and countries. This political program, in terms of competitiveness, was adopted by the Heads of State and Government in March 2000. It is known as the 'Lisbon strategy', and its ambition was to turn the European Union into the 'most

---

[3] 'This event was attended by over eighty senior representatives of national governments, European Union institutions and the business sector' (ERT, 1996: inside front cover).

competitive knowledge-based economy in the world by 2010' (European Council, 2000: §5). These ideas of the 'knowledge-based economy', 'full employment' and 'boundless prosperity' – as unrealistic as they may seem today – were in the air at that time. On the other hand, what was striking at that time was the new method of co-ordination that would replace the traditional Community Method. Since its inception, European integration has proceeded from the production of Community Law.

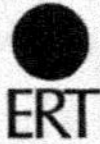

BENCHMARKING FOR POLICY-MAKERS IN A NUTSHELL

BENCHMARKING is looking at "the best in the class", learning from this experience, and then trying to do as well or better.

BENCHMARKING is a tool that many companies and some governments are already using with great success as a means to improve their performance.

BENCHMARKING is a powerful source of information for action, not an end in itself but a process... and a powerful motor of change and motivation.

BENCHMARKING works well in companies, but how well is it suited to public policy?

Some interesting **BENCHMARKING** initiatives already exist at national level : for example, in the Netherlands and Australia.

The political advantage of the **BENCHMARKING** approach to public policy is that it allows governments to work towards some common understanding of what needs to be done - and then to decide for themselves which way to go. In that sense, **BENCHMARKING** is policy-neutral.

The Maastricht Criteria are powerful **BENCHMARKS** that have spurred individual governments to make hard decisions in order to reach common European goals.

The ERT calls upon the Council of Ministers and the European Commission to make **BENCHMARKING** a key tool in EU public policy.

ERT

EUROPEAN ROUND TABLE OF INDUSTRIALISTS
113 avenue Henri Jaspar • B-1060 Brussels • Tel.: 32 2/534 31 00 • Fax: 32 2/534 73 48

'Benchmarking for policy-makers in a nutshell' (ERT, 1996)

In order to carry out the Lisbon strategy, a new methodology was designed and named 'Open Method of Coordination' (OMC). Unlike traditional methods, the OMC was neither legal, nor compulsory, but soft and incentivising. It was supposed to help Member States to progressively develop their own policies. How so?

- First, by 'fixing guidelines for the Union combined with specific timetables for achieving the goals which they set in the short, medium and long terms'.

- Second, by 'establishing, where appropriate, quantitative and qualitative indicators and benchmarks against the best in the world and tailored to the needs of different Member States and sectors as a means of comparing best practice'.

- Third, by 'translating these European guidelines into national and regional policies by setting specific targets and adopting measures, taking into account national and regional differences'.

- Lastly, through 'periodic monitoring, evaluation and peer review organised as mutual learning processes' (European Council, 2000: §37).

Of course, comparing statistical indicators and exchanging best practices were not unprecedented. But it remains that implementing such a disciplined and systematic way of coordinating national policies by means of comparable statistics, quantified targets and scoreboards, marked a turning point in the history of the European Union and of sovereign states. According to Jens-Henrik Haahr, the OMC is the European manifestation of advanced liberal government. It enables European policy-makers to 'contract, consult, negotiate, create partnerships, empower and activate forms of agency'. But, at the same time, these very practices also bring about 'norms, benchmarks, performance indicators, quality controls and best practice standards, to monitor, measure and render calculable their performances' (Haahr, 2004: 216). Needless to say, this methodology was not invented from scratch. As one may notice, the OMC approach is broadly in line with the four-stage process of benchmarking (see above). In short, the OMC is nothing else but a benchmarking exercise applied to countries – as meaningless as it is.

The case of the research policies is particularly emblematic. From the very beginning, 'establishing a European Area of Research and Innovation' was at the top of the Lisbon agenda (European Council, 2000). That is why benchmarking national systems of research and innovation was prioritized by the European Council. And as soon as 2002, a benchmark of '3%' had been established:

> In order to close the gap between the EU and its major competitors, there must be a significant boost of the overall R&D and innovation effort in the Union, with a particular emphasis on frontier technologies. The European Council therefore agrees that overall spending on R&D and innovation in the Union should be increased with the aim of approaching 3% of GDP by 2010. (European Council, 2002: §47)

It is worth noting that 'Two-thirds of this new investment should come from the private sector' (ibid.), that is to say essentially from companies which are induced to do so through tax credits for example.

This is in keeping with the overall project that aims at building a market, a 'knowledge market' with the sacrosanct principle of property. It's written in black and white in the magazine published by DG Research, which spoke of nothing less than achieving a 'cultural revolution'[4]. In order to populate this 'knowledge market', entrepreneurs are needed. More precisely, the scholar, the scientist, the committed intellectual should move over and let 'the researcher-entrepreneur' take care of knowledge in Europe[5]. By the same token, universities are subjected to the same transformation, insofar as they are caught in the crossfires of the Lisbon strategy and the Bologna process.

In short, the Lisbon agenda projected a 'knowledge market', populated with 'researchers-entrepreneurs', 'innovative teachers' and 'mobile students-consumers', who embodied the neoliberal subjectivities. Now everyone agrees that the Lisbon strategy ended in failure. Obviously, the 3% benchmark, like the Lisbon strategic goal as a whole, is still far from being achieved. As

---

[4] 'The days when knowledge acquired in academic scientific circles was handed down and available for all are well and truly over. In today's knowledge circles, acquisition goes hand in hand with protection and exploitation. Patents and, more generally, intellectual property rights (IPR) are very much the "hot topic" in the world of public research' (European Commission, 2002b: 16).

[5] 'The time when universities and businesses regarded each other with mutual suspicion is well and truly over. In recent years, the symbolic figure of the researcher-entrepreneur has become central to the organisation of research' (European Commission, 2002a: 6).

expected, the European Union is not 'the most competitive knowledge-economy in the world', and the spending on R&D has even been declining for the past ten years. As a matter of fact, it was no big surprise. European leaders were perfectly aware of that from the outset. A string of assessment reports kept sounding the alarm since the mid-term audit (European Commission, 2004). Nevertheless, no doubt was ever cast over the method itself. Benchmarking was never challenged, quite the opposite. The Open Method of Coordination has been streamlined; lists of indicators have been reduced to focus on even fewer benchmarks.

The new strategy, 'Europe 2020', emphasises further the key role of benchmarking in monitoring results and thereby sustaining the drive of competition. Why this? Why such obstinacy since the device has been ineffective so far? Because the '3% objective' – like the overall goal of competitiveness – was not made to be attained, but to spur policy-makers on to greater efforts towards economic reforms and social 'modernization', especially towards a 'knowledge market'. Plainly, the very function of benchmarks is to be unreachable: they are fugitive targets. In other words, benchmarks are like the dangled carrot that the donkey can never reach. And the stick is the subtle discipline of peer pressure, as well as of public opinion when league tables hit the headlines and your country lags behind in the ranking. The Lisbon strategy aims at coordinating national systems through an endless cooperation through competition, to which managers refer as 'co-opetition'. It plays on the 'indefinite discipline' of competitiveness.

Why indefinite? Because the norm of competitiveness is endogenous to the endless competition in which benchmarking engages its users. The benchmark, i.e. the reference point identified as a goal, is a moving target that cannot be reached once and for all. It is ideally fugitive, and hence unattainable, set only to be caught up and replaced by the latest 'best performer'. Setting competitiveness as the aim to achieve by means of benchmarking, which precisely consists in measuring gaps of performance so as to close them, amounts to strive to reduce a distance while reproducing it in(de)finitely. This expression of 'indefinite discipline' is taken from Foucault who coined it to refer to 'a procedure that would be at the same time the permanent measure of a gap in relation to an inaccessible norm and the asymptotic movement that strives to meet in infinity' (Foucault, 1995: 227). It captures very well how 'cognitive capitalism' condemns social creativity to overkill, just like other common resources[6].

---

[6] I elaborated on this in Bruno (2009).

11

Theorizing Regimes of Surveillance/Exploitation

Joanna Bednarek

1. Hardt and Negri: Controversy around Immaterial/Biopolitical Labour

The concept of biopolitical labour, introduced by Hardt and Negri in the *Empire* trilogy, seems to be the most promising for contemporary anticapitalist struggles, as it brings to light the fact that life as such, in its various manifestations, is a productive force. However, it is precisely this all-encompassing character and universality that is the source of the controversies it raises and of its potential limitations. One of the most important and controversial aspects of Hardt and Negri's stance in *Empire* is the thesis of the unification of the social factory, caused by the passage from Fordism to post-Fordism. The hegemony of immaterial/biopolitical labour – a form of labour that has as its basis cooperation and communication – constitutes the autonomy of the production process and the unity of the working class or multitude that provide the objective conditions for communism (Hardt and Negri, 2000: 31-34; Hardt and Negri, 2004: 107-115). The power of living labour is the consequence of its status as the most advanced form of production that renders obsolete other forms, deprived of its political potential.

This nexus of the notions of hegemony, degrees of advancement of the forms of labour and productivity of life itself is so tightly intertwined that it's not possible to use one of the concepts separately. And this is precisely what should be achieved, because not all parts of this nexus are equally useful.

Some – and I mean especially the concept of the unity of the multitude on the basis of the traits of the production process – seem to be nothing other than dead ends from the perspective of working class struggle.

My thesis is that in order to make the category of biopolitical labour, introduced by Hardt and Negri, more useful (theoretically and practically), it should be supplemented with the analysis of the internal diversity of the social factory – a feature that was underlined by Harry Cleaver in his *Reading Capital Politically* (2000: 70-71, 113) – and with the description of the particular forms of surveillance/exploitation in different economic sectors.

This attempt will also amount to the necessity of modifying the thesis, maintained by certain advocates of cognitive capitalism, on cognitive labour as the most advanced form of production. As I claim, it would be better to perceive it as a form specific to the centre of the world economy. The condition of its existence and its higher status is exploitation of the periphery (understood not only geographically, as regions of the capitalist world-system, but also structurally, as less advanced forms of labour).

Following George Caffentzis and Silvia Federici, I will maintain that we cannot describe tendencies of contemporary capitalism through the lens of the most advanced sectors of production. Caffentzis and Federici stress that establishing hierarchies between sectors of the economy and between geographical regions, as well as the creation of underdevelopment, are vital for capitalist accumulation:

> True, we need to identify the leading forms of capitalist accumulation in all its different phases, and recognize their 'tendency' to hegemonize (though not to homogenize) other forms of capitalist production. But we should not dismiss the critiques of Marxian theory developed by the anti-colonial movement and the feminist movement, which have shown that capitalist accumulation has thrived precisely through its capacity to simultaneously organize development and underdevelopment, waged and un-waged labour, production at the highest levels of technological know-how and production at the lowest levels. In other words, we should not dismiss the argument that it is precisely through these disparities, the divisions built in the working class through them, and the capacity to transfer wealth/surplus from one pole to the other that capitalist accumulation has expanded in the face of so much struggle. (2009: 127)[1]

---

[1] See also De Angelis (2007).

I would make an even stronger statement: the most advanced sectors do not embody the tendency of the system; they cannot serve as a model for the explanation of the evolution of the whole system. It is a practical/political mistake to conceive the capitalist system in terms of the linear order of sectors, from the most backward to more advanced.[2] Instead, we should always look at the system as a whole and the place of certain sectors in it, as well as their divisions and hierarchies.

The thesis on the exceptional role of knowledge production can strengthen existing hierarchies of the labour force, as it maintains the physical-intellectual labour distinction – a distinction that from the earlier stages of capitalism served to establish hierarchies, introduce divisions and occlude common experiences, and in consequence to set parts of the working class/multitude against each other.

The hypothesis of the passage to social capital should then be detached from the concept of immaterial labour. Therefore we could assume that immaterial/biopolitical labour as we experience it every day does not constitute the common and does not provide in itself the basis for communism.

The dominant trait of the capitalist system today is the imposition of precarity; however, it takes on diverse forms and is implemented by means of different techniques of surveillance/exploitation, depending on a given sector's position in the global economy. It may consist in the exploitation of creativity, but it can also take the form of a traditional disciplinary regime; the presence of these 'underdeveloped' forms of surveillance/exploitation is necessary for the system to function. I will demonstrate the importance of this diversity by referring to four examples of militant research, undertaken in different sectors of the social factory. These are: research on factory production by Pun Ngai; research on services (call centres) undertaken by the collective Kolinko; the analysis of some trends in the sector of intellectual

---

[2] The strategic role of the university is a fact, but, as Caffentzis and Federici comment with respect to the edu-factory project: 'We are concerned, however, that we do not overestimate this importance, and/or use the concept of the edu-factory to set up new hierarchies with respect to labour and forms of capitalist accumulation' (2009: 126).

labour in the traditional sense by Ursula Huws and Michael McNally; and research on precarised care workers by the collective Precarias a la Deriva.

I will focus on the following criteria:

- terms of employment (flexible contracts);

- privatization of the costs of reproduction as a form of control; and

- techniques of surveillance/exploitation in the workplace (disciplinary regime, exploitation of knowledge and affect).

The analysis of techniques used in each of the sectors reveals common features, the existence of similar tendencies that is nevertheless realized by means of different techniques. What is most striking in these examples (and what was the reason for choosing them) is the fact that they demonstrate the extent to which Fordist/Taylorist techniques of management are used in diverse sectors of our supposedly post-Fordist economy.

2. Surveillance/Exploitation

As we have learned from Foucault, techniques of control are productive. This productivity is, primarily, not economic, but rather, metaphysical. Taking into consideration the fact that Negri underlines the importance of Foucault's method for his own work[3], we could expect to find traces of this important motif in it. But despite these declarations the influence is not clearly visible. The interview in which Negri admits this influence is an example of his persistent attempt to describe Foucault's work in terms of a one-dimensional passage from modernity to postmodernity, from discipline to control:

> However it is true that even though Foucault uses thereafter the model of biopowers in his attempt to outline a critical ontology of the present, you will seek in vain analyses devoted to the development of capitalism and to the determination of the passage from the *Welfarestate* to its crisis, from the

---

[3] Negri writes: '… to assume the Foucauldian perspective also entails putting a style of thought, identified as the genealogy of the present and always open in so far as it deals with the production of subjectivity, in touch with a given historical situation. And this given historical situation is a historical reality of power relations' (Negri, 2004; see also Hardt and Negri, 2000: 23).

Fordist to the Post-Fordist organization of labour, from the Keynesian principles to those of neo-liberal macro-economic theory. But it is also true that in his simple definition of the shift from the regime of discipline to that of control at the beginning of the XIXth century [sic! – J.B.], we can already understand that the post-modern does not represent a withdrawal of the State domination on social labour, but it is rather an improvement of its control over life. (Negri, 2004)

Moreover, Negri openly disposes Foucault of his main thesis: that of the productivity of power, in favour of the statement of the autonomous organization of production. This is partly because Negri replaces a Foucauldian perspective on biopolitics, as a nexus of techniques of power, with a Deleuzian notion of biopolitics as a productive unfolding and self-organization of life itself. But it is certainly not Deleuze who is responsible for the use that Negri makes of this concept, stating that life/living labour is unified and autonomous due to the form it takes in the era of immaterial/biopolitical labour. As Nicholas Thoburn stated in *Deleuze, Marx and Politics*, Deleuze underlines that life is always already alienated; resistance rests in its ability to cross, by means of lines of flight, the boundaries and limitations established earlier (Thoburn, 2003).

The source of Hardt and Negri's stance can be situated mostly in Negri's earlier work from the 1970s, where he formulated the thesis that the passage to the stage of social capital amounts to the end of the validity of the law of value. In consequence, capital ceases to be productive and transforms into a principle of repression: 'at a certain level of capitalist development, capitalist command ceases to be necessary', '… [t]he form of value is pure and simple command, the pure and simple form of politics' (Negri, 1991: 159,148).

The effect of this unfortunate combination of Deleuze's theory and Negri's earlier theses from *Marx beyond Marx* is the idea that living labour organizes its production autonomously, with no need for the help of capital. The latter becomes merely an obstacle to the full development of the multitude's productivity – a parasite.

Here the question emerges: what is actually the status and nature of the capitalist mechanisms of exploitation? Are they really merely repressive? At this moment appears the possibility (and the need) of introducing the category of surveillance/exploitation. My inspiration here is the concept of the fractal-panopticon, introduced by Massimo De Angelis (2001a). The fractal-panopticon is a single regime that organizes the entire capitalist system. De Angelis states that the world market operates according to the rule of fractal-panopticism, whose features are:

- individualization – isolation of individuals

- modular character

- prices as indicators of productivity

- limitation of knowledge: no subject has the complete knowledge of the whole process, yet the system is supposed to work in perfect harmony

The function of the fractal-panopticon is the extraction of labour from the entire social field, as well as the disciplining of individuals/economic subjects. This will be especially important to me, as I am preserving from De Angelis' article only the basic intuition that there exist mechanisms whose function is at the same time surveillance, discipline or control and the extraction of surplus value. I'm also proposing something much more modest than De Angelis' concept, more limited in scope and more down-to-earth: a description of some tendencies of the capitalist system of surveillance/exploitation, based on selected examples of militant research.

3. Pun Ngai: The Dormitory Labour System as a Foucauldian Disciplinary Regime

Pun Ngai is a researcher and a founder of the Chinese Working Women Network, an organization whose goal is the empowerment of the migrant women workers. I will refer to the participative research undertaken by her in the 1990s in the Shenzhen Special Economic Zone in Southern China. This research is a testimony of profound changes in class composition in this country: the replacement of the Maoist working class with the *dagong* class (migrant rural workers):

> … the global process shatters the China's old socialist pattern of industrial ownership and China's old workforce composition, the latter of which has constantly been under restructuring since the mid 1990s. (Ngai, 2005: 2)

Ngai's research is a proof that discipline is not something obsolete and belonging to the previous stage of the development of capitalism. On the contrary, it is vital for the expansion of the sector of industrial production in China. What we might call the Fordist model of production is still important for the modern economy. It is, however, supplemented and transformed by a specifically 'post-Fordist' feature: the imposition of precarity.

This imposition is visible first of all in the legal status of the workers. They have no possibility of getting permanent residence in the city they work in (because residence is connected to the place of birth); they only have the entitlement to temporary residence, connected to the workplace, without the right to marry or to register a child (obviously, they also have no possibility of going on maternity leave). Although the workers are not supposed to marry or have children, the management often refers to the ideal of femininity in order to pacify them. No paid sick leave is allowed:

> Employers provide no paid sick leave, despite the fact that most employees contribute their share to social insurance – the central insurance fund contributed to by both employers and employees at the city level. (Ngai, 2005: 10)

Permanent health damage, which occurs very often, is to be dealt with after the girls stop working and return to the countryside (which they are supposed to do, though they would rather stay in the city).

The temporary character of work is inscribed into the legal system of Chinese Special Economic Zones: 'This newly forming working class is permitted to form no roots in the city' (*ibid.*: 4). The system is organized in such a way as to ensure that reproduction of the labour force is completely externalized (Ngai, 2004).

The second trait of this regime is the detailed management of life by means of discipline. The workers live in dormitories that belong to the company employing them. Since housing and employment are provided by the same subject, and the workplace is at the same time 'home', a detailed organization of their lives becomes possible. Life itself can be organized and managed in such a way as to limit the possibility of subversion: activities comprising the work process are decomposed into small and simple components, and timetables predetermine most of the possible activities.

This factory/dormitory discipline, combined with the privatization of the costs of reproduction of the workforce, is a powerful testimony to the fact that Fordist techniques of management are still one of the most important ways of organizing and exploiting of work.

4. Kolinko: Taylorization of Services in the Call Centre Sector

The second case will be an inquiry undertaken by the German collective Kolinko in the years 1999-2002. The reasons for starting the inquiry were the strike at a Citibank call centre as well as the expansion of the sector in Europe in the 1990s. The researchers describe call centres as 'communication assembly lines' and see them as a part of a more general process of deskilling of the labour force:

> especially in the banking sector the new work organisation of a call centre made it possible to attack the white collar employees' position. The tasks of a 'formally highly qualified' bank worker with several years of training are now executed by call centre workers, after two days of training, for about two thirds of the white collar wage and subject to much stricter controls as well as much higher workloads. ... The problem for management is that often they are not able to see what is really happening in complex workflows and thus are not able to measure, control, and ultimately increase the amount of work delivered. Therefore they have to divide those complex processes into simple single tasks. *The transition from artisans to the factory went like that, and it's no different in the call centre, even if customer cases are being processed, rather than metal or wood.* (Kolinko, 2002, emphasis added)

The members of the collective state that the same processes take place in industrial and in service sectors. No wonder they are very sceptical about the concept of immaterial labour, seeing it as a part of capitalism's attempt of presenting deskilling as a passage to the 'new economy':

> There has been a lot of ideological drivel concerning call centres.... they re-packaged capitalism as a 'service society' and emphasised how much we need call centres as a 'new kind of service'.... call centres were sold as a kind of new economy for the unskilled. (Kolinko, 2002)

Workers – human interfaces between a database and the customer – are subjected to insecure working conditions: time-limited contracts, sometimes one-day contracts (as in Audioservice in Berlin) or even, as in the case of Atesia in Italy, imposition of self-employment. The fluctuation of staff prevents the exchange of knowledge and the building of solidarity. The call centre sector is also feminized (about 60% of the employees are women).

Call centres use technologies that ensure both the control of workers' activities and the intensification of work; they prescribe the pace of work, as well as determine the sequence of steps undertaken by the worker:

> The connection of computer- and telephone devices allows a higher call rhythm and a strict control of the workers (through statistics on the call amount, breaks, etc.). The computer-software only allows us certain operations and a certain chronological order which we have to perform them in. The calls are automatically put through to our phones ('Automatic Call Distribution, ACD' – [central, computer-controlled telephone machine]), sometimes even without us picking up the phone – straight to the headset ('direct-to-ear'). That way they want to prevent us having any control over the amount of calls we accept. In outbound, after finishing one call, often the computer starts dialling up the next customer so we have no time to take a breath ('power dialler').… Many call centres… register every step the worker does on the phone – accepting the call, duration of the call… – and the worker has to push buttons on the 'Call Master', a kind of telephone with loads of buttons. There is a button for every kind of break: official break, loo, training, post-processing. (Kolinko, 2002)

The double task of surveillance and the maximization of productivity is also facilitated by performance quotas that entail: arbitral set ratios of calls per hour or per day and statistics used to create new norms; personal statistics of each worker; and daily statistics displayed in the workplace. In addition, workers are inspected individually by way of mystery calls. The organization of work serves the same purpose. Teamwork, for example, makes employees control each other:

> the teams are just a way to form smaller, 'easy-to-control' units out of the mass of workers. That way the management has less difficulties getting through measures to intensify work. Teams are formed to channel conflicts and, if possible, to sweep them under the carpet. (Kolinko, 2002)

The concentration of workers in one place is also part of the surveillance/exploitation system. Technically, call centre agents could work at home; but concentration, making training and surveillance easier, is eventually better than isolation, which could amount to granting them too much autonomy. It also enables direct cooperation between workers and between workers and management – but this applies only to some call centres; in others direct communication between workers is not needed and therefore kept down.

Creativity is not well received in most call centres; the workers are supposed to use standard phrases or the script prescribing the content of the whole conversation: 'A conversation is supposed to be ninety percent pre-phrased from the script. Not only the words are pre-phrased but also what you emphasise, how you raise and lower your voice' (Kolinko, 2002).

This is problematic, as in many cases the employees feel forced to diverge from the scripts, not only because using them is unnatural and embarrassing, but also because it leaves a bad impression with the customer. A 'natural' way of talking is perceived by them as a better way of establishing a relation with the customer. Scripts seem to be counterproductive, serving only to limit workers' creativity. This phenomenon seems to support Hardt and Negri's thesis on the autonomy of biopolitical labour. Still, many call centres persistently rely on standard phrasings; this may indicate that it is an important feature of the productivity of this sector. Why? The answer could be the following: the requirement of using standard phrases and the script, besides being the most efficient way of guaranteeing that the employee will present the whole offer to the customer, are a part of the brand identity, and this identity, in addition to the particular goods or the advice, is what is really sold by the call centres.

There are exceptions to this picture: creativity and the interest in software are encouraged in some of the call centres (mostly in those that belong to software producers); even private activities are tolerated to some extent:

> Everyone is surfing and e-mailing but it's not forbidden either. After all, it's part of your 'training'.… A lot of people do it because they're interested in it... or because they want to show the team leaders that they're interested... or to pass time. (Kolinko, 2002)

But sometimes this private interest in software is used to limit the communication between employees:

> In the call centre where I work lots of workers loaded PC games onto their computers or surfed the internet during breaks or wrote private e-mails or stuff like that. That didn't necessarily make the breaks shorter so management restricted the use of the internet to certain sites and deleted all games from the computers. The only thing they left was some paint program. First we wondered why they left us a fucking paint program that we really don't need for work. Then you could see that during the breaks a lot of people played with the paint program thus remaining at their desks, while others loitered

around the coffee machine talking to each other. That showed us why. (Kolinko, 2002)

5. Huws and McNally: The Taylorization of Intellectual Labour

Michael B. McNally (2010) provides an analysis of Enterprise Content Management (ECM) systems, a type of software that focuses on unstructured content and makes possible the coordination of all the steps in the production of documents. He interprets the introduction of these systems using Harry Braverman's thesis of the deskilling of the industrial and, later, white-collar labour force:

> While an employee may have been free to perform a wide range of tasks before the deployment of an enterprise content management system, such software ultimately casts the employee's role within a narrow range of simple, scheduled functions. (McNally, 2010: 367)

ECM systems make possible the decomposition of the work process into small simple steps; they also offer the possibility of tracking every change in a document's history. The ability to access the documents can be predetermined by management. It is also possible to set automatic expiration dates; every simple task can be assigned a deadline. The Taylorization of the work process made possible by ECM is openly praised by its producer:

> IBM uses Taylorist language such as, 'processes can be broken down into their component parts for subsequent analysis',… and 'BPM's graphical process definition provides consistent, comprehensive view of the processes under management' … in promoting their ECM software. (McNally, 2010: 363-364)

As a consequence of the introduction of ECM, workers are deprived of a broader knowledge of the work going on within their own institutions: 'Knowledge is taken and separated from employees and reified into capital in the form of the ECM system' (*ibid.*: 365).

Generally, ECMs implementation entails three dimensions of deskilling: loss of skill; loss of knowledge about the work process and loss of tacit, private knowledge. As McNally stresses, it is precisely the capture of this knowledge that was the main goal behind the project of ECM:

> an intellectual worker's most important resource, his or her own knowledge, is transformed from tacit knowledge, which is theirs exclusively, to the legally

protected property of the employer. The ability of ECM systems to capture tacit knowledge is one of their primary attributes, with IBM noting that their system can, 'capture critical undocumented information from the aging workforce'. (McNally, 2010: 364)

ECM has the power to deskill workers and control them, as well as to facilitate the creation of an intellectual assembly line. This has, as McNally observes, disastrous consequences for intellectual work, because it contributes to the reification of the human process of content creation.

Of course, ECM implementation also requires the upskilling of some employees, especially those in IT departments, or the system administrators; but this is tantamount to the introduction of hierarchy that privileges small groups at the expense of the disempowerment of the many. As McNally remarks, theoretically some features of ECM could transform employees that use them intp a 'collective worker' – but in reality this rarely is the case. And even with this proviso, they remain profoundly ambiguous:

> While a review of the technical literature on ECM systems identifies the potential for deskilling, there also exists a potential for upskilling and using the collaborative features of such software including blogs, wikis and instant messaging, to make work more social, though workers must remember that even new mechanisms for social exchange created by information systems can fall under the panoptic control of management. (McNally, 2010: 368-369)

Ursula Huws in the article *Expression and expropriation: The dialectics of autonomy and control in creative labour* (2010) describes current trends in the restructuring of knowledge-based work. The main change consists in the intensification of the pace of work. The trends become exacerbated by the global division of labour (as an example from the fashion industry shows: the longer the transport from the countries where the manufacturing takes place takes, the less time is left for creative work). The dominant trend is also standardization (the fashion industry again: the pressure to use image processing software packages forces the designers to choose between standardized shapes instead of creating them).

The imposition of precarity onto the creative workers is visible in the increase of the requirement to work in response to customer demands and the expectation that they absorb the impact of customer dissatisfaction. Flexibility is here something that constrains rather than empowers the workers, and can be understood only in a negative way. Huws also points toward the emergence of two-tier structures, with small numbers of specialists and great numbers of easily replaceable generic workers.

The overall conclusion from McNally's and Huws' research would be the following: capital has to standardise some aspects of creative work in order to increase efficiency. This limitation of creativity definitely contributes to productivity:

> The management of creative workers is widely recognised as a challenge for capital. A recent *Economist* article put it like this: 'Managing creativity involves a series of difficult balancing acts: giving people the freedom to come up with new ideas but making sure that they operate within an overall structure, creating a powerful corporate culture but making sure that it is not too stifling'. (Huws, 2010: 517)

6. Precarias a la Deriva: Precarity as Existential Category

Spanish collective Precarias a la Deriva ('Precarious Women Workers Adrift') takes inspiration from the tradition of autonomist feminism and feminist economy. They also use drift, a practice taken from the Situationists, as an exercise in militant research. Theirs is a modified, 'situated' drift that concentrates on daily routes of the workers.

According to the members of the collective, nowadays precarity becomes a condition of life: it concerns life in general, the whole of existence, not only the terms of employment; moreover, it concerns the whole of society, not only the poorest. Instability, popularity of fixed-term contracts and deterioration of the social networks that ensure care become the norm.

Precarias introduce the notion of the sex-care-attention communicative continuum: its function is to elicit the common traits of different forms of care work. The goal that Precarias set for themselves is to underline, in their practice as well as theory, the continuity between the work of language teachers, migrant domestic workers and sex workers; to stress the aspect of creativity in care labour, as well as the phenomenon of exploitation of life in its mental and bodily capabilities. This 'continuum' is of course a political, not merely descriptive, category: the common of these all types of work has to be articulated.

Precarias emphasize the everyday and omnipresent character of affective labour, as well as the fact that it consists of activities that were traditionally assigned to women; as they remark, women always were precarious workers (Precarias a la Deriva, 2003). Biopolitical labour is at the same time material, emotional and intellectual – all three dimensions are intertwined. Precarias also turn our attention to the corporeal character of communication that is the basis of affective labour: 'these three elements (sex, attention and care) create relationships; they are modes of corporeal communication' (Precarias a la Deriva, 2006).

At the centre of the collective's research practices is the present crisis of care, connected with neoliberal restructurisation. Their attention is focused on two important aspects of this process. The first one is the specificity of the commodification of attention in the so-called service society:

> attention as a differentiated activity constitutes a new element. This capacity of listening and empathy, just as associated with models of femininity but also with the concrete activities historically reserved for women (in the areas of care as much as in sex), is isolated as a specific function and put to work for the nascent attention industry, in its different variants: telemarketing, telesales, teleassistance, customer service… In this manner, attention, exchanged for money in function of a temporal pattern of measure, is separated from incarnated communication, that which produces lasting relations, trust, and cooperation, and turns to a functionalized and uninvested exchange of codes (words and gestures). (*ibid.*: 35)

The second one is the commodification of domestic work, and, more broadly, the phenomenon of the 'externalization of home', imposed by the decline of the welfare state. As they notice, the necessity of outsourcing of domestic labour tasks, combined with the global division of labour, bring about the generalized instability of the conditions of living: 'Uncertainty for periods of illness and old age, above all for those who do not have the money to buy care at the market prices' (*ibid.*: 38).

Despite the emphasis put on the similarities, Precarias also point towards the internal divisions present in the sex-care-attention continuum. One can identify in it three types of care labour, each of whom has its specific goal and form of resistance or struggle:

- Repetitive work – telemarketing, supermarkets, form of resistance: absenteeism

- 'Fulfilling' precarious jobs like nursing or teaching: demand for change of form and content, conditions of labour

- Invisible work: domestic workers, sex workers: struggle for recognition (Precarias a la Deriva, 2004)

Surprisingly, Precarias a la Deriva refer to Negri in a positive way, treating him as a critic of the limited notion of immaterial labour – which is quite rare among feminists. Quoting Hardt and Negri, they suggest that one of the biggest errors of such an analysis of immaterial labour resides in:

> the tendency… to treat the new labouring practices in biopolitical society only in their intellectual and incorporeal aspects. The productivity of bodies and the value of affect, however, are absolutely central in this context. (Hardt and Negri, 2000: 29-30)

But, contrary to Hardt and Negri's thesis on the autonomous organization of production in the stage of social capital, Precarias a la Deriva state that care and 'biopolitical labour' understood as the precarisation imposed by the present system represent two opposing logics and thus stand in direct opposition. The present regime, operating through the isolation of individuals and the privatisation of the activities necessary to sustain life, is a combination of macropolitics of security and micropolitics of fear, whereas the bases of care are interdependence and affective virtuosity. The latter category was introduced as a means of conceiving of care not as private service, but as work requiring certain qualifications and skills (but not commodified work in capitalist sense).

7. Conclusions

The tendencies in surveillance/exploitation that I have tried to reconstruct consist at least of two dimensions: the Taylorization of the labour process and the imposition of precarity (the privatisation of reproduction costs).

The labour process is not open to employees' creativity and initiative; on the contrary, it subjects workers to very precise rules of performance. Workers' autonomy and creativity is rarely valued in itself; even in the case of intellectual labour the norm is its standardisation and subjection to rigid rules concerning efficiency as well as provided content. Certainly, creativity is valued in some limited, relatively small sectors, where it is a condition of the valorisation of capital. The examples can be art, the media sector or the activities of internet users. But techniques of surveillance make even the freedom present in these sectors questionable.

Flexibility does appear in this regime, but entirely concerns the status and the desired behaviour of the workforce: people are forced to accept the demand of flexibility, mobility and social insecurity, and to cover the costs of reproduction of themselves and their children (as feminist economists, like Rachel Kurian, Lourdes Beneria and Spike V. Peterson for example, have already stated some time ago).

Now the key question is: do the Taylorist techniques described by Pun, Kolinko, McNally and Huws contribute to the increase of productivity? Or are they only means of controlling the working class, disempowering it, ensuring its obedience to capital? This is not merely a metaphysical question whose aim is to at introduce some scholastic differentiation – or, to be more precise, it is a metaphysical question, but one that can have interesting practical consequences. If the latter was the case, we should agree with Hardt and Negri's statement that the labour of the multitude directly produces the common, and that capital, with its regimes of surveillance, only controls and exploits living labour, without contributing in any way to its productivity. But, as the examples I referred to above demonstrate, capital frequently uses techniques that either stifle creativity and cooperation or mould it in such a way as to ensure that it would serve the valorisation of capital and not of the working class. Thus,from this perspective we cannot speak of the productivity or creativity of the working class as of something autonomous; and even less as of something that leads to its self-valorization.

Taking this into consideration, we can conclude with the statement that two interpretations of Hardt and Negri's thesis are possible. The following distinction between these interpretations will be introduced by using the Deleuzian distinction between the virtual and the actual (see Deleuze, 1990; Deleuze and Guattari, 1987):

1. The multitude/working class organizes its work autonomously: this should be understood literally, as applying to work in its actual dimension, in present conditions, conceived of empirically. The work process as we experience it is the outcome of living labour's *potentia*.

This interpretation is not only counterintuitive, but also has rather upsetting consequences for resistance and politics. This is because the cooperation we now experience in the work process is the final form of the organization of the multitude, there is no such thing as exploitation, and alternative forms of labour are unthinkable. The interpretation of the autonomy of living labour as actual leaves us with the reality of work as it is under capitalism (as the imposition of efficiency and productivity) as the ultimate horizon.

One of the examples of militant research quoted earlier provides us with remarks that can cast some light on this problem. Kolinko write about call centre workers complaining about the software used, the management or the organization of work not letting them perform their work properly:

> Most workers want to help the customer, but they fail due to the work-organisation and required work speed… If the information the customer demands is not available the worker has to start improvising, lying or trying in other creative ways to wriggle themselves out of the sticky situation. This determines how a lot of call centre-workers relate to their 'service': 'I can't change the organisation of work. Some things just don't work and I'm the fool who has to compensate for them by talking!' (Kolinko, 2002)

But, as the inquiry makes obvious, the organization of work is not bad by accident; the company is not supposed to provide genuine advice given by experts; what is sold is rather the illusion of such advice. A similar observation was made by Barbara Ehrenreich, who writes in *Nickel and Dimed*:

> I was amazed and sometimes saddened by the pride people took in jobs that rewarded them so meagerly, either in wages or in recognition. Often, in fact, these people experienced management as an obstacle to getting the job done as it should be done. Waitresses chafed at managers' stinginess toward the customers; housecleaners resented the time constraints that sometimes made them cut corners; retail workers wanted the floor to be beautiful, not cluttered with excess stock as management required. (2001: 116)

The possibility of efficient organization of work by the employees themselves appears here as a constitutive illusion of exploited workers; an illusion that enables the internalization and subconscious acceptance of the capitalist dictate of efficiency.

It is very hard to find in the realm of the actual any unequivocal confirmation of the thesis on the multitude's self-organization in the work process. The only thing we do find is this illusion of pure efficiency that stifles its power of resistance. What then about the second possible interpretation?

2. Autonomous production exists virtually, not actually: it is involved in the actual form of work processes. It is accessible under certain special conditions, but not in our everyday experience of work, which is, as our intuition rightly gives us a hint, organized by and for capital.

The virtual has no other being than the forms in which it is actualized. But, though it is always present in the actual, it also is inaccessible for us under normal circumstances; we can access it only by way of certain practices. And these practices are, in our case, nothing other than the practices of resistance, or workers' struggles (against work). This is completely congruent with the basic assumption of *operaismo* (an assumption that Hardt and Negri sometimes seem to forget about) that work is never a neutral, purely technical process, but always a place of struggle. It could then be stated, in good, old school 'refusal of work' style, that the work process is the proper space in which we could seek the political potential of the working class only if it is, at the same time, conceived of as a process of resistance.

PART FOUR:
RESISTANCE

12

The Artistic Mode of Revolution: From Gentrification to Occupation

Martha Rosler

A discussion of the struggles, exoduses, and reappropriations of cognitive labor, especially in the field of visual art, and especially when taken as the leading edge of the 'creative class,' while critically important, is trumped by the widespread, even worldwide, public demonstrations and occupations of the past year, this year, and maybe the next. I would like to revisit the creative-class thesis I have explored in a recent series of essays (published in *e-flux* journal [Rosler, 2010; 2011a; 2011b], and republished as part of the volume *Culture Class* [Rosler, 2013]), in order to frame my remarks in light of these occupations and to make a few observations about the relationship between artists, the positioning of the creative class, and the Occupy movement. in order to frame my remarks in light of these occupations and to make a few observations about the relationship between artists, the positioning of the creative class, and the Occupy movement.

Even before 'the multitude' became a common touchstone for dreams of revolution, there was, famously, Seattle 1999, when anti-corporate protests brought environmentalists and community activists together with organized labor to block a meeting of the World Trade Organization, a scenario repeated at multiple locations in several countries in the years since.[1] It is not

---

[1] The movement generally pegged as anti-globalization is more properly referred to by its members and supporters as the 'alt-globalization' movement or some variant of that term and is anti-corporate more than alter-globalization – although globalization is a term derived from its enthusiasts; see the discussion of Theodore Levitt below.

news that the processes that go under the name of globalization, which center on the flows of capital, goods, and labor, create a unity that does not always serve the interests of capital or the capitalists.

Nouriel Roubini (2011a), channelling Marx, wrote in 'The instability of inequality' that 'unregulated capitalism can lead to regular bouts of over-capacity, under-consumption, and the recurrence of destructive financial crises, fueled by credit bubbles and asset-price booms and busts.'[2]

Roubini is saying that capitalism tends toward catastrophic collapses – no news here. But the point is that neoliberalism and its rampant financialization have created a capitalism that eats its young. Roubini goes on to remind his readers that even before the Great Depression, the enlightened bourgeoisie realized that worker protections and a redistributive system providing 'public goods – education, health care, and a social safety net' were necessary to prevent revolution.[3]

Roubini (2011) remarks further that the modern welfare state grew out of a post-Depression need for macroeconomic stabilization, which required 'the maintenance of a large middle class, widening the provision of public goods through progressive taxation, and fostering economic opportunity for all'; but all this went under during the massive Reagan-Thatcher deregulation, which Roubini – no Marxist after all – traces in part to 'the flaws in Europe's social-

---

[2] See Roubini 2011a, 2011b. Roubini begins the blog post of October 14, 2011, by alluding to 'social and political turmoil and instability throughout the world, with masses of people in the real and virtual streets': 'The Arab Spring; riots in London; Israel's middle-class protests against high housing prices and an inflationary squeeze on living standards; protesting Chilean students; the destruction in Germany of the expensive cars of "fat cats"; India's movement against corruption; mounting unhappiness with corruption and inequality in China; and now the 'Occupy Wall Street' movement in New York and across the United States.' (Roubini, 2011b)

[3] I addressed this issue in an essay of 1981 on documentary photography ('In, around, and afterthoughts: on documentary', first published in *Martha Rosler: 3 Works* [Halifax: Press of the Nova Scotia College of Art & Design, 1981]).). I was pointing out that ideological images were employed in the United States, during the Great Depression, to mobilize support for the very poor under the Roosevelt Administration, with the understanding that alleviating suffering would forestall revolt.

welfare model [...] reflected in yawning fiscal deficits, regulatory overkill, and a lack of economic dynamism.' (*ibid.*)[4].

Roubini, unlike most, goes on to proclaim the failure of this 'Anglo-American economic model' of embracing economic policies that increase inequality and create a gap between incomes and aspirations, accompanied by the liberalization of consumer credit and thus rising consumer debt, as well as public debt because of decreased tax revenues, all of which is then followed by counterproductive austerity measures. This is precisely the financial model that seized the imagination and drove the policies of former Eastern bloc governing elites, many of whom in implementing the prescribed austerity measures, are destroying their present and future middle classes (see Latvia)[5], as is neo-Thatcherite Great Britain.[6]

---

[4] I am using Roubini here as a convenient figure, since one might quote from quite a few other economists, particularly Joseph Stiglitz, Dean Baker, Paul Krugman of the *New York Times,* or Simon Johnson, former chief economist of the Internatiomal Monetary Fund, to outline the fears of the left-liberal wing of Western economists.

[5] Latvia, a tiny Baltic country that (like the other two Baltic states, Estonia and Lithuania) broke free of the collapsing Soviet Union in the early 1990s, is so far the sharpest example of this syndrome; one might also cite Ireland and possibly Greece, Spain, and Portugal in the coming year – all of which stand in contrast to the course of Iceland (the tiniest economy of all of these, but, as luck would have it, not a member of the Eurozone), which was promptly to reject any terms imposed by international financial agencies and instead defaulting on its debt and pursuing their top bankers for criminal fraud. In the early 2000s, Latvia's center-right government instituted aggressive neoliberal measures in large part to join the Euro and escape the dominance of Russia. After the financial crisis of 2008, Latvia experienced the most precipitous financial decline of any nation, losing about a quarter of its GDP in 2 years. Its government then applied stringent fiscal austerity, including slashing pensions and wages. The budding middle class, in a familiar story, had been induced to buy homes on cheap credit, but this mortgage debt (owed largely to Swedish and German banks) cannot be repaid, while property values have also plunged. The austerity measures have failed to improve Latvia's balance sheets but has sent the middle class, not to mention the poor, into subsistence mode – or emigration. Tens of thousands of Latvians have left, and unemployment stands at or above 20 percent A reference from 2010 is http://www.counterpunch.org/2010/02/15/latvia-s-road-to-serfdom/;   and

In the United States, Citibank, which required two US government rescues after the financial crisis of 2008, posted record quarterly profits of \$3.8 billion in the fall of 2011, a 74% increase over the previous quarter, while its CEO, Vikram Pandit, expressed his sympathy with the Occupy Wall Street protesters and offered to meet with them.[7]

The ongoing round-the-world occupations, which have drawn inspiration from the uprisings across the Arab world in 2011, are driven by the frustration of the young educated middle classes – in the Arab case fairly new ones – confronting societies controlled by hugely rich ruling elites but having little hope of a secure future for themselves, despite their university educations. These are societies that had made no effort to create modern welfare or even neoliberal states, nor to control corruption, bureaucratic indifference, and flagrant nepotism, nor to institute more than the appearance

---

from 2011, http://krugman.blogs.nytimes.com/2011/07/18/lats-ofluck/. Yet, like Ireland, Latvia is bizarrely hailed as a successful example of austerity budgeting. (Krugman [2011] writes: 'A few more successes like this and Latvia will be back in the Stone Age.')

[6] The European Commission in 2011 voted in 'the six pack' – a group of measures that overrides member states' abilities to control their budgets, reinstituting the Maastricht Treaty's limit of 3 percent on deficits and 60 percent of GDP on debts, beyond which large fines will be levied, among other penalties. According to economist Susan George , the Commission is also engineering a shift in worker protection leading to longer work weeks, lower pay, and later retirement. See Susan George, 'A Coup in the European Union?' *CounterPunch*, Oct. 14, 2011, online at http://www.counterpunch.org/2011/10/14/a-coup-in-the-european-union/. The still-developing situation in regard to Greece (which will have EC monitors in place enforcing austerity measures) shows the antilabor direction, a hallmark of neoliberalism, of the European financial governors.

[7] See http://www.businessweek.com/news/2011-10-12/panditsays-he-d-be-happy-to-talk-with-wall-street-protesters.html; http://money.cnn.com/video/news/2011/10/12/n_vikram_pandit_protesters.fortune/; and for JPMorgan Chase's CEO Jamie Dimon, making essentially the same point, see http://video.foxbusiness.com/v/1450365871001/dimon-policies-made-recovery-slower-and worse/?playlist_id=87247.

of democratic governance. Protesters in the developed world are aware of sharing conditions that are functionally quite similar.[8]

Such protests – as in France in 2006, which saw widespread mobilization against 'precarization', as well as the subsequent uprisings in the Paris *banlieues* or in England in August 2011 – also reflect the anger of working-class youths, especially their rage against racist police violence. In the English case, these young people were out there smashing and looting together with young

---

[8] Although Western European protests in response to the prospect-less future, such as the *indignados* or *encampados* in Spain and the many demonstrations in Greece's Syntagma Square, were critical examples, and the uprising in Tunisia was ultimately at least a partially successful one, the sheer scale and unlikely success (similarly only partial) of the occupation in Cairo's Tahrir Square made it the touchstone for the movement, and it remains so regardless of its as-yet unfulfilled aims. In recognition of its role, veteran occupiers of Tahrir Square sent a message to Occupy Wall Street: 'The current crisis in America and western Europe has begun to bring this reality home to you as well: that as things stand we will all work ourselves raw, our backs broken by personal debt and public austerity. Not content with carving out the remnants of the public sphere and the welfare state, capitalism and the austerity state now even attack the private realm and people's right to decent dwelling as thousands of foreclosed-upon homeowners find themselves both 'home- less' and indebted to the banks who have forced them on to the streets. So we stand with you not just in your attempts to bring down the old but to experiment with the new. We are not protesting. Who is there to protest to? What could we ask them for that they could grant? We are occupying. We are reclaiming those same spaces of public practice that have been commodified, privatized and locked into the hands of faceless bureaucracy, real estate portfolios and police "protection". Hold on to these spaces, nurture them and let the boundaries of your occupations grow. After all, who built these parks, these plazas, these buildings? Whose labor made them real and liveable? Why should it seem so natural that they should be withheld from us, policed and disciplined? Reclaiming these spaces and managing them justly and collectively is proof enough of our legitimacy.' (Comrades from Cairo, 2011). [http://www.guardian.co.uk/commentisfree/2011/oct/25/occupy-movement-tahrir-square-cairo]

As we go to press in late 2013, the Egyptian revolution is in the process of complete collapse, and the country has fallen back under military control; revolutionary processes are inherently unstable.

members of the middle class. Some of the latter group had mobilized months earlier – as young Chileans are doing still – thanks in no small part to crushing increases in school fees driven by the Tory/Liberal Democrat governing coalition. The protests of these groups, these classes, have been fired by the recognition that there are likely no secure jobs for them, or perhaps any employment at all.

But precarization is not a necessary consequence of any particular form of labor.

Precarization now joins mechanization (the replacement of workers with machines), delocalization (capital's worldwide search for the weakest labor and environmental regulations), and financialization (the maintenance of excess value in the stock market as opposed to surplus value extracted from manufacturing) as one of the great strategies used to restore profitability since the late 1960s. These strategies supplement the more widely noted assaults on the welfare state and worker's rights (Marazzi, 2010b). Many of the protesting students and young postgraduates, for their part, were preparing for jobs in what we have come to call the knowledge industries, or, more recently, the creative industries, a branch of the former.

1. University as engine, lifeways into lifestyle

Let me step back a bit, to the consolidation of this sector in the newly dawning information age of the early 1960s. Clark Kerr, labor economist, first chancellor of the University of California's elite Berkeley campus, and then president of the entire UC system, saw the university as a site for the production of knowledge workers. In 1960 he oversaw the creation of an expansive Master Plan for growth into the twenty-first century that harmonized the state's higher education institutions and organized them into three tiers: research universities, state colleges, and two-year 'junior colleges' (renamed 'community colleges'). This 'benchmark' plan acknowledged a need to unify the training and administration of the entire knowledge sector, from the elites to the working classes, in a politically divided world. In his widely influential work, *The Uses of the University* (1963), Kerr called the university a 'prime instrument of national purpose', and he envisioned the 'knowledge industry' (his term) as eventually supplanting the industries surrounding new modes of transportation – railroads in the nineteenth century and automobiles in the twentieth – in unifying the nation, acting as its economic masthead, and serving as the motor of US world dominance.

The foundational student protest movement of the 1960s, Berkeley's Free Speech Movement, was triggered in part by Kerr's educational and managerial policies and goals. It was a movement of a leading sector of the middle class who were destined to become the elite workers of the new knowledge industries, if not their leaders. Ironically, today the UC system is almost broke, confirming the exemplary use of college campuses by Apple's dictionary, in defining the term 'bellwether', that 'college campuses are often the bellwether of change.'[9]

In contrast, the 1970s Britain punk subculture was arguably a working-class response to a diminished future, despite its partial traceability to art school, which in any case was a newly experimental repository for working-class misfits. As Dick Hebdige described it:

> Despite the confident assurances of both labor and conservative politicians… that "we never had it so good" class refused to disappear. The ways in which class was lived, however, the forms in which the experience of class found expression in culture, did change dramatically. The advent of the mass media, changes in the constitution of the family, in the organization of school and work, shifts in the relative status of work and leisure, all served to fragment and polarize the working-class community, producing a series of marginal discourses within the broad confines of class experience. (Hebdige, 1979: 78)

Punk was anti-commodity and anti-corporate, and followed a tactic of uglification and self-mutilation, a *fuck you!* response to bourgeois culture; the fact that it was quickly commodified and heavily promoted in the music industry is beside the point… until, at least, it became the point. For the post-1970s generations, lifestyle politics became almost indistinguishable from either politics or daily life, and that frame of reference has now spread around the world.

Indeed, lifestyle has been intensively developed as a major marketing point for consumer goods. In a prime nugget of lifestyle marketing analysis offered in 1984 (when the thinking was new), Theodore Levitt, Harvard professor of business administration and marketing, commented on the failure of the

---

[9] *The New Oxford American Dictionary* has since 2005 come installed on Apple computers using version OS X.

Hoover corporation to sell washing machines in Europe: 'It asked people what features they wanted in a washing machine rather than what they wanted out of life'[10]. Levitt, editor of the *Harvard Business Review*, is credited with popularizing the term 'globalization'. In *The Marketing Imagination*, his bestseller of 1983, Levitt pointed out that as a result of media expansion worldwide, the United States was in a unique position to market its goods everywhere, making its so-called high touch goods – jeans and Coca-Cola – right up there alongside high tech ones (and integrally, along with them, Americanism and the English language) into the world's most desirable possessions.

> A powerful force drives the world toward a converging commonality, and that force is technology… . Almost everyone everywhere wants all the things they have heard about, seen, or experienced via the new technologies. (Levitt, 1984: 2)

In short, without naming it but simply placing it under the rule of the 'imagination', Levitt defines the new key to marketing dominance as a wholesale subordination of rational product claims to universalized Bernaysian psychological modeling, which is the basis of lifestyle marketing. Levitt refers to homogenization as both the means and the result of globalization.[11] He differentiates multinationals from the more forward-thinking global corporations, which, he says,

> sell standardized products in the same way everywhere – autos, steel, chemicals, petroleum, cement, agricultural commodities and equipment,

---

10 Levitt (1984: 13) writes, in distinguishing what he considers a multinational mind set from a global one: 'The Hoover case illustrates how the perverse practice of the marketing concept and the absence of any kind of marketing imagination let multinational attitudes survive when customers actually want the benefits of global standardization. The whole project got off on the wrong foot. It asked people what features they wanted in a washing machine rather than what they wanted out of life. Selling a line of products individually tailored to each nation is thoughtless. Managers who took pride in practising the marketing concept to the fullest did not, in fact, practise it at all. Hoover asked the wrong questions, then applied neither thought nor imagination to the answers.'

11 In the homogenizing world market, certain goods, such as pizza, tacos, and bagels, become near-universal signifiers of difference.

industrial and commercial construction, banking and insurance services, computers, semiconductors, transport, electronic instruments, pharmaceuticals, and telecommunications, to mention some of the obvious. (*ibid.*: 4)

Thirty years on, we have placed many of these categories in Levitt's rather jumbled array under the rubric of the knowledge industries, including the management of Fordist industrial production (of 'autos, steel, chemicals, petroleum, cement, agricultural commodities and equipment,… computers, semiconductors, [...] electronic instruments, pharmaceuticals'). Thirty years on, lifestyle politics, as both a unifier and a differentiator, help determine how we live or are supposed to live. People form alliances based on taste, above all via the tribalism of appearance-as-identity. Commodified lifestyle clusters include not merely possessions but persons, achievements, and children, and they tend to be costly to acquire and maintain.

Punk is now another lifestyle choice, albeit an urban romantic one. Along with Goth and other ways of life associated with New York's East Village, punk also provides the preferred uniform of suburban and small-town mall-dwelling malcontents, while the 'Bronxish' hip-hop style, which is popular worldwide, does the same for working-class people of color. In this taxonomy, hipsterism is the lifestyle of arty types – the triumph of surface over substance – and is a direct consequence of the easy availability of cultural goods through technological means.

But there are times when the professionalization of art training in colleges and universities, combined with the capture and branding of artist-led, artist-run initiatives – the ones which used to reside outside the purview of art institutions – can broaden the social network and the vocabulary of action. It is a commonplace that in a post-industrial economy virtually all work falls in some sense under the reign of language and symbolic behavior. Certainly, all cultural products are flattened into 'information', mashing together writing, research, entertainment, and, of course, art. The popular reception of art and its greatly expanded audience have allowed, in the present moment, a mutual visibility between artists and other underemployed groups, both educated and undereducated.

Or perhaps more directly, looking for a series of master texts, the newly professionalized discourse of artistic production settled on Continental theories of aestheticized capital. How else to explain the peculiar position of artists at or near the vanguard of capitalist organization? Thus, even if the tendency may be toward the professionalization and *embourgeoisement* of artists, along with other members of the symbolic sector, when the future hits a brick wall, those ideas and alliances *in potentia* can have revolutionary consequences. The artists and artist-run groups, and others belonging to the creative-class demographic – which often overlaps with the group of those who identify as grass-roots activists, whether or not they have been to art school – have been at the center of instituting, strategizing, and energizing the Occupy Wall Street movement at New York's Zuccotti Park – renamed Liberty Park.

A way of life that relies on virtue and secular good living, as sold to a generation raised on school and media campaigns promoting civic responsibility and morality – such as Just say No to Drugs[12], Smoking Kills, and Save the Earth – is no doubt more likely to be adopted by urban art-school grads than any other demographic group. These are young urban professionals, perhaps, but not the 'yuppies' of the past (though I am interested to see that the term has returned). The latter were high-earning lawyers, ad-agency honchos, and magazine editors, while these new young urban professionals are low-level workers and wannabes in their field. City life appeals to members of these industries, which themselves are made up of networks of small shops that benefit from face-to-face relations and the excitements of the urban environment.

2. The new creative city

This wave of renewed preference for the city can be traced to the postwar economic boom in Western industrial democracies – I am looking at the United States – which led to the rising affluence of the middle class. Immediately after the war, many city dwellers, having gained some measure of financial security, migrated to small towns and freshly built suburbs, causing urban shrinkage[13]. One effect of this depopulation was the evacuation

---

[12] Drugs, that is, not considered part of the approved Big Pharma formulary. This is important because among other things it allowed adolescents to make distinctions between good and bad drugs, but often based on criteria other than legality.

[13] I am minimizing the all-important role of capital flight and runaway shops here.

of many city business centers and the failure of many urban industries. But the direction of migration began to be reversed as bored children of the suburban middle class (along with corporate managers and the newly defined yuppies) were drawn to the organized pleasures of city life, not least the museums and theatres, as well as the dizzying mixture of anonymity, community, diversity, and possibility that fills the urban imaginary. To point out the obvious, the stultifying, homogeneous experience of life in the suburbs, with its identical malls and fast food joints, doesn't offer the would-be creative much in the way of identity formation; and insofar as the local exists today, it is found either in the city or in rural small towns, not in fenced-in suburbia.

This repopulation and transformation of cities – from spaces bereft of shops and manufacturing, starved of resources, and inhabited by poor and working-class people or squatters living in ill-maintained housing stock, into spaces of middle-class desire, high-end shopping, and entertainment – took at least a generation. It also required the concerted effort of city leaders. New York's Soho and East Village had proved, by the late 1970s, that the transformation of old warehouses and decaying tenement districts into valuable real estate could be accomplished by allowing artists to live and work in them – if nothing else, city government recognized or identified with such people and understood their needs. Those elected officials who might, in an earlier era, have supported organized labor, found that such constituencies were fading away. Artists, in addition, were not going to organize and make life difficult for city governments. In the following decades, the Soho model became paradigmatic for cities around the world. (Another popular tactic was to attract small new industrial shops, mostly high tech ones.) But no matter how much the arts (whether the performing arts or the institutionalized visual arts in museums) have been regarded in some cities as an economic motor,

---

Since racism was an important motivator, the resulting urban shrinkage is often attributed in no small part to 'white flight'. Small towns often became dormitory towns for city workers. The small town has remained the preferred location of US residents for most of its history and was idealized during the high point of American sociology that spanned the Second World War.

that remedy is not applicable everywhere, and not every city has proved to be a magnet for the arts. A new urban theory was required.[14]

The civic usefulness of educated but often economically marginal young people was first popularized by a young professor of urban planning at Carnegie-Mellon University in post-industrial Pittsburgh. What Professor Richard Florida saw around him in that declining city was neighborhoods made cozy and attractive by the efforts of recent grads, who were setting up coffee shops and small businesses in low-rent locations. The customer-friendly environment – friendly to middle-class customers – emphasized shared tastes passed down since the mid-1960s via schools, music, movies, and magazines, tastes that define a particular niche among the educated, professional middle class. Elements of what might ironically be seen as suburban virtue, from recycling to gardening to arts and crafts (perhaps rescued from the lore of small-town Edens by nostalgic lifestyle magazines), were now being brought back to decaying city neighborhoods.

Professor Florida developed a new theory based on selling these congeries of young, generally underemployed people – as well as such subcultural categories as gays, who also tended to congregate in what used to be called bohemian neighborhoods – to urban planners as a sure-fire remedy for urban desuetude. (Or apparently selling them, for there is a bait and switch tactic at work here.) His book (Florida, 2002) *The Rise of the Creative Class: And How It's Transforming Work, Leisure, Community, and Everyday Life* offered a crafty new turn in business evangelism, creating a catchy new way of thinking about city marketing as lifestyle marketing – much as Theodore Levitt had done for brand marketing – and throwing a lifeline to often desperate city managers.[15] With his apparently systematic analyses, Florida parlayed his popular book into a new job and a consulting career. He is now the head of the Martin

---

[14] Although the demonization of working-class and poor residents in areas ripe for real-estate harvesting is a tactic of long standing, the in-coming 'good people' have only recently been granted a profile of their own; previously, class privilege was taken for granted as a deserved entitlement.

[15] Florida did not come up with the idea of the creative class, but he did populate it with statistical categories. According to his thesis, the creative class makes up about 30 percent of U.S. workers, but as we shall see, the groupings he uses are problematic.

Prosperity Institute at the University of Toronto, and he is consultant to cities, corporations, museums, and nonprofits around the world. Prosperity, like the lovely name Florida, is a keyword. His website says

> The Creative Class Group is a boutique advisory services firm comprised of leading researchers, communication specialists, and business advisors. CCG combines a pioneering approach of global thought leadership and proven strategies offering clients worldwide the market intelligence critical for competitiveness and greater economic prosperity[16].

I have addressed Florida's 'creative class' thesis in a series of earlier articles (see Rosler, 2013); here I offer an abbreviated digest, to flesh out the argument. There is a certain irony to revisiting this matter now, as the long-term financial downturn has cast some doubt on the appeal of creative-class theorizing in the areas under financial strain, but the thesis has had a decade to catch hold, and catch hold it has.[17] Florida's analyses have struck a chord with city managers by appearing to promote diversity in ways that often replicate what is already in place. Many who have scrutinized his data have demonstrated the insufficiency of his analyses and thus his conclusions.[18] Critics point out that in relying on standard census categories, he sweeps into the creative class all knowledge-industry workers, from those in call-centers

---

[16] Creative Class Group, 2013, http://www.creativeclass.com/.

[17] Toronto, Florida's base, is currently afflicted by a mayor with a take-no-prisoners, right-wing populist style, complete with racist and anti-gay pronouncements and actions. In repudiating the previous government's agenda, Toronto's suburbanite Mayor Rob Ford has cut funding for bike lanes and light rail. Asked about Florida's response, Torontonians with whom I spoke said that he has been largely silent but has quietly complained that the city was cutting all the things that made Toronto 'his city'.

[18] Recently Florida has been criticized again for sloppy interpretation and aggregation of polling data and economic statistics in his article 'Why America keeps getting more conservative' published in the venerable magazine *The Atlantic* (these days politically center-right), where he is one of 19 editors (Florida, 2012). Many other commentators read the data quite the opposite way and claim that the US electorate is, on the contrary, growing increasingly liberal in its beliefs while US politics, thanks to the radicalization of the Republican Party, have moved to the right. See Alterman (2012), Jaffe (2012).

to professional data analysts, scientists, and mathematicians – hardly artists.[19] A consensus on his conclusions is that they amount to the well-established 'human capital' thesis of urban development placed within new linguistic frames, and most importantly with the 'creative' moniker generously washing over everyone in the knowledge industries. A small, relatively poor group of urban dwellers, the ones offering consumer friendliness and local color, becomes the face of the other, larger, richer, but basically invisible members of Florida's 'supercreative core' grouping.[20] In his shell game, creatives are defined under one shell as people whose mental engagement is at the heart of their work and under another as people who know how to live nicely, decoratively, and cheaply, and under yet another as primarily a high-earning, tax-paying economic grouping. As policy follows prescriptions, inconvenient, poorly accoutered working-class people are marginalized, pushed further out to the edges of the city or to the suburbs, while in the newly reclaimed city precincts, bourgeois predilections – of ego-centered, commodified, and mediated rituals – enfold every milestone in life, from

---

[19] Florida ingeniously includes in his mix a statistically small bohemian group, which includes gay people, but as Harvard economist Edward Glaeser has reluctantly noted, his data regressions suggest that in only two cities – in, yes, the state of Florida – does the gay population help the economy.

[20] '[T]o harness creativity for economic ends, you need to harness creativity in all its forms. You can't just generate a tech economy or information economy or knowledge economy; you have to harness the multidimensional aspects of creativity. [...] there are three types of creativity: technological creativity [...]; economic creativity, [...] turning those things into new businesses and new industries; and cultural and artistic creativity, [...] new ways of thinking about things, new art forms, new designs, new photos, new concepts. Those three things have to come together to spur economic growth. The creative class is composed of two dimensions. There is the supercreative core, [...] scientists, engineers, tech people, artists, entertainers, musicians – so-called bohemians that are about 12 percent of the workforce [...] the supercreative core is really the driving force in economic growth. In addition to the supercreative core, I include creative professionals and managers, lawyers, financial people, healthcare people, technicians, who also use their ideas and knowledge and creativity in their work. I don't include people in service or manufacturing industries who use creativity in their work' (Florida and Dreher, 2002).

birth to premarital stag and hen parties, weddings, baby showers, births, communions, and maybe even deaths.

3. The limits of creativity, and of liberalism

Many critics naively fail to realize that Florida, like Clark Kerr, is a social liberal. Like most neoliberals, he is out there on the rhetorical barricades arguing for tolerance, subsidies, and the right of the creative class to perform the work of the patrician class for little or no compensation. In a strange way, then, he can be taken as the collective projection of a certain branch of the liberal elite. Liberals are happy to celebrate artists, or even better, 'creatives' — that amorphous group of brewers, bakers, urban farmers, and baristas — as long as their festivals and celebrations can be sponsored by banks, corporations, and foundations and their efforts civically branded. Architectural institutes hold meetings and publish newsletters touting 'livable' cities. Arts institutions benefit from the attention of governmental agencies and foundations, but the costs are also worth considering.

Artists, already complicit (wittingly or unwittingly) in the renegotiation of urban meaning for elites, were called upon to enter into social management. Real-estate concessions have long been extended to artists and small nonprofits in the hopes of improving the attractiveness of 'up-and-coming' neighborhoods and bringing them back onto the high-end rent rolls. The prominence of art and 'artiness' allows museums and architecture groups, as well as artists' groups, artists, and arts administrators of small nonprofits, to insert themselves into the conversation on civic trendiness.

Artists are hardly unaware of their positioning by urban elites, from the municipal and real estate interests to the high-end collectors and museum trustees. Ironically, perhaps, this is also the moment in which social engagement on the part of artists is an increasingly viable modality within the art world and young curators specialize in social practice projects. Many artists have gone to school in the hopes of gaining marketability and often thereby incurring a heavy debt burden. Schools have gradually become the managers and shapers of artistic development; on the one hand, they prepare artists to enter the art market, and on the other, through departments of 'public practice' and 'social practice', they mold the disciplinary restrictions of an art that might be regarded as a minor government apparatus. These programs are secular seminaries of 'new forms of activism, community-based practice, alternative organization, and participatory leadership in the arts' that explore 'the myriad links between art and society to examine the ways in which artists… engage with civic issues, articulate their voice in the public realm'[21].

To look again at the United States – but not only there – arts and architecture institutions are quite pleased to be swept along by the creative-class urban-planning tide. The distinctly old-economy, luxury-vehicle maker BMW has joined with the Guggenheim Museum to create 'a mobile laboratory traveling around the world to inspire innovative ideas for urban life', with the names of some high-profile artist and architect attached.[22]

The 'Lab' firmly ties the corporation, the museum, architecture, art, and entertainment to the *embourgeoisement* of cities. Urban citizenship has replaced other forms of halo-polishing for so-called corporate citizens. By the way, they all like bikes. As does Urban Omnibus – which also likes 'Art as urban activator'. The Urban Omnibus is an online project of New York's venerable Architectural League and is funded by foundations, the city of New York, and the federal government.[23] Its recent feature, 'Civic action: A vision for

---

[21] These quotes are from a job announcement put out by a department at a major university that offers 'a Master's Degree in Arts Politics which treats, in an activist key, the nexus between the politics that art makes and the politics that make art'. Despite my skepticism, I don't want to dismiss the potential of such training and network formation; the problem lies in the short life span that such initiatives can have before the institution render them zombies. See the latter two installments of my *Culture Class* essay for a discussion of the culturalization argument of Fredric Jameson and its adoption by George Yúdice to argue that art that can be framed as social practice may put the artists in the position of unwittingly serving the aims of the state and, by focusing on melioration, of abandoning the possibility of critique. See also footnote 4, above.

[22] See http://www.bmwguggenheimlab.org/ (accessed 24.04.2012). There was an unsuccessful effort by artists to occupy the lab during a day of artists' actions.

[23] See http://urbanomnibus.net/ (accessed 24.04.2012). Urban Omnibus is funded by the Rockefeller Foundation's New York City Cultural Innovation Fund, the National Endowment for the Arts, the New York City Department of Cultural Affairs, and the New York City Council. The Architectural League was founded

Long Island City', describes a new venture, developed by two local contemporary art museums, that 'invites artist-led teams to propose visions for the future of Long Island City', a neighborhood in the borough of Queens, New York, that is a post-industrial ruin with new high-end waterfront residential development. Another feature, 'Making Room', is 'a research, design, and advocacy project to shape New York's housing stock to address the changing needs of how we live now'[24]. In March 2012, as I was writing this section, there was a feature on the site in which a freelance writer described an open house at the newly renovated jail, The Brooklyn House of Detention, an event designed to placate the neighborhood gentrifiers that all will be well (Sohn, 2012). I am here using the Lab and Urban Omnibus to represent the myriad efforts of city agencies and elite institutions – and some free-standing ones or those attached to public universities that still follow a non-corporatized path, to adopt the now virtually naturalized creativity and hipster-friendly memes posed in terms of imagination, design, and advocacy, just as in some respects I am using the name Florida to represent the creative-class thesis that his work has helped turn into dominant policy lingo.

The Florida version of the Soho urban transformation model, as I have argued, fails to capture the agency of the actors in his transformational scenarios. Just as science has been seen in the capitalist mind as a necessary steppingstone to technology (a business term), creativity is regarded as the necessary ingredient of 'innovation'. The creative classes as constructed by Florida operate strictly within the world view pictured by the capitalist imaginary; even those who are not simply employees in high tech firms are seen to be instituting small businesses and learning to deliver retro boutique services that bear echoes of pre-war American neighborhood shops and delicatessens or even nineteenth-century 'purveyors' (next up, the milk wagon and the seltzer-delivery man!) or idealized French or Italian shops in cities and villages. They have no agency outside the application of their imaginative abilities to the benefit for the gentrifiers and the well-to-do. They have no agency in respect to large-scale political and social transformation. It is true

---

in 1881 by Cass Gilbert and has long sought to recognize the importance of the arts in relation to architecture.

[24] The phrase 'how we live now' evidences a predictable set of assumptions about who constitutes the 'we'.

that the Florida model is not strictly interested in those whom the present readership recognizes as artists. But here the picture of agency is even worse in respect to the market artists whose potential social worth is quite directly to serve the interests of the international clientele inhabiting the most rarefied income heights, a service role to which several generations of artists have been trained to aspire.

But this is not the picture of ourselves that most of us artists, curators, critics, wish to recognize. Like other participants in the movements taking place around the world, and like participants in earlier ones, artists tend to want to lend themselves and their energy and abilities to social betterment and utopian dreaming, but not necessarily as participants within the sanctioned institutionalized frames. The artistic imagination continues to dream of historical agency. In a protracted economic downturn such as we are experiencing now, while the creative-class thesis is showing its limits in respect to saving cities, it becomes clearer that artists and other members of the art community belong to the pan- or non-national class whose composition is forged across boundaries and whose members are inclined, as the cliché demands, to think globally and act locally.

Political movements are perpetually dogged by accusations of 1960s nostalgia and even Luddism, a result of the antimodernism of much 1960s counterculture. People on the left are routinely derided by the Right as dirty fucking hippies, and once the occupations began, the Right was not slow to use this picture to discredit the occupiers. But the constellations of dissent have largely changed since the 1960s. If people are aiming to secede from modernity, they do so with a different range of continental theorists to draw upon, and without the three-worlds model of political contestation, in which the land-bound peasant figured strongly as an ideal, or the tribal nomad for those not inclined to socialist revolution. Revolution now looks more anarcho-syndicalist, or perhaps council communist, than Marxist-Leninist. The city is not simply the terrain to be evacuated, nor is it the site of guerrilla warfare; it is a conceptual puzzle as well as a battleground in which the stakes are slow-motion class war, and farming is brought to the city not by dreamers in homespun clothing but by those who might adopt the garb of the professional landscape architect or beekeeper. 'Creatives' may bring not only training in design and branding, and often knowledge of historical agitprop and street performance, but also the ability to work with technological tools in researching, strategizing, and implementing actions in virtual as well as physical spaces. Actually or functionally middle class, they are at ease with the discourses and modes of intellectual endeavor required in higher education, or in college prep. Craft and skill are enfolded in a framework that differs significantly from their earlier understanding; but the hegemonic role of the knowledge industries and the 'devices' of electronic production and communication render that framework near-ubiquitous.[25] The often flexible schedules of artists and other members of the precarious sectors of Florida's creative/bohemian classes also permits a freedom to come and go at encampments and meetings, an ability to shift time and work commitments that is not available to all.

---

[25] The most prominent sign of technological sophistication is the frequent visual reference to Anonymous, an amorphous group of hackers, or hacktivists (of which one small international groupuscule, LulzSec, was arrested in February 2012), in the form of the Guy Fawkes masks from the V for Vendetta franchise (worn by protesters and occupiers and used on signage). 'Anonymous' apparently has carried out denial-of-service attacks against the websites of the governments of Tunisia, Egypt, and Bahrain during the attempted revolutions there, and it has expressed or enacted support for Occupy. See: http://www.youtube.com/watch?v=l6jdkpQjueo&feature=g-vrec&context=G27aba48RVAAAAAAAACg (accessed 24.04.2012).

I do not have the space here to dissect further the possible role of this pointedly anarchic, often playful, assemblage of hackers. But in more workaday fashion, a range of technological ease is suggested by the facility with which the Occupy movement has made use not only of the widely know popular media sites such as Facebook and Twitter but also of less well known ones, sites such as Vibe, the older IRC, the now indispensable Livestream, Reddit, or internet relay chat, according to *PC Magazine* (see Strange, 2011) as well as Tumblr and Google Docs. See: http://mappingthemovement.tumblr.com/ (accessed 24.04.2012).

To quote an early assessment: 'We set up shared google docs so we could communicate [...] and we set up google voice numbers for everyone. [...] One Tumblr page, *We Are The 99Percent* (http://wearethe99percent.tumblr.com/) reveals the plight of people who see themselves as far outside the top 1 percent of Americans' (in Emspak, 2011). See http://news.discovery.com/tech/occupy-wall-street-timblr-111006.html.

We can see the occupation activists as staking a claim, creating a presence, setting up a new public sphere, demanding the reinstatement of politics by refusing to simply present demands to representative governments and instead enacting democracy themselves. (Democracy has long been part of the American particular brand, albeit usually combined with double-barreled neoliberalism – or neoimperialism.) While welcoming the new, I can't resist pointing back to the old, not to the eighteenth-century demands for self-governance led by a group of bourgeois colonial rebels in the American colonies but to the American Civil Rights Movement and one of its children, the Free Speech-inspired, anti-war, worldwide student movement of the 1960s, for which democracy – direct democracy, without representation – was a foundational idea, at least as the degree zero of the movement in the early years.[26] In this current iteration, the contributions of celebrity artists such as Shepard Fairey (made famous by his Obama/Hope campaign poster of 2008) have been politely greeted but are beside the point, as it is not hard to see the occupations themselves as grand public works of process art with a

---

[26] Here I am looking not only to the town meetings of the early days of the American colonies but explicitly to the model of nonviolent participatory democracy propounded by one of the groups central to the Civil Rights Movement, the Student Nonviolent Coordinating Committee, or SNCC. Many of the young student activists had joined SNCC's Freedom Rider campaign to disrupt racial segregation in the American South, which influenced the principles outlined shortly after in the Port Huron Statement, a foundational document of the student/antiwar movement. Naturally enough, the history, origins, and influences of these movements are more complex than I can sketch out here. The widely noted, galvanizing speech of Berkeley student leader Mario Savio, delivered in the Berkeley campus quadrangle on Dec. 2, 1964, during a stand off with university police, includes the following in its preamble: 'I ask you to consider – if this is a firm, and if the Board of Regents are the Board of Directors, and if President Kerr in fact is the manager, then I tell you something – the faculty are a bunch of employees and we're the raw material! But we're a bunch of raw materials that don't mean to be – [to] have any process upon us. Don't mean to be made into any product! ... Don't mean to end up being bought by some clients of the University, be they the government, be they industry, be they organized labor, be they anyone! We're human beings!'

cast of several thousand.[27] The vast majority of artists – forming the core of the underpaid, unpaid urban army whose activities Florida acolytes wish to harness – live in a state of precarity that may lead them to seek social solutions in new and unexpected ways. This is where the so-called artistic mode of production comes in.

Urban sociologist Sharon Zukin, writing in 1982, identifies this precariousness of bohemian life as one of the five major ways in which this artistic mode of production affects the urban environment. The others include the 'manipulation of urban forms [and] the transfer of urban space from the old world of industry to the "new" world of finance, or from the realm of productive economic activity to that of nonproductive economic activity'; diminishing expectations about the provision of housing resulting from the substitution of 'bohemian' living arrangements for contemporary housing; and, finally, the ideological function:

> While blue-collar labor recedes from the heart of the financial city, an image is created that the city's economy has arrived at a post-industrial plateau. At the very least, this displaces the issues of industrial labor relations to another terrain. (Zukin, 1989: 180)

If the creative-class thesis can be seen as something of a hymn to the perceived harmony between the 'creatives' and the financiers, together with city leaders and real-estate interests, guiding the city into the post-industrial condition, perhaps the current grass-roots occupations can be seen as the eruption of a new set of issues related to a new set of social relations of production. The mode of production, we remember, includes the forces of production but also their relations, and when these two come into conflict, a crisis is born. If the creative-class thesis can been seen as something of a hymn to the harmony between the creative forces of production and the urban social relations that would use them to the benefit of cities bereft of industrial capital, perhaps the current grassroots occupations can be seen as the inevitable arrival of the conflict between the creatives and the city that uses them. It is interesting, in this respect, that the battle cry has been

---

27 Artists' groups are increasingly making this point, for good or ill; see Fellah (2011), Schwendener (2011). See, for example: http://newamericanpaintings. wordpress.com/2011/11/09/the-art-ofoccupation and http://www.villagevoice. com/2011-10-19/art/what-does-occupy-wall-street-men-for-art.

'Occupy' (which echoes Florida's similar injunction to gentrify), that is, to occupy space, to occupy the social and political imagination, in a way analogous to the way previous movements radicalized freedom into emancipation, republic into democracy, and equality into justice. Florida says gentrify, we say Occupy.

That leads us to the next step, now under way. What the occupations have done is to make members of disparate groups – neighborhood advocacy groups, immigrants'-rights groups, and working-class labor groups, both organized and not, visible to each other – and in Occupy's first phase put them into temporary alliances. It is these alliances that form the nuclei of the occupation of the present and future.

13

The Composition of Living Knowledge: Labor, Capture, and Revolution

Gigi Roggero

0. From Struggles to Struggles: Situating the Concepts

Starting from the struggles and coming back to the struggles: only in this movement are concepts embodied, becoming an expression of the creative *potentia* of the multitude. This means that there is no theoretical practice outside political practice. From a revolutionary point of view, there is no production of knowledge that is not immanent to the composition of living labor and its historical determination. We will shortly focus on three of these concepts that are part of a collective experience: 1) autonomy of living knowledge; 2) communism of capital; and 3) institutions of the common.[1]

In the global crisis, our thesis is that the latest transnational struggles over the last years are determined by the convergence and differentiation of a downgraded middle class and a proletariat whose poverty is directly proportional to its productivity: they are put in common by the irreversible end of the progressive promise of capitalism, the definitive collapse and exhaustion of the school and university as an elevator for social mobility and the generalized perception of precariousness and indebtedness as a permanent condition. Be careful: talking of a common composition of the global struggles does not at all refer exclusively to Europe. In Tunisian and

---

[1] These collective experiences have, first of all, the names of UniNomade (uninomade.org), Commonware (www.commonware.org), and edu-factory (www.edu-factory.org). This is the reason why in the text I will use the plural first person.

North African insurrections, as well as in the Chilean movement or Occupy Wall Street, the central subject is exactly the young, highly educated (in a formal or informal way, i.e. full of knowledge), and impoverished person. From this point of view, in contemporary capitalism, the Marxian definition of the poor comes true: the poor is living labor, the form of life that produces the others' wealth and its own poverty. In fact, in struggles within the global crisis, cognitive labor is becoming a political subject, or it is becoming class — if we define class not in economist terms, but as the formation of the collective subject in the struggle within social historically determined relationship. To use Mario Tronti's (2008) words: there is no class without class struggle. And it is becoming class immediately on a transnational plane, because today there is no possibility of political action limited within the nation-State borders: this is a fact.

On this base, we want to make the opposing aspects of our analysis explicit right away. On one side, there is a picture of global capital through the re-proposition of the dialectic between centre and periphery, for which the former shows the image of its own future, according to a progressive line of development. The corresponding idea of class is founded on homogeneity, for which the subject most advanced in the capitalist hierarchies is, in a deterministic way, the most advanced one in the struggles. On the other side — we are thinking mainly of the constellation of the postcolonial studies — there is a correct critique of this historicist idea, belonging to the tradition of socialism and orthodox Marxism, showing heterogeneity as a constitutive element of the composition of contemporary living labor. But this correct critical approach often risks concluding the impossibility of the common composition of the differences, that is to say, the impossibility of breaking with capital and the construction of a new social relationship.

Therefore, we could say against the first pole: differences are irreducible to homogeneity; and against the second: but they can compose themselves in the common. Because the common is the base and the product of differences and multiplicity. In fact, if they are separated from the common, differences become fetishes, continuously translated in the language of value: this means making capital the only active subject of history, homogenous and empty, abstract and normative. So the risk is to fall again into the historicist trap that was originally put into question. In other words, universalism is never a starting point, as imaged by the Enlightenment and socialist traditions, but it is always what is at stake in the struggles and the product of living labor cooperative's *potentia*.

We should briefly clarify what this means for cognitive capitalism and cognitive labor. It does not refer to a new stage of the historical process, marching towards the transition beyond capital, its *Aufhebung*. And cognitive labor does not identify a sector of the technical composition of labor, as the 'knowledge workers' or the 'creative class', or the forms of labor in specific areas of the world. Cognitivization (becoming cognitive of labor) is a process through which we can read the new quality of capital's relations and the specific forms of exploitation and class antagonism today: in this process, knowledge is not only a source, but also a means, of production. In its production, we can qualify the forms of accumulation and the contemporary class composition on a global level. To use Marx's *Einleitung*, the cognitivization of labor is a 'general illumination which bathes all the other colours and modifies their particularity. It is particular ether which determines the specific gravity of every being which has materialized within it' (Marx, 1973: 107). If we do not grasp this general illumination, we cannot understand the specific elements, new or old, that are determined or re-determined.

1. Autonomy of Living Knowledge

Over the last years, within university movements and transnational networks[2], we have elaborated the concept of living knowledge that rose from the *operaista* analysis of the 1970s on the transformations of class composition (Alquati, 1976). We want to immediately give a warning about a populist interpretation of this category: in Italy, for example, some groups use it as an idea synonymous with knowledge 'from below', in opposition to academic knowledge, 'from above'. There is nothing more subaltern than this idea of below and above.

Instead, in Marxian terms, living knowledge indicates the new quality of the composition of contemporary living labor. The process of formation of living knowledge is rooted in the struggles over education, against waged

---

[2]   See the activiy of the edu-factory collective. For in depth analysis, see Roggero (2011).

labor and in the flight from the chains of the 'Fordist' factory, in the anti-colonial movements and global migrations. So the concept of living knowledge points out not only the central role of science and information in the contemporary productive process, but above all its immediate socialization and embodiment in living labor. This means that today the classical relationship between living labor and dead labor becomes a relationship between living knowledge and dead knowledge. In this process, on one hand, living knowledge is valorized by capital, on the other hand, it tends to become autonomous with regard to the automatic system of machines. This leads the general intellect to no longer be objectified in dead labor, at least in a stable way. This means that knowledge cannot be completely transferred to machines and separated from the worker: the traditional process of objectification nowadays is overthrown, and living knowledge embodies many aspects of fixed capital, producing and regenerating the machine uninterruptedly. Living labor/knowledge needs to be vivified with a rapid temporality, from which there is a continuous excess of living and social knowledge. 'The primary fixed capital becomes man himself', affirms Vercellone (2007: 29), paraphrasing Marx. From this standpoint, the telematics network is an obvious and illuminating example.

In this context, the necessity to reduce living knowledge to abstract knowledge, or the imperative of the measure of labor despite the crisis of the law of value, forces capital to impose completely artificial units of time. To use Marx's words, it is for capital a *'question de vie et de mort'*. To reassure Marxist intellectuals and philologists, we can add that the crisis of the law of value does not coincide with its disappearance: however, it becomes not only a bare measure of exploitation, but an immediately empty and artificial measure of command. This is the political point. Therefore, capital has to capture the value of the production of subjectivity, to interpret in the double sense of its genitive: on one hand as the constitution of living labor, on the other hand as its productive *potentia*, not only for capital but also autonomously (Read, 2003). All in all, capital has to capture the production of the common in its double statute: it is, at the same time, the form of production and the horizon of a new social relationship, it is what living knowledge produces and what capital exploits. On this plane of tension between the autonomy of living knowledge and capitalist capture, we can find the space and time of antagonism today.

At this level, we have to re-think the relationship between the technical composition and political composition of class, i.e., the relationship between the capitalist articulation and hierarchization of the workforce and the process of its formation as an autonomous subject. These concepts were elaborated by *operaismo* in a specific phase, marked by the struggles of the workers in the relationship between the Taylorist factory and Fordist society. Nowadays, with the tendential overlapping between labor and life, there is also a sort of overlapping and confusion between technical and political composition. When production is based on the common, we could say in a certain sense that political composition comes before technical composition. Or technical composition is the block and segmentation of political composition. We have to elaborate a new concept of *common composition*: this exactly what is at stake.

2. Communism of Capital

The term communism of capital was used some years ago also by milieu close to *The Economist*, explicitly going back to the expression of 'socialism of capital' through which Marx described the rise of stock companies. Nowadays, the communism of capital (Marazzi, 2010a) is the form of the capitalist social relationship in the age in which it is based on the capture of the common. In other words: less and less does capital organize the social cooperation upstream, like in the phase of industrial capitalism; more and more must it organize this capture downstream. The corporate figure of the cool hunter can be an example here. If in the 1920s Henry Ford said 'buy the car that you want, the important thing is that it's a Ford Model T', summarizing the (impossible) capitalist dream to induce the needs from above, the cool hunter acts directly downstream, trying to capture and translate the excess of forms of life and expressions of subjectivity into the language of the value. The 'centre' is forced to go into the 'periphery' in order to capture the production of the common.

In this context, the classical distinction between profit and rent is quite problematic: when capital appropriates a social cooperation that mostly takes place without its direct organization, these two terms overlap. So rent becomes the form of capitalist command that captures the autonomous production of living labor/knowledge. The Schumpeterian entrepreneur is definitely dead. Today the form of the enterprise is the organization of the 'hunters of the common'. A quick joke: if the Bolshevik party overthrew the highest level of the *potentia* of the associated living labor productive force – the factory – in subversive enterprise, today we could say that capital is forced to overthrow the highest level of the *potentia* of the associated living labor productive force – the network – in the form of the enterprise.

This analysis allows us to understand why many contemporary liberal and neoliberal scholars have exalted the characteristics (free cooperation, centrality of non-proprietorial strategies, horizontality of relations and sharing, etc.) that are the patrimony of critical media scholars and activists. For example, Yochai Benkler (2006), starting from the description of the cooperative and self-organized practices in the web, hypothesizes the emergence of a horizontal production based on the commons. The well-known jurist of Yale University illustrates the passage from a system based on intellectual property to a system increasingly based on open social networks, in which open source and free software are entirely valorized[3]. From Benkler's analysis, it's simple to observe that the production of the common is at the same time extreme resource and mortal threat for contemporary capitalism. And if intellectual property risks blocking not only the autonomous power of the productive forces but also the dynamics of innovation that innervate production relations, then capitalism has to become 'property-less'. This is the clash between Google and Microsoft, or the alliance between IBM and Linux. This is the web 2.0, that is to say, the response to the autonomy of the living knowledge of autonomous networking.

But to recompose command and govern social cooperation downstream, capital is continuously forced to block the productive *potentia* of living labor/knowledge with various means – from intellectual property to precariousness. This constitutes the new form of the contradiction between productive forces and production relations and therefore the base of the contemporary global economic crisis, i.e. the crisis of the communism of capital. So, against the interpretation of the crisis that re-proposes the contraposition between the real economy and the financial economy, we can

---

[3] For an important critique of the digital utopia and its developments, see Pasquinelli (2008).

define financialisation as the real and concrete form, although perverse, of capitalist accumulation in a system that must capture value that cannot be measured without command, that is as violent as well as empty and artificial as its capacity of organization.

On this base, we can also say that we have to question and re-think the cyclical nature of the capitalist process (crisis – restructuration – expansion – new crisis, and so forth). Since the communism of capital is based on the capture of what it cannot organize and what structurally exceeds it, i.e. the production of the common, the crisis assumes a permanent dimension. Let's think back to the crises of the last fifteen years: from the collapse of the South-East Asian markets, to the crash of Nasdaq, up to the subprime crack and, recently, the explosion of public debt; we witness an exceedingly rapid succession of bubbles with deep global effects – from net economy to debt, and maybe the next one will be the ecological or social network bang. The question is: what is inside the bubble? There's the Internet and networks, i.e. social cooperation; there is the debt, i.e. welfare and social needs – education, communication, houses, healthcare, and mobility; there is life, i.e. the production of the human being through the human being. The flesh and body of the bubble-financial economy is the common. Therefore, temporality is completely unstrung: the crisis is no more a specific phase of the economic cycle and a structural horizon, but the permanent and impassable condition of capitalist development. In other words: the communism of capital is capture without organization, block without development, and accumulation without progressive promise.

3. Institutions of the Common

As we have said, the common is both extreme resource and mortal threat for a capitalism in permanent crisis. The Keynesian or neo-Keynesian recipes, aiming at re-starting the economic cycle through public government, have failed. Indeed, the communism of capital is not only a permanent crisis, but it also represents the irreversible end of the dialectic between public and private. The institutions of the communism of capital are beyond classical juridical definitions. Let's take the example of the contemporary transformations of the university, summarized in the formula of corporatization. It does not refer only to the intrusion of private money in a public institution, and it is not tied to the juridical status of single universities. In the American case, the paradigmatic model of the full development of the corporatization trend, public universities are funded by corporate money, and private institutions receive vital state and federal funds. The definition of the corporate university is independent from the representation of itself as public or private. The process points out how the university itself must become a corporation, based on: the calculus of costs and benefits, inputs and outputs; the cuts to the workforce costs and its precarization; on profit/rent to capture; and rating agency evaluations in order to compete in the global educational market. The corporatization of the university means precisely dissolving the dichotomy between public and private.

Then, let's take the connected topics of debt and the central element of the contemporary crisis as a standpoint to investigate the interweaving between the cognitive economy and financialization. To follow the example of education, it would be a mistake to think that increasing university fees – a common transnational trend, now becoming more and more dramatic with the crisis – mean the return of the classical mechanisms of exclusion. In fact, we can see a trend of increased enrolment, seemingly strange due to the increasing level of precarization and impoverishment. How is this possible? Through the system of debt: in the context of the absence or structural dismantling of welfare policies, debt is used by millions and millions of proletarians and downgrading middle class as a tool to access higher education. Debt is a selective filter and a reduction of the social wage, often before the access to a monetary wage. It represents an exemplification of what we call 'differential inclusion', or financialized inclusion to the welfare.

But the use of the credit – against the moralist judgments of the statist left, as well as catastrophist and liquid modernity's sociology – also highlights the incompressibility of the social needs conquered by the multitude and its struggles, from housing to healthcare, from mobility to communication and knowledges. The debt system is a *dispositif* of individualization of these social needs, and capture that is produced in the common in the mechanisms of financialization. But it also shows the fragility of contemporary capitalism: the increasing non-repayment of debt, the right to bankruptcy practiced by the proletarian, precarious, downgrading middle class and the working poor, is one of the subjective roots of the crisis, and it is a tool to re-appropriate social wealth. It's not by chance that this students' and precarious workers' 'right to bankruptcy' became a central claim in the global day of action of 15th October 2011. In fact, we can say that the struggle over credit-debt in cognitive capitalism is the functional equivalent of the struggle over salary in industrial capitalism.

Now, we are at the point that the struggles raise: the processes of financialization and corporatization cannot be faced and defeated on the field of the public, because this is simply an articulation through which those processes work. The battlefield is immediately based on the re-appropriation of social wealth, and therefore its constitution in commonwealth; this happens on the plane of the construction of institutions of the common, i.e. the collective creation of common normativity immanent to the composition of living labor and social cooperation. The institutions of the common are not 'happy islands' or utopian spaces protected from capitalist accumulation, but the organization of collective autonomy and the destruction of apparatuses of capture.

Here we face a first important question: what is the relationship between the public and the common? This is a strategic issue for the struggles and its forms of organization. Let's take another recent example from the Italian context where, in Spring 2011, a great mass mobilization lead to the victory of the referendum against the privatization of water. The slogan 'water is a common good' is extraordinarily important and quite problematic. It is important because it indicates that the issue and the desire of the common have become hegemonic. But it is also problematic for a couple of reasons. On one hand, beneath the concept of common good there is a naturalistic idea of the common, an uncontaminated space outside subsumption and to be defended from the intrusion of capital. It is what we call a Polanyian idea of the commons. But – following Marx – what makes the common the common is not the so-called nature of it, but living labor and social struggles. There is no common outside production and relationships of power: water becomes common when social cooperation appropriates it. To be brief: the common does not exist in nature, but it is always instituted. On the other hand, following this naturalistic vision of the common good, or the commons (plural), it coincides with the public, that is to say, State management. Because we know that, in the modern capitalist era, the public is what is produced by everybody but belongs to nobody, that is to say, it belongs to the State. From this point of view, the case of water in Italy shows that its re-publicization changes very little of concrete collective life, because public companies are completely inside corporate parameters, financialization processes and competition in the private market. Therefore, the challenge rising from social struggles is how to transform the mobilizations over the public into the organization of the common. This is the political point.

Then, there is a second important question: what is the relationship between the communism of capital and the institutions of the common? Does the communism of capital mean the objective premise of its overcoming, the linear passage from the communism of capital to communism beyond capital? Is the full development of cognitive capitalism the key to going to the next stage? Again: this is not a metaphysical problem, but it is related to the choices of strategic political options. For example, in the Italian university movement there are some groups – in this case in implicit alliance with the liberal or neoliberal opinion makers – that try to convince Italian capitalists that investment in the so-called knowledge economy is in their interest; they do not understand that Italian capitalists do not invest because they know their interests very well, and their role in the hierarchies of the global market of cognitive capitalism! Therefore, to answer, we could paraphrase Lenin: the 'proximity' of such capitalism to communism should genuinely serve the living knowledge as an argument proving the proximity, facility, feasibility, and urgency of the common revolution, and not at all as an argument for tolerating the repudiation of such a revolution and the efforts to make capitalism look more attractive –something which all reformists are trying to do.

So, the institutions of the common are not the opposite of capital's command but its destruction: the destruction of the apparatuses of capture and blockage of social cooperation. It is not the affirmation of a new measure, but its radical negation. We have to defeat every neo-socialist temptation: reforming capital is impossible. Socialism cannot run again to save capital from its crisis: the failure of the European left is in this. Michael Hardt and Toni Negri are right: the one divides in two (2009: 290-296). The idea of transition in terms of historicist linearity is our enemy: the transition can only mean, exclusively, the hegemony of the common and the actuality of revolution.

4. Movements of the Common and Constituent Plan

To conclude: rupture and constituent separation, this is the node. The process of collective re-appropriation of the wealth that is frozen in the dialectic between public and private means, in fact, the creation of new institutions. Also in this case, these are very concrete issues that are immediately translatable into keywords. This means that there is nothing to defend: the challenge of the movements of the common is immediately on a constituent plane, as social struggles clearly show. The occupation of squares (that contagiously bounces from Tahrir Square and Tunis' Casbah to Puerta del Sol and Occupy Wall Street, going through Athens and arriving on 15th October) is not a simple protest, there are not demands to address to the government or visibility in the supposed public opinion: it indicates the immediate creation of a new space, an embryonic form of metropolitan production and organization of life in common. Squares and networks are not the public space dreamed up by Habermas, but they become common space: communication and decision are unified by the constituent *potentia* of the multitude.

At the beginning of the text we sketched the convergence and differentiation of a downgraded middle class and a proletariat with no more illusions of 'social redemption' in the current system. The subjects of these struggles find almost only the function of control without material benefits in public welfare. The uprising in the Paris *banlieues* or the recent riots in England are not the *jacquerie* of the excluded people, but a revolt against the subaltern inclusion of the poor productive multitude. Between the downgraded middle class and the 'no future' proletariat, there could be frictions or latent fragmentation; but we cannot avoid this risk through a politics of alliances based on the exhausted mechanisms of representation. If there is a mass perception of capital as a purely parasitic block against the cooperative *potentia* of living knowledge, the political question is the construction of common composition, i.e. new institutions of the common in revolt.

Between 2007 and 2008, when the UniNomade and edu-factory collectives were developing our analysis of the global economic crisis (Fumagalli and Mezzadra, 2010; edu-factory, 2010), we could not see the emergence of new cycles of struggles, or it is better to say, those new cycles were only fragmented in character. Today we can say that — in the permanent crisis of capitalism — we have to question and re-think the idea of cycle from the point of view of struggles, too. They assume a new temporality: the struggles wait and attack the enemy where it is the weakest; they act contagiously and explode like bubbles. But these bubbles are not metaphysical events, they are full of flesh and blood of the organization processes of living labor/knowledge, i.e. they are full of the common. How is it possible to construct continuity and sedimentation in the 'bubbles', and can they be transformed into a constituent process? How can we avoid the double risk of accumulative determinism (the linear development of the processes without events) or, symmetrically, of the messianism of the Event, i.e. the metaphysical re-proposition of an idea of revolution disembodied from the historical determination of class composition and struggles?

These are the urgent political questions. All in all, in the time when the desire of the common becomes majority in the struggles, we can reformulate the classical definition of the revolutionary situation: the ruling elites of the global capital *cannot* live as they did in the past; the workers, the precarious, the students, the poor, the productive multitude *do not want* to live like they did in the past. But we also know that a revolutionary situation does not lead to revolution in a mechanic movement, and that the ruling elites will not fall if we do not push them down. This is our task.

14

Free Labour Syndrome. Volunteer Work and Unpaid Overtime in the Creative and Cultural Sector

Precarious Workers Brigade and Carrot Workers Collective

Free labour has been finally confirmed as a widespread syndrome in the cultural sector. Its negative symptoms include, but are not limited to: the drive or compulsion to undertake unpaid internships and voluntary work placements; the tendency to work beyond ones' physical and mental limits; the incapacity to resist unpaid overtime, as well as a generalised sense of frustration, isolation, worthlessness and insecurity. Early diagnosis is often made difficult by the positive sensations that accompany the desire to work for free: aspirations, hopes, promises, an ephemeral sense of belonging to a world of glamour and disinterested intellectual and artistic beauty. Subjects experiencing early symptoms of the free labour syndrome are often unable to identify the source of their anxiety due to their education and their rejection of empathic identification with workers in similar situations across other sectors. Some specialists have called this denial of subjects' own material and immaterial needs, such as food, shelter and emotional support, the 'labour of love' – with reference, presumably, to the proverbial blindness that is associated with this feeling.

Environmental factors determine the development of the syndrome in those who are culturally predisposed. Due to the withdrawal of public funds from both the education and the cultural system, unpaid internships are perceived and promoted as the only way into paid employment and/or meaningful occupations.

1. Views from the Floor

The collective voice that authors this piece emerges from a constellation of groups that we are a part of. Hence we are variously implicated in the many histories of different groups that have been reinventing themselves at different points and with varying speeds. The 'we' (our group subject) began about five years ago, and it very much started as a space to think about changes going on within the cultural sector. We felt the need to link that with a critique of the creative industries in a way that would enable us to articulate in a self-reflective manner, an understanding of what cultural labour meant and what our political positions were. The collective process started by sharing testimonies of what our different practices were and meant, and we invited more people into the process that slowly coalesced around various activities, processes and occasions. Based in London, the first moves of our collective practices have been very much inspired by those who have worked on similar campaigns – e.g. *Intermittents du spectacle* and the White Masks in France; *Serpica Naro* in Italy, etc. The names we used for our collective processes have changed too at various moments, to match different modalities of thinking and acting together, different contexts of intervention, and varying numbers of people involved. As many other collectives, we realise that organising around labour legislation does not account for the desires that bring people to work for free. Akin to the question raised for women's wages in the home, the issue of wages alone did not seem sufficient as a mobilising strategy. We came together to ask questions about the forms of life we want to inhabit, facing our own gestures of complicity and imagining possibilities of disobedience and refusal.

To understand and mobilise around the expanding phenomenon of free labour in the creative and cultural sector, we started by asking ourselves – as current and ex-interns, and precarious workers in London's art, culture and education fields – 'to tell it like it really is', and to collect testimonies and evidence from the floor. Since we started this process in the middle of the 2000s, the context for the discussion of free labour has evolved.

1) The paradigm of free labour has expanded well beyond the field of culture and the instances of internships that were the initial focus of our research. Free labour, in its various guises, appears as the condition of work within the late capitalist economy. In the early 2000s, the issue of free labour

was discussed mainly in relation to the 'free' production of content by users participating in online platforms (Terranova, 2000). Since then, the debate has expanded to include:

- free labour across the entire service industry (increasingly linked to critiques of immaterial, feminised and precarious labour);

- the rise of internships as a compulsory passage between formal education and the job market, transferring the cost of training from the sector and the education system to the individual;

- a radical outsourcing of research and innovation by the corporate world, towards the academy, pushing the self-exploitation and risk-absorption of cognitive workers to a new threshold;

- the becoming reality of brutal regimes of workfare that just a few years earlier were only a menacing cloud on the horizon. These regimes force the unemployed to work free of charge, often for mega-corporations and superstores.

2) There has been a lot of quickly evolving terminology used to advertise and describe unpaid work in the cultural sector. When we began working together, we focussed on the figure of the intern. Yet, many organisations are now advertising their internship positions as 'volunteer' because various campaigns – including a recent union case won by BECTU[1] and the National Union of Journalists' victory in its Cash for Interns Campaign[2] – proved that what some organisations have been calling 'internships' are legally defined as work. The National Minimum Wage legislation says that everyone working in the UK is entitled to at least a minimum rate set by the law[3]. An exemption from the legislation means the 'voluntary workers' are not entitled to the NMW[4]. Yet, the category allows for many profit-making arts and cultural

---

[1] The UK's media and entertainment trade union.

[2] See http://www.journalism.co.uk/news/nuj-chalks-up-first-victory-in-cashback-for-interns-campaign/s2/a544128/.

[3] See http://www.direct.gov.uk/en/Employment/Employees/TheNationalMinimumWage/DG_10027201.

[4] Also from the above website: 'Voluntary work: You're classed as doing voluntary work if you can only get certain limited benefits (e.g. reasonable travel or lunch expenses) and you're working for a: charity, voluntary organisation or associated fund-raising body, statutory body.'

institutions, drawing on funding from the private sector and operating like businesses, to rely on these kinds of unpaid work.

3) The 'Creative Industries' have lost centre stage both as governmental strategic framework and as social promise. Its critiques revealed that while populations are encouraged to become more creative, only a few are allowed to 'cash in' on cultural capital produced in common. The creative industries paradigm has to rely upon an intense community of exchange that fosters ideas and clusters of collaboration, to then single out and enclose the 'best' ones, or those fittest for marketisation. As argued by Andrew Ross (2003), competitive collaboration and exploitation mark the very way in which the creative industries work, rather than being a contradiction that is about to be resolved, or a systemic failure that could be dealt with through reforms. But the creative industries are not only the label of an economic policy; they also point to a set of strategies of governance that collide with the processes of increased scarcity: of jobs, services, rights, and wealth. The acquisition of soft skills and the flexible mind-set promoted through the figure of the creative global worker sugar-coats many of these scarcities by making them coincide superficially with social desires.

Many of us have experienced choosing a career or a 'study pathway' when the framework of the 'Creative Industries' was still in full force. Within the UK, but also other areas of the European Union, the creative sector was being shaped through discourse and investment, and began to emerge as the desired future edge of the Old Continent's economic strategy. No longer competitive in terms of cheap labour costs, countries like Great Britain began repackaging themselves as producers of everything new and cool. It is hard to say how much of New Labour's discourse about creative education – 'everyone can be creative' – has influenced the many teenagers and young adults who decided to train and work within the creative and cultural sectors in the 1990s and 2000s – for sure the numbers of students in the field have been soaring since then[5]. Projections however show that the service sector, not the cultural or creative sectors (the difference between those was never

---

[5]   The number of students enrolled in creative arts and design courses went up from 87,170 during the academic year 1996/97 (4.9% of total HE student population in the UK) to 173,825 (6.9% of total) in 2009/10. Source: Higher Education Statistics Agency, http://www.hesa.ac.uk.

clear anyway), is expected to be the largest employer in the next two decades. 'Austerity' has replaced 'creativity' as the political catchphrase of the moment, accompanying the driving down of real wages. That brief parenthesis during which it was plausible to imagine the artist as being the new successful and affluent entrepreneur has now closed. The currently multiplying creative quarters, showcase festivals and start-up hubs clearly show themselves to be a mix of corporate social responsibility projects, big-politics opportunism and exploitation of precarious work – and have nothing to do with people making a decent and self-determined living via culture. The current situation has us confronting a bundle of desires that are no longer being addressed, not even nominally, by policymaking – how to evade the humiliation of the relationships at work, how to positively contribute to society with one's job, how to carve out our own spaces?

There is of course no reason to be nostalgic. Yet, to describe what has changed we must pass through what has been 'a shattering of hope' (Beuret, 2011). Indeed, as we carried a large 10ft long papier-mâché carrot to parliament at one of the student demonstrations, a young student came up to us and said – 'but there are no carrots any more'. And it is indeed refreshing to see how this shift has registered as a sharp political awareness with the young people that we work with.

2. The Carrot

One of the symbols we adopted for this research upon our condition is that of the carrot. One of our collective names includes it too: Carrot Workers Collective. But what is the carrot? The carrot is an ambivalent image that represents both a false promise and a genuine desire that are prevalent in free labour. It marks the subtle but important shift that occurs in going from 'working for a very bad salary' to 'working for free' (or for symbolic or in-kind reimbursements), as the economy of the exchange becomes completely based on social capital. The carrot symbolises the promise of paid work, meaningful experience, success and stability that in the cultural and creative sectors, more often than not, is never actually kept. The carrot signifies the hope that we might organise our work around 'creativity' rather than drudgery; an aspiration that is used to prompt, cajole and sometimes blackmail workers into long-term and recurring periods of free and precarious labour. The carrot becomes a disciplinary device that taps into our aspiration to live and produce creatively, to manage our own time, to be social, in order to string us along. The carrot, in short, is the compound of promises and hopes that mobilise subjective and collective becomings when they are put to work as a tool of governance and production of surplus value. To examine how it operates as a device is compelling, because it forces us to scrutinise the ways in which our own desires are traversed by the forces we want to combat. To do so however, is not to engage in an exercise of self-blame; nor does it mean ending our critique with a cynical posture that laments that everything can and will be recuperated. On the contrary: it demands that we seek collective solutions to the conditions of life and work that we share to begin with, but that we often confront in isolation.

Following from this, the carrot has also become an image that we use during a variety of actions. We have been dangling carrots from sticks during demonstrations, we have 'returned' giant papier-mâché carrots to various institutions that promote aspirational narratives while withdrawing social support; and we have been using carrots as props to begin conversations with strangers. The withdrawal of satisfaction and stability that runs as a constant across all the various positions of precarity implicated in cycles of cultural production is made tangible through the symbol of the carrot.

Despite career advisors' claims to the contrary, for many young people there is no linear progression, no process in which the subject smoothly moves along from studentship, to internship, to precarious and finally, full employment. Within the cultural and creative sectors, a condition of constant oscillation is perpetuated; a process that bears some resemblance to the mode of governance of migrant labour. The mainstream discourses on migrant labour often attempt to split this population between good, hardworking, legal migrants and the bad, criminalized, illegal ones. In fact, these two figures are often the same person, someone who enters the country illegally, engages in illegal labour for a period until she finds a regular employment contract that allows her to obtain a temporary visa, only to go back to illegality and cash in hand work agreements when such a contract expires (Mezzadra, 2006). It is not a straightforward progression, but a state of permanent oscillation between precarious roles that creates an infinite pool of cheap and free labour.

Similarly, the high degree of precariousness in the cultural and creative sectors creates a reserve pool constantly threatening to expel the worker from her network of socialization that revolves around 'the scene' (Gielen, 2009). In this case, the career is not a progression, but a constant oscillation between gigs one does for money, more stable contracts, and unpaid projects one does out of passion or necessity for visibility. In what follows we will look at a few of these positions or moments within the cycle of free labour in the cultural sector. We have been thinking about each position not according to a psychological profile, but to the contrary, in an attempt to de-psychologise the sense of self in order to personalise the sense of power, by emphasizing the dispositives that determine the emergence of certain dispositions.

3. The Intern

The figure of the intern appears paradigmatic as it negotiates the collapse of the boundaries between Education, Work and Life. Whilst remaining a very specific example of a worker, the intern has come to expose the broader economic tendency of free labour conditions and precarity beyond the cultural sector, in which the carrot and the stick increasingly regulate our present: from student loans, 'personal development' pathways, to the things we tell ourselves to get through the day.

The internship in itself embodies a certain reversal that is at work within the cultural and artistic sectors, the creative industries, and more broadly in a number of professions where labour of passion comes about through a desire to be emancipated from the drudgery of labour itself. Furthermore, the cultural sector is often considered to be the paradigmatic model of organisation for all labour (Virno, 2004). Interns have become the norm, but also a structural necessity, de facto masking the collapse of the cultural sector, hiding the exodus of public resources from these activities and thus preventing the general public from perceiving the unsustainability of the situation. For instance, according to a survey conducted by the National Union of Journalists (NUJ), 25% of interns claimed to work for media organisations that would not be able to function without interns (National Union of Journalists, 2008: 3). Another survey published by the Arts Council in 2006 exposed that there are two unpaid workers and one freelancer for every three regular employees in the visual arts sector. In this landscape, interns offer both a solution and a threat. They fill in the ever-widening gaps between ambitions and cash, but they also legitimise the exploitative nature of cultural work – reminding those who are employed in the sector that there is always someone ready to do your job for free (if they can afford to).

Furthermore, internships function as an access filter to professions perceived as desirable, a regulatory valve that replicates the most classic lines of class division. According to the same NUJ survey, on average interns are undertaking work placements in at least three different organisations; one in five for three months or more, with some working for more than six months unpaid (National Union of Journalists, 2008: 3). In order to be able to work for six months for free, the intern/volunteer needs to have the economic possibility of doing so. Increasingly, the internship is reiterated and repeated not to satisfy a desire for further training, but to postpone the moment of unemployment and eviction from 'the scene'. The affiliation with cultural institutions, even when not remunerated, allows for the carrot to be preserved.

As part of our engagement with the question of internships, we began to hold a series of regular meetings where people would gather to study together, discuss and share personal anecdotes. We held a few public events where participants could choose to give testimony while wearing donkey masks, so as to protect their privacy (the donkey of course being also an ambiguous symbol of self exploitation and complacency). We also carried out some photo-romance workshops, where participants could construct a common story out of their various personal experiences.

Another action involved the staging of a 'Creative Job Fair' for the cultural sector. In the UK many such recruitment fairs exist, targeting recent graduates but mostly offering unpaid or precarious positions. At our fair, instead of the usual corporate desks, participants found peers offering legal advice, future mapping, tarot card reading, debt forgiveness, competitions for the fastest envelope-stuffer and recommendation letters. We found that the presence of stands dedicated to the various aspects of free labour was an effective dispositive as it allowed for long face-to-face encounters and discussion to take place.

Out of these various initiatives, two main situations emerged as the most common negative experiences. In the first scenario, the intern is deployed by the organisation to carry out mundane tasks that require very little skills: invigilating an exhibition space or an event; stuffing envelops and attaching stamps to correspondence; making coffee and reorganising archives are typical examples. The second kind of experience leans toward the opposite pole. Here, interns are given great responsibilities, such as project managing entire events or programmes, or carrying out research for the organisation; writing texts and making contact with stakeholders. The issue here is that often the intern is not credited for her contribution, and/or ends up handling responsibilities that match those of a highly skilled employee.

4. The Student

The figure of the student has become politically charged once again. Surely, most of the student protests and actions (beginning in 2009) stemmed from the announced cuts to the education sector and a three-fold increase in university fees in England. However, this situation also renewed the continuity and overlap between the positions of the intern, the student and the worker. Many students alternate periods of work in low paid jobs in the service sector with voluntary placements within the field of study. Summer internships are seen as the only way to boost one's CV. Career services in many universities actively encourage students to spend their summers doing internships or working for free. Graduate recruitment fairs hosted on many campuses are full of stands advertising unpaid positions. However, often no critique of this model is offered to students as part of their educational experience – why it appears to have to be this way and how the system has changed radically over the last ten years.

The school and the university, rather than protecting their students take up the role of gatekeepers for accessing job placements and brokers of talent for major corporate interests that, in turn, can offer donations and lend brand credibility to the expensive courses on offer. The experience of free labour, narrated as job placements, is often written into the curriculum of very expensive graduate and postgraduate courses. Many postgraduate courses showcase their corporate internship partners on their advertising materials, as it is a selling point to entice potential customers. Increasingly, a job appears as something you buy, and the monopoly seems to be in the hands of education providers.

On the other hand, post-graduate and research students also work as teachers within their universities. Low-paid teaching positions are often what supports workers in the creative professions through periods of unpaid labour with other cultural institutions. However, here again the situation indicates a spiralling dynamic: PhD students cost less than accredited professionals. Graduates are told repeatedly that they don't have enough experience. While this notion of experience, one of the most complex philosophical notions to date, is never fully explained, an artificial scarcity of it has been created. Implicitly, experiences are also arranged into hierarchies: the willingness to work extra hours for no compensation, for instance, is translated as 'commitment', and has a higher currency than being engaged in, say, community gardening.

During the recent season of protests against the cuts to (among other issues) higher education in the UK (2008-2011), we mobilised as students, teachers and cultural workers. We became involved in moments of demonstration, occupation and direct action working together with other groups and collectives in a mood of joyful rage. Among other things, we created a Protest Lab where people could meet to design banners, props and slogans together prior to the various demonstrations. A series of placards used the sign of equivalence (=) to debunk myths around cultural labour, aspiration and education. The signs, cut out in the form of speech bubbles, said for instance 'the big society = you are on your own'; 'education? = £40,000 + of debt'; 'internship? = infinite free labour'. Some of the signs were left blank and could be completed by others during the demo.

We also made a fake edition of the *Evening Standard*, a popular free London evening newspaper. Our version, renamed *The Evening Substandard*, comprised only a back and a front cover, so that it could be conveniently wrapped around existing newspapers. The front page was covered with utopian good news about increased social benefits and expanded opportunities for education, a very simple way to show alternatives and debunk the inevitability of the cuts. The newspaper was a way to engage with others, as we started to become more and more concerned about what happens at the margins of a demonstration. The slogans that most people chant going through the streets are often inaudible to those on the edges, and it gave us an opportunity to talk to them. *The Evening Substandard* was also an effective prop because when opened up, it created a kind of a space for interventions. Obviously, we do not fetishize the paper as an object, but the experience of producing, circulating and using it made us more aware of the ways in which creative skills can contribute to the movement.

5. The Cultural / Creative Worker

We are told that the creative worker has become a symbolic economic figure, driving growth, setting lifestyle trends and reshaping urban environments. This does not only come from a post-autonomous form of analysis, but also from the discourses of management: 'The way artistic labour is organised makes artists arguably a prototype not just for work organisation, but for innovation in the rest of the economy', reads the report of the governmental consultancy NESTA (2008). The 'self-actualising' and infinitely flexible (and exploitable) 'creative' work becomes the ideal towards which all work should strive, serving as an example and encouraging a series of expectations around non-waged labour that infiltrate the entirety of productive and social relations (Carrot Workers' Collective, 2011).

In the 1990s, a phenomenon emerged in which, when presented with the ever-banal chat up line 'what do you do for a living?' people working across a number of creative areas responded: 'do you mean my real work, or what I do for money?' This distinction tells us something about the contingency of free labour or 'unreal' wage labour. Three out of five cultural workers have a job outside the cultural field that actually supports their work (Arts Council England, 2010). In this perceived unreality of a second job there is an evacuation of all aspiration and identification, making this group more easily exploitable.

The day-to-day work within cultural production is often made possible through the enforced dedication of the workers in the field. Most of this work is not creative at all, but it has to do with administrative tasks (increasingly demanding, as the funding bodies require higher levels of bureaucracy than in the past), endless grant applications, or technical executions of projects conceived by others. Cultural workers are often split between the necessity of using free labour (their own and that of others) and the awareness that free labour is worsening their own conditions (being replaced by an intern or someone who can work more hours).

Often, cultural workers do not perceive themselves as workers and do not talk about what they do as work but as 'practice'. This lends currency to a widespread perception that work in culture is a middle class occupation. However, this assumption, still popular within many left wing circles, is problematic for a number of reasons. First, the very idea that creative professions should be a remit of the middle and upper classes should be challenged, and doing so requires a redefinition of what counts as culture, as well as a realisation that the sector excludes those with fewer resources. Second, since the hype around the Creative Industries in the 1990s, the idea of a career in culture has become a much more widespread aspiration. Third, if we understand class in terms of income, recent reports have shown that cultural workers earn as an average 60% less than the national median of all UK employees, and 75% of them don't have a pension (Arts Council England, 2010).

To make matters worse, the UK's new coalition government's introduction of the notion of 'The Big Society' after the recent elections in 2010, which is an ideologically-driven (mis-)appropriation of cooperative working/living and alternative economies, and its plans to impose regimes of forced labour on the unemployed disguised under the slippery title of 'workfare', are symptomatic of an even stronger emphasis on the necessity of labour as indicative of personal wealth, placing great value in overworked bodies, self-investment and hyper-responsibility. While the state appears to hand back its power to the public, state funding is being violently withdrawn and masked by new troops of unpaid volunteers in the guise of self-disciplined, socially responsible and committed individuals and communities.

Another set of questions for us concerned our relationships with institutions of various kinds. This includes cultural institutions, and refers to the portion of institutional support we may receive for our practices – support that comes from public spending, and is thus directly caught up with politics with a capital P; but it also includes the educational institutions that may host us or employ us; and also perhaps some kind of institutionalised modality of being 'critical'. Our line of inquiry has led us to become more aware of the implicit demands and expectations that come with these settings, and what might be our points of leverage.

In 2010, we received an invitation by one of the art institutions in London to do a short residency as part of a seasonal programme that promised to showcase political and critical artistic projects. In an attempt to answer the question of how to inhabit a cultural institution in a radical manner and in solidarity with broader social issues, we decided to open up this invitation. A call out to others critically involved in the cultural sector in London included a series of questions related to the role of institutions and the ways other practitioners thought about their involvement. It was very much an attempt to animate and bring together the cultural scene in turmoil because of the announced cuts and reforms. Would other creative workers take the risk to form an alliance?

A series of meetings and processes that involved more than 60 people at times followed our call. Other responses were articulated in the familiar tone: 'I would not go near this kind of mainstream cultural institution', usually from those that rarely get involved in any kind of practice that does not involve writing. The initial group that later came to operate under the name of Precarious Workers Brigade, came together under this pragmatic premise of wanting to do something meaningful with the (little) money, space and time offered by this cultural institution. Soon enough, this invitation became to be perceived as a pretext. The much more urgent questions that drove the process included: is there enough will and capacity right now to building a broad and strong movement of cultural workers that intersects with other new and emerging groups in the city? Is it possible to connect the struggles of cultural workers beyond the so-called creative class to build solidarity with other workers and to organise around the more systemic issues that we all face? How can we develop sustainable ways of organising that take into account the overworked, transient, underfunded and precarious nature of many of our lives?

The process started in August 2010 as a series of facilitated discussions and rounds of introductions, mapping out the concerns and desires people were bringing to the table, and what they thought should happen next. It was quite interesting to notice how there was never an issue about accommodating one desire over another, as one may expect working with very diverse groups. Finally, we ended up with a series of subgroups that would develop specific interests, but there was a real moment when anything that had enough support would be collectively sustained towards realisation. Hence the original invitation worked out to be simply an excuse, a carrot, to create an energy that then went in another direction and proliferated in a way that we couldn't have expected beforehand. On this occasion, somehow we were able to claim back this investment, this cultural capital handed to us by the institution, and use it for other purposes. The project became an opportunity to renegotiate how we generate value and self-value, which in a place like London, where sociality is very fast and very atomised, is a pressing problem.

While the group was deliberating proposals for what could be done next (a seminar, debates about the discourses of the Big Society and its relation to culture, making objects and carrying out performances) the cultural institution that offered to host us put on the brakes. Two weeks before the event was scheduled, they called and asked us to postpone to a later moment. As this was happening in November 2010, rescheduling would have severed our project from the context of on-going protest that created a necessity for it in the first place. In a way this was the best that could happen – we realised that we wanted to go ahead anyway and that the cultural value of the institution did not matter to us.

The project evolved into the People's Tribunal on Precarity[6]. Its form allowed us to map the systemic nature of our concerns regarding our working practices of our own and that of the institutions we work with, share testimonies and gather evidence, as well as identify culprits. Our success came in the form of a coherent, collective analysis. An experiment with tools of collective research became a platform for addressing institutional and personal collusion within the free labour paradigm and opened a space to think possible remedies and recommendations.

Closing Remarks

Many groups of militant researchers are reticent about sharing what they actually do as their practice. There are strong theoretical reasons for this approach that stem out of mistrust for universalising methods, which we also share. At the same time, we find that there are other pedagogical reasons that call for the sharing of anecdotes and precedents, also in written form. This is not a matter of compiling DIY books with recipes to follow or 'best

---

6   See   http://precariousworkersbrigade.tumblr.com/post/3999720634/precarity-the-peoples-tribunal.

practices', but it has to do with what we could call 'engagement tools' that is, the more visible, perceptible components of a practice. This line of questioning involves not taking for granted the practicalities and materialities involved in organising direct actions or co-investigations, hosting events or making time based performances. We became interested in tools as something you can touch, feel, break; objects that we might make as we make ourselves into a group. While we want to avoid producing a trademark approach or a methodology, we do cultivate a set of questions to do with the very nature and modality of the 'we', the collective, the notion of a having a collective 'practice': what is an exteriority and an interiority of an open group practice? how we sustain ourselves? how can we maintain a group ecology? how do we relate to each other across the different group experiences that keep proliferating? Within our group process we share a very intimate space of friendship. It is the collaboration with each other that holds this space together.

Of course, this is positive because it would be unlikely that any of us would be willing to be in this intensive collective process without getting an affective return, having a sense of intimacy with each other, a shared history as well as a reciprocal learning process. On the other hand, this leads to questions about the way a group is held together. In a situation like ours, where we operate through such strong affective ties, the danger is that it also becomes very demanding, so that the core group has shrunk at different moments. We have been thinking about the advantages and disadvantages of this modality, what does it mean for us as a group not to be adopting the very strict protocols of meetings that you may find in plenary assemblies for instance. Of course, we do have a minimum set of procedures for keeping the group and the process open and accountable, we do take notes and make agendas. However, there is a dimension of familiarity and quotidian informality among some of us that may become difficult for people to fully come into and inhabit the group process. But then again, some other people who become involved really loved this intimacy and the idea of becoming part of a collective process that offers more then a dry 'contractual institution' (Wills, 2011).

What does it mean to practice, to practice collectively, is a question we are keen to reclaim back from the predicament of free labour.

15

Art strikes and the metropolitan factory

Stevphen Shukaitis

> The unrest of change, assuming theatrical form as a spectacle, transforms the city into a penultimate opportune occasion for mastering unrest itself… The impermanence of the city affirms the active capacity of the collective to be self-fashioning and, simultaneously, its anomic recognition of the perishable character of all that comes to be, showing in this way the limits of a finitude which is typically celebrated for its works and achievements, while being denigrated for its failure to master creation itself.
>
> Alan Blum (2003: 232-233)

Gazing down upon the city, looking at the development of the metropolis, one is struck by many things. Perhaps one the more obvious, regardless of what one thinks of the process that led to its development, is that it's often rather ugly. Not just in the way it looks (jungles of concrete and steel), but even more so in what it does: how the city operates as a factory, isolating people from each other, channeling social relations into prescribed routes and preventing other from forming, transforming our relationship with nature, and so on. David Harvey, the renowned Marxist geographer, responded to this observation with the comment that it was 'really quite a strange thing that the bourgeois has no imagination', no sense of creativity that can devise anything more appealing in its domination and transformation of the social space and the urban environment. This may seem a minor point or trite observation. What does it matter how aesthetically appealing, how well designed or not, an area is, when there are more crucial questions and ongoing issues of communities being displaced, workers being exploited, and the nature of social life being shaped by the needs of capital? This is true enough to a degree. But what is interesting about such an observation is the process it hints at and what this can tell us about the development of capitalism today and our struggles to shape social life and interactions otherwise.

Whether or not the bourgeoisie has any creativity is debatable (Marx himself marveled at the inventiveness of the ruling class in transforming social reality, albeit usually for the worse), this is not so important, precisely because it is so skilled at stealing the imagination and creativity of others. And this is precisely what the history of the transformations of the city and society more generally show us. Social and political movements, new artistic developments and quarters, as soon as they arise (or even before they arise sometimes) are seized upon by real estate developers, urban planners, and policy makers, to create the image of a new 'hip' district that will boost real estate prices, attract 'more desirable' residents, and so forth, in a virtuous spiral of capitalist development. This process of gentrification led by or inadvertently spurred by developments in artistic and social creativity, is an old one. When Albert Parry wrote his history of Bohemia in the US (1960) he paid close attention to the relation between artists and the rise of the real estate market in the 60s and 70s. But in Parry's case the decades in question were the *1860s* and 70s rather than the rise of loft living, to borrow Sharon Zukin's description of the reshaping of lower Manhattan during the 1960s and 70s (1989). The point of raising this is not to sulk over this process or mourn that so much creative energy fermented by often-antagonistic social movements gets turned into mechanisms for further accumulation. Rather the question is making sense out of it, and making sense in a way that further clarifies this process for political and social organizing.

In recent years there has emerged within radical theory and organizing coming out of Europe, Italy and France specifically, a focus on the metropolis as both a space of capitalist production and resistance to it. This is based on an argument developed over many years within autonomous social movements that we live in the social factory, that exploitation does not just occur within the bounded workplace but increasingly comes to involve all forms of social interactions that are brought into the labor process. In the social factory our abilities to communicate, to relate, to create and imagine, all are put to work, sometimes through digital networks and communications, or through their utilization as part of a redevelopment or revitalization of an area based on the image of being a creative locale. Given this argument it becomes possible to look at the rise of the discourse of the creative city and the creative class, most popularly associated with its development by Richard Florida, and then seized upon by large numbers of urban planners and developers. The rise of the idea of the creative class is not just a theorization of the changing nature of economic production and social structure, it is, or at very least, has become a managerial tool and justification for a restructuring of the city space as a factory space.

But to read Florida's arguments, such as in *The Rise of the Creative Class* (2002) or *Cities and the Creative Class* (2005), is to encounter a very strange managerial tool. It is quite strange in that while on face value his work seems to describe empirical phenomena, namely the development of an increase in prominence of forms of labor that are primarily premised on creating new ideas and forms rather than physical labor, whether that is actually the case or not is not the main issue. The creative class is not a homogenous or unified whole but is itself, even in Florida's description, marked by an uneven development of the forms of creative labor engaged in (for instance in distinguishing between a 'super creative' core of science, arts, and media workers from the 'creative professionals' and knowledge workers who keep the necessary organizational structures running). It is not then that they necessarily describe an empirical reality or condition, the existence of the creative city, but rather as a form of mythological social technology of governance: to bring it into being by declaring its existence. In other words, the question is not whether the creative class exists as such, but rather what effects are created through how it is described and called into being through forms of governance and social action based upon these claims. Planning and shaping the city based around a certain conceptualization of the creative potentiality of labor, or the potentiality of creativity put to work, is not an unprecedented or unique development, but rather is the latest example of capital's attempt to continually valorize itself through recuperating the energies of organizing against it.

The argument that all of society and social relations are being brought into economic production leaves out a crucial question, namely what are the particular means and technologies through which social relations are made productive. How are aspects of social life outside the recognized workplace brought into the labor process? What are the technologies of capture that render the metropolis productive? This is precisely what the creative class is, a social position that formalizes the process of drawing from the collective wealth and creativity of the metropolis, and turns it into a mechanism for further capitalist development. It is what Zukin describes as the advent of an 'artistic mode of production' where mixed residency and industrial space usage is accompanied by the intermingling as art through life, and work all throughout life. In the industrial factory it was generally very easy to clearly distinguish between those who planned and managed the labor process and those who were involved in its executions, between the managed and the managers, the owners, professionals, and subordinate labor workers who were of interest only for their ability to work and not their ideas. But in today's post-industrial service economy these distinctions become increasingly hard to make. The passionate and self-motivated labor of the artisan increasingly becomes the model for a self-disciplining, self-managed form of labor force that works harder, longer, and often for less pay precisely because of its attachment to some degree of personal fulfillment in forms of work engaged in (or a 'psychic wage' as Marc Bousquet [2008] refers to it).

To use the language developed by autonomist movements, what we see in the rise of the creative class both as empirical description and as discourse for the management and shaping of the city, is a shifting of class composition. Class composition is made of two characteristics: technical composition, or the mechanisms and arrangements capital uses for its continued reproduction; and political composition, or the ability of ongoing struggles and movements to assert their own needs, desires, and shape the conditions of the existing economic and political reality. The rise of the creative class is formed by a convergence of a set of dynamics including demands put forth by workers for more fulfilling kinds of humane and engaging labor rather than repetitive meaningless tasks. The rejection of the factory line and factory discipline that emerged during the late 1960s was met during the 1970s by managerial attempts to create jobs that were more fully engaging for the worker, but in doing so also more fully exploited the laboring capacity of the worker. Similarly, campaigns of community organizing and neighborhood renewal undertaken by social movements around the same time (such as in the lower east side of New York) were then used by financially backed real estate speculation to kick start a renewed process of capital accumulation based on land values. The point of identifying and analyzing these relations of social contestation and capitalism is not to lament them, but rather, when one thinks about them compositionally, which is to say looking at the relation between contestation and accumulation, understanding how the city functions as an expanded factory space broadens the terrain for disrupting capitalist domination of social life.

What this comes down to is the realization that capital depends on a certain kind of glide for its continued development. Capital is not real, it has no body and certainly no imagination – it can create nothing on its own. Rather what capital increasingly relies on today is the movement of ideas and creativity through networks of social relations, cooperation, and communication that are already in existence. What capital needs is a process through which this dispersed creativity already in circulation can be harvested and put to work in the renewed production of surplus value. The bourgeoisie then exists not in the form of the factory owner, the one who owns the means of production, but rather the figure that renders the diffuse productivity of the metropolitan factory into forms that can be exploited. Capital is reproduced through profit making that has become rent: by attempting to restrict access to this social creativity rather than through its ownership. The creative class and its dispersal through the rise of the creative city/cluster is the process through which the siphoning off of social imagination is managed, the way that the pleasure of being in common becomes the labor of living together.

Understanding how capital attempts to turn its glide through social space into capturing profits does not mean that there are no options left for interrupting and breaking these circuits of accumulation. If anything the number of points where capitalism is open to disruption have multiplied exponentially. In so far as we are engaged in the labor of circulation and imagination necessary to keep a parasitic economy alive, we are also located precisely at the point where it is possible to refuse to continue to do so. The subversive potentiality of any creative art or artistic production then is not simply its expressed political content, but rather the potentiality it creates for interrupting the circuits of capitalist production that it is always already enmeshed in. In the metropolitan factory the cultural worker who thinks that she is autonomous simply because there is no foreman barking orders is just as capable of having her passionate labor co-opted, perhaps all the more deeply in so far as the labor discipline is self-imposed and thus made partially imperceptible. Through understanding the social technologies of rendering the city as a unified social fabric of production it becomes possible to develop further strategies of refusal and resistance that finds avenues for creative sabotage and disruption all throughout the city.

Reconsidering the Art Strike

> The art of the future is not connoisseurship, but labor itself transfigured.
>
> Nikolai Tarabukin (Quoted in Kuric 2010: 242)

What then, is to be done, when it seems that there is nothing to be done? That is, how is it possible to recompose strategies for social movement and subversion within the space of a metropolitan factory that has found ways to turn the practices of antagonistic cultural production into levers of further accumulation of capital? Perhaps then the question becomes less one of what is to be done and more of what is to be undone, or action through antagonistic not doing: in short, to reconsider the notion of the strike for cultural labor.

Everyone is an artist. This would seem a simple enough place to begin; with a statement connecting directly to Joseph Beuys, and more generally to the historic avant-garde's aesthetic politics aiming to break down barriers between artistic production and everyday life. It invokes an artistic politics that runs through Dada to the Situationists, and meanders and dérives through various rivulets in the history of radical politics and social movement organizing. But let's pause for a second. While seemingly simple, there is much more to this one statement than presents itself. It is a statement that contains within it two notions of time and the potentials of artistic and cultural production, albeit notions that are often conflated, mixed, or confused. By teasing out these two notions and creatively recombining them, perhaps there might be something to be gained in rethinking the antagonistic and movement-building potential of cultural production: to reconsider its compositional potential.

The first notion alludes to a kind of potentiality present but unrealized through artistic work; the creativity that everyone could exercise if they realized and developed potentials that have been held back and stunted by capital and unrealistic conceptions of artistic production through mystified notions of creative genius. Let's call this the 'not-yet' potential of everyone *becoming* an artist through the horizontal sublation of art into daily life. The second understanding of the phrase forms around the argument that everyone *already* is an artist and embodies creative action and production within their life and being. Duchamp's notion of the readymade gestures towards this as he proclaims art as the recombination of previously existing forms. The painter creates by recombining the pre-given readymades of paints and canvas; the baker creates by recombining the readymade elements of flour, yeast, etc. In other words, it is not that everyone will become an artist, but that everyone already is immersed in myriad forms of creative production, or artistic production, given a more general notion of art.

These two notions, how they collide and overlap, move towards an important focal point: if there has been an end of the avant-garde it is not its death but rather a monstrous multiplication and expansion of artistic production in zombified forms. The avant-garde has not died, the creativity contained within the future oriented potential of *the becoming-artistic* has lapsed precisely because it has perversely been realized in existing forms of diffuse cultural production. 'Everyone is an artist' as a utopian possibility is realized just as 'everyone is a worker'. This condition has reached a new degree of concentration and intensity within the basins of cultural production; the post-Fordist participation-based economy where the multitudes are sent to work in the metropolitan factory, recombining ideas and images through social networks and technologically mediated forms of communication. We don't often think of all these activities as either work or art. Consequently it becomes difficult to think through the politics of labor around them, whether as artistic labor or just labor itself.

The notion of the Art Strike, its reconsideration and socialization within the post-Fordist economy, becomes more interesting and productive (or perhaps anti-productive) precisely as labor changes articulation in relation to the current composition of artistic and cultural work. The Art Strike starts with Art Workers Coalition and Gustav Metzger and their calls to withdraw their labor. First the AWC called for a strike in 1969 to protest the involvement of museum board members and trustees in war related industries, as explored brilliantly by Julia Bryan-Wilson (2009). Gustav Metzger then called for a strike of a minimum of three years, from 1977-1980, although he notes that almost no one noticed (which perhaps is not so surprising when you go on strike by yourself). Metzger and the AWC's formulation of the Art Strike was directed against the problems of the gallery system. This conception was picked up by Stewart Home and various others within the Neoist milieu who called upon artists to cease artistic work entirely for the years 1990-1993. In this version, the strike moves beyond a focus on the gallery system to a more general consideration of artistic production and a questioning of the role of the artist. In the most recent and presently emerging iteration, Redas Dirzys and a Temporary Art Strike Committee have been calling for an Art Strike currently as a response to Vilnius, the capital of Lithuania, becoming a European Capital of Culture for 2009. The designation of a city as a capital of culture is part of a process of metropolitan branding and a strategy of capitalist valorization through the circulation of cultural and artistic heritage. (In Vilnius this has played out through figures like Jonas Mekas, George Maciunas, the legacy of Fluxus, and the Uzupis arts district.) In Vilnius we see the broadening of the Art Strike from a focus on the gallery system to artistic production more generally, and finally to the ways in which artistic and cultural production are infused throughout daily life and embedded within the production of the metropolis.

The Art Strike emerges as a nodal point for finding ways to work critically between the two compositional modes contained within the statement 'everyone is an artist'. An autonomist politics focuses on class composition, or the relation between the technical arrangement of economic production and the political composition activated by forms of social insurgency and resistance. Capital evolves by turning emerging political compositions into technical compositions of surplus value production. Similarly, the aesthetic politics of the avant-garde find the political compositions they animate turned into new forms of value production and circulation. The Art Strike becomes a tactic for working between the utopian not-yet promise of unleashed creativity and the always-already but compromised forms of artistic labor we're enmeshed in. In the space between forms of creative recombination currently in motion, and the potential of what could be if they were not continually rendered into forms more palatable to capitalist production, something new emerges. To re-propose an Art Strike at this juncture, when artistic labor is both everywhere and nowhere, is to force that issue. It becomes not a concern of solely the one who identifies (or is identified) as the artist, but a method to withdraw the labor of imagination and recombination involved in what we're already doing to hint towards the potential of what we could be doing.

Bob Black, in his critique of the Art Strike (1992), argues that far from going on a strike by withdrawing forms of artistic labor, the Art Strike formed as the ultimate realization of art, where even the act of not making art becomes part of an artistic process. While Black might have meant to point out a hypocrisy or contradiction, if we recall the overlapping compositional modes of everyone being an artist, this no longer appears as an antinomy but rather a shifting back and forth between different compositional modes. While Stewart Home has argued repeatedly that the importance of the Art Strike lies not in its feasibility but rather in the ability to expand the terrain of class struggle, Black objects to this on the grounds that most artistic workers operate as independent contractors and therefore strikes do not make sense for them. While this is indeed a concern, it is also very much the condition encountered by forms of labor in a precarious post-Fordist economy. The Art Strike moves from being a proposal for social action by artists to a form of social action potentially of use to all who find their creativity and imagination exploited within existing productive networks.

But ask the skeptics: how we can enact this form of strike? And, as comrades and allies inquire, how can this subsumption of creativity and imagination and creativity by capital be undone? That is precisely the problem, for as artistic and cultural production become more ubiquitous and spread throughout the social field, they are rendered all the more apparently imperceptible. The avant-garde focus on shaping relationality (for instance in Beuys' notion of social sculpture), or in creative recombination and *detournément*, exists all around us flowing through the net economy. Relational aesthetics recapitulates avant-garde ideas and practices into a capital-friendly, service economy aesthetics. This does not mean that they are useless or that they should be discarded. Rather, by teasing out the compositional modes contained within them they can be considered and reworked. How can we struggle around or organize diffuse forms of cultural and artistic labor? This is precisely the kind of question explored by groups such as the Carrotworkers' Collective, a group from London who are formulating ways to organize around labor involved in unpaid forms of cultural production, such as all the unpaid internships sustaining the workings of artistic and cultural institutions.

In 1953, Guy Debord painted on the wall of the Rue de Seine the slogan '*Ne travaillez jamais*', or 'Never work'. The history of the avant-garde is filled with calls to 'never artwork', but the dissolution of the artistic object and insurgent energies of labor refusal have become rendered into the workings of semiocapitalism and the metropolitan factory. To renew and rebuild a politics and form of social movement adequate to the current composition does not start from romanticizing the potentiality of becoming creative through artistic production or working from the creative production that already is, but rather by working in the nexus between the two. In other words, to start from how the refusal of work is re-infused into work, and by understanding that imposition and rendering, and struggling within, against and through it.

15

Economists Are Wrong!
The Warsaw Manifesto 2011

Freee Art Collective

Freee produces manifestos and holds group readings of manifestos with the aim of generating discussion. Participants are requested to read the given text and make their own minds up about what they believe. When present at the group reading, the participants only read out the words of the manifesto they agree with. The reading then becomes a collective process in which individuals publicly agree, as well as disagree, and declare their commitment to Freee's manifesto. While the use of a specific text by Freee is a given, the text itself can be used and reworked by those who read it to formulate their own opinions, just in the same way Freee has reworked it from the original. Freee acknowledges that ideas are developed collectively through the exchange of opinion. In this way, Freee offers a text that they produced but one that then becomes the basis for further critical thinking.

The content of Freee's manifestos are an explicit call for the transformation of art and society and Freee readily takes and uses existing historical manifestos, speeches and revolutionary documents, such as *The Manifesto for a New Public* (2012) based on Vladimir Tatlin's *The Initiative Individual in the Creativity of the Collective* (1919), the *UNOVIS, Program for the Academy at Vitebsk* (1920) and the *Freee Art Collective Manifesto for a Counter-Hegemonic Art,* based on the *Communist Manifesto* by Karl Marx and Friedrich Engels (1848).

Economists are Wrong

Is art an economic activity? Should art be independent of economic pressures? Is the value of art to be determined separately from its value as a commodity? Can we apply the Marxist labour theory of value to art? To consider the question of value in art from a Marxist perspective is, on the face of it, to invoke two kinds of philistinism. Marx tells us that value is twofold, with use-value and exchange-value forming a contradictory unity of value. There is no third kind of value. So, if art is supposed to be useless and priceless, how can a Marxist engage seriously with art with only use-value and exchange-value as tools?

Art and Labour

When an economist says a 'work of art often arrives on the market because of one of the famous *'three D's'* (divorce, death, or debt)', it is clear that cultural economics places its emphasis on consumption and the secondary market. From a Marxist point of view, it is utterly absurd for a product to 'arrive' on the market without being produced. Even if we could press the economist to start an economic analysis of art with its arrival for sale on the primary market, we would have arrived too late. No Marxist could knowingly subscribe to such a belated economic analysis. Artworks themselves cannot be a given, as it is for mainstream economics, but must be identified as the object of economic analysis.

Errors are made by not knowing what precisely Marx's labour theory of value sets out to explain. Andrew Kliman tells us, 'Marx's value theory [...] pertains exclusively to commodity production, that is, to cases in which goods and services are 'produced for the purpose of being exchanged', or equivalently, produced as commodities'. This is important for a Marxist economic analysis of art because, as he goes on to say, 'if the products have been produced for a different purpose, that of satisfying the producers' and others' needs and wants, they have not been *produced* as commodities'. Kliman explains:

> a key reason for distinguishing between commodity production and non-commodity production is that prices or rates of exchange are determined differently in the two cases. When things are not produced as commodities, the rates at which they exchange may depend exclusively upon the demand

for them, or upon normative considerations, or [...] upon customary rules. It is only when products are produced for the purpose of being exchanged that their costs of production become significant determinants of their prices.

Not all production is commodity production. Not all production is production for financial exchange. Not all production is determined by supply and demand. Economics is not the best method of examining non-economic production. Economists give artists bad advice.

If artists increase and decrease production according to demand and alter the production of their work according to market preferences (e.g. halting production of this version of their work and expanding production of that version of their work), they must be in the business of producing commodities. At the same time, of course, we must insist that if artists do not increase and decrease production according to demand and do not alter the production of their work according to the preferences of the market, then they are demonstrably not in the business of producing commodities. If art is produced as a commodity, that is to say produced for the purpose of being exchanged, then it is the kind of product that Marxist economics explains. If art is not produced as a commodity, but rather to satisfy aesthetic and cultural needs and wants, then it is not. There is no shortcut to this kind of economic examination, no general rule, no standard economics of art in the age of consumerism, or the changing economic status of the artwork in the society of the spectacle. We can look at art's apparent commodification only by asking on a case by case basis whether, as Kliman puts it, 'their costs of production become significant determinants of their prices.'

Mainstream economists will argue that the labour theory of value is mistaken. This is partly based on the fact that mainstream economists are not interested in the source of value at all (they have no alternative explanation to the Marxist argument). It is also partly based on the fact that mainstream economics takes for granted the key elements of capitalism (supply and demand, prices, profit, wages, etc.), whereas Marxism calls all these into question. Marxism shows us the limits of economic thought and the limits of a social system based on market forces. Marx was right. Capitalism inexorably leads to crisis. Economists tell us, on the contrary, that supply and demand is a self-correcting mechanism.

Economists are fucking wrong!

Following the labour theory of value, we would expect to determine whether art is produced as a commodity from an analysis of artistic production, not by examining the behaviour of its consumers or its systems of distribution and display. If we find that art production does not correspond to the model of commodity production, then no matter how art is subsequently brought into the circulation systems of capitalism, *art is not converted into a commodity in its consumption*. The labour theory of value proceeds from the value of labour, so we need to ask whether the price of artworks are determined by the value of the labour in their production.

The labour theory of value, which explains how value is produced within capitalism, states that *labour* is the source of value. This value is then broken down into three types: the transfer of value, absolute surplus value and relative surplus value. Machines, for instance, transfer their value to the product; labour-power produces absolute surplus value, that is to say, value on top of the wages paid for it. Relative surplus value is produced by the division of labour, automation and so forth, which through increases in productivity and efficiency do not produce value in itself but increases the proportion of surplus-labour in relation to wages.

We can test the question of the price of artworks as determined or not by the cost of labour in production by observing the means of production. In capitalist commodity production, capitalists increase absolute surplus-labour (and thereby surplus value) by attempting to extend the working day, the working week, the numbers of days worked in the year, and the number of years worked in a worker's life. Second, capitalists increase relative surplus value through the use of technology and supervision, which play an effective part in driving down labour costs through the division of labour, deskilling and increasing productivity.

If the price of artwork is set by the labour that goes into it, then we would expect that the prices of artworks would vary according to the average labour that goes into producing them. When the price of an artist's work goes up, this is not because the labour producing it has gone up, that the assistants have managed to have their wages increased or their hours reduced. Also, when the price of an artist's work drops, this is not due to the efficiencies of competitors in the market who have managed to lower their production costs. No, the prices of artworks does not fluctuate according to the cost of labour, technological efficiencies, or increases in productivity. Art prices are not determined by 'socially necessary labour-time'. Mainstream economists might argue that art's high prices disprove the Marxist labour theory of value, but what is shown here is that art is typically not produced as a commodity governed by supply and demand.

Of course, assistants are wage-labourers. But this, in itself, is not proof that artists generate surplus value from them. If assistants do not produce surplus value then they are to be regarded as luxuries, like domestic servants in the nineteenth century. Marx derived the distinction between productive and unproductive labour from Adam Smith. Smith's definition of unproductive labour still stands today: *labour not exchanged with capital but directly exchanged with revenue*. There is no such thing as productive or unproductive labour in itself. The difference is between labour that produces profits and labour that consumes revenue. In the 19th century, this distinction was clearly illustrated with the contrasting ways in which the capitalist paid two kinds of wages: one to the workers in a business enterprise and the other to domestic servants in their homes. The former was productive because it produced surplus -labour and the latter unproductive because it used up revenue. Another, clearer, way of understanding the distinction between productive and unproductive labour is to examine whether the capitalist or the labourer owns that labour.

If we retain our focus on artistic labour, rather than its products, the test of Smith's definition of unproductive labour provides clear results. Is artistic labour exchanged with capital or directly exchanged with revenue? Since artists are not wage-labourers employed by capitalists, but own their means of production as well as the products that they produce, we are forced to conclude that *artistic labour is unproductive labour* even if certain capitalists, such as gallerists, dealers and, later in the process, investors, earn a profit from trade in the *products* of artistic labour.

Normally, unproductive labour does not produce products that are luxury goods; normally the unproductive labour is the luxury good itself. Art isn't usually unproductive labour that is not a luxury in itself but produces luxuries without first producing commodities. Studio assistants are wage-labourers, but if they are unproductive labourers, like domestic servants, then they do not produce surplus value.

Yet, if the value of labour does not determine the price of artworks, what does? The variations of price of an artwork are not due to underpaying or overpaying in relation to the actual value, nor is it due to an increase or decrease in the average cost of the means of production. A collector does not pay less than the value of a work by a young artist only to realise its true value once they become a mature artist. Both the relatively cheap price and the relatively expensive price are the true value of the work at two different points in time. Art appreciates. However, while investments normally appreciate because a firm for which one owns shares is profitable, or is perceived to be so – that is to say, by drawing on or anticipating the production of surplus value in production – this is not the case in the appreciation of artworks. The relative cheapness of a work by a lesser known artist or 'early work' is based on the risk that the artist will never develop a significant career; the relative expensiveness of the same work later on is based on the subsequent rarity of 'early work' and the price of the mature work, which retrospectively sets the pace for prices of earlier works. Just as skilled workers are paid more than unskilled workers because this kind of labour costs more to reproduce, the cost of reproducing a successful, mature, reputable, established artist with hundreds of important exhibitions and a bibliography to match is expressed in the price of their works.

However, this explanation, which can be found partly in Diederichsen, presents an immediate difficulty, which Diederichsen misses. The reputation of an artist is not a quality that is contained in their labour, is not produced by them, and is not under their control. The reputation of an artist is ascribed to their work by others. So, if we are to explain the high prices of artworks in terms of the reproduction of labour-power that produces them, we need to consider the labour-power of those who contribute to the value of the work's reputation, namely art critics, theorists, curators and art historians.

Formal and Real Subsumption

How might we test, from a Marxist point of view, the common complaint that art has been incorporated into capitalism?

Marx's distinction between *formal* and *real subsumption* is part of his explanation of the incorporation and transformation of particular spheres of production by the capitalist mode of production. We must remind ourselves that Marx did not theorise the subsumption of commodities. For Marx, the incorporation and transformation of spheres of production occurs with the formal and real *subsumption of labour*.

The formal subsumption of labour takes place when the capitalist takes financial control of production – owning the means of production, paying wages for labour-power, extracting surplus labour and surplus value. Before production a market relation is established between the capitalist as a purchaser of labour and the worker as a seller of labour, and within production these same individuals are put in a conflictual relation with each other in which the capitalist struggles against the workers to extend the working day, increase productivity and so forth, while the workers struggle against the capitalist to reduce the working day, improve working conditions and so on.

The real subsumption of labour goes further than this, establishing a capitalist mode of production with the division of labour, the employment of machinery, the centralisation and intensification of production on a large-scale and the transformation of the production process into a conscious application of science and technology. In short, everything that is implied with the idea of industrialisation. Formal subsumption is presupposed by the real subsumption of labour, but only the latter can be described in terms of what Marx calls the continual revolution of the means of production and relations of production in capitalism.

In order to determine whether artistic labour has been subsumed, we need to ask ourselves, therefore, two questions. First, whether artistic labour has been converted into wage-labour, and second, whether the production of art has been transformed by the processes of industrialisation. The producers of art still own their means of production. Unlike in the capitalist mode of production, the product of the production of art is invariably owned by its producer. Artists have not been converted into wage-labourers, employed by a capitalist. Gallerists have nothing to gain from extending the working day of artists and technological developments are not implemented to increase productivity. The gallerist does not establish a relationship with the artist along the lines of the capitalist-worker relationship. There is no labour market separate from the market for artworks produced by artistic labour. Dealers do not employ artists. In addition, since no gallerist takes ownership of the means of production for art or engage individual artists to operate those means of production, consequently the gallerist, unlike the capitalist, does not own the product. The gallerist enters the marketplace of art with capital and leaves the marketplace with profit, but they do this without formally subsuming artistic *labour* under capital, but by converting commodity-capital (artworks) into money-capital. This is why there can be no real subsumption of art.

Wake up to the fact: the subsumption of labour can only take place with *productive labour*, i.e. with labour that is capable of producing surplus value directly for the capitalist.

The Mainstream Economics of Art

Hans Abbing proposes that art is economically *exceptional* because it is 'sacred'. Abbing says talking about money in relation to art is 'taboo': 'profit motives are not absent, they are merely veiled, and publicly the economic aspect of art is denied'. The reference to taboo is a deliberate strategy to associate the uneconomic in art with irrationality. When he recounts the values of the art community, he frames them in terms of 'myth', 'taboo', 'ritual' and 'the sacred'. He is convinced of the rationality of the economic, while subscribing to the idea that the arts promote an alternative 'value system', 'the gift sphere' or 'the gift economy', an idea that he derives from the abstruse anthropological ideas of Lewis Hyde. The concept of the 'gift economy' allows Abbing to register these so-called irrational values without them coming into conflict with economics and economic value. In fact, this apparent irrationality is a cover for economics. In art, he says, 'anti-market behaviour can be profitable'. Economic value trumps the values of art every time. This is the precise opposite of the Marxist critique of political economy. From a Marxist point of view (i.e. the *critique* of political economy), art's antagonism to economics is not a 'taboo' but a clear-headed defence of art's value from its dangerous liaison with sales, markets and business. Abbing's economics of art alerts us to the controversial encounter between the values of art and economic value, but it does not analyse this antagonism as an instance of the abiding contradictions of capitalism itself.

Mainstream economics has been developing what it calls Cultural Economics for several decades. From 1966 onwards, with Baumol and Bowen's pioneering work on the 'economic dilemma' of the performing arts, mainstream economists have increasingly come to think of art as an almost standard economic sector.

If you insist that art is an economic activity like any other, then tell us: is the artist part of the proletariat, producing value through labour, or is the artist the capitalist or entrepreneur who makes artworks specifically for sale, advancing capital to pay the wages of assistants from which the artist makes profit?

The debates on the funding of the arts from the late 1960s through to the 1980s, between Baumol and Bowen, Richard Musgrave, Alan Peacock, William Grampp, Gary Becker, David Throsby and others, has followed a clear pattern in which the case for the public funding for the arts was increasingly shot down by the case against subsidies. We are now feeling the full force of this theoretical shift in the cuts to the arts. In this period, arguments have been presented for art to be regarded as a Veblen good, a luxury good, a public good, a merit good and an information good, among others. The debate has narrowed severely in recent years, resulting in the apparent victory of a neoliberal agenda for the arts. 'Despite the special position that art occupies in the fabric and culture of societies,' Clare MacAndrew says,

> the reality is that art is produced, bought, and sold by individuals and institutions working within an economic framework inescapable from material and market constraints. The economic case is clear: the market for works of art functions at least as well as many others (albeit imperfectly and with certain special features), as it allows market transactions by voluntary consent, in which buyers and sellers mutually benefit.

It is interesting to note that economists do not agree what kind of good art is. The question of whether art is a *public good* keeps resurfacing despite neoliberal economists' best efforts. The persistence of the question has sound economic grounds. Technically speaking, a public good is a good that is *non-rival* and *non-excludable*, i.e. that the consumption of it by one person does not prevent others from consuming it and that nobody can be excluded from consuming it. This seems to fit certain patterns of 'consuming' artworks (viewing them in galleries, museums, reading about them in books and magazines in libraries, online etc.) but does not adequately account for artworks 'consumed' as singular or unique objects by collectors and investors. In some respects, artworks also exhibit the characteristics of *information goods*, and in other respects they exhibit the characteristics of a *Veblen good*. On the other end of the scale, Richard Musgrave includes art among his list of *merit goods* – i.e. products that individuals ought to have regardless of their ability to pay for them. As such, for most of us, artworks are distributed and displayed as public goods, not commodities.

It is rare – perhaps unique to art – for a product to have all these economic properties. Art does not belong to one category of good alone. Even the most expensive artwork exists within several distinct economic categories. This means that it is impossible to prevent art from spilling out of these economic categories, even when it seems to be exemplary of that category. This is the case in the relationship between art and luxury goods.

Art and the Economics of Luxury Goods

In mainstream economics, a luxury good is a good for which *demand increases more than proportionally as income rises*. What this refers to is the fact that even if the wealthy buy more expensive and higher quality bread, cheese and other necessities, they do not increase their consumption of bread and cheese *proportionally* to their relative wealth; their consumption of sports cars and designer clothing increases at a greater rate, becoming an increasingly large proportion of their expenditure. The formula seems sound enough, but it leaves out two entire branches of commodities that are not luxuries but which increase more than proportionally as income rises: firstly financial goods (investments, bonds, shares, etc.), and secondly expenditure on labour and machinery by the owners of firms, which also increases disproportionately to income. Nevertheless, the formula is at least good enough to account for certain consumption practices in relation to artwork. Roman Kraeussl makes the standard case: 'Art is a luxury good. If aggregate levels of wealth are high, the demand for art may also be expected to be high, as investors may spend part of this excess of wealth in the arts. Changes in income are therefore likely to have a significant effect on the demand for art and the prices paid for works of art.'

The art market is indeed a vast luxury trade. But art is not a standard luxury in terms of its production. Unlike *haute cuisine, haute couture* or *fine and rare wines*, there need be no high quality within the product. At $15 million, Damien Hirst's stuffed shark is one of the most expensive artworks by a living artist, but it is technically inferior to comparably preserved animals. One could purchase a *better* stuffed shark at a fraction of the price of Hirst's. Artworks do not have to exhibit any qualities of the luxury trade in their raw materials, skills, technology, or any other intrinsic quality.

Despite the conspicuousness of art's luxury trade, artworks do not conform in many respects to the conventional economic pattern of consumption of a luxury good. Luxury goods such as sports cars are often purchased, as Thorstein Veblen observed, in part to exhibit them. However, the display aspect of luxury goods means showing off goods that are not normally consumed in their display. Nonetheless, when a non-owner of an artwork looks at it, she consumes it without purchasing it. This is why artwork is naturally seen as a public good as well as a luxury good. Sports cars and jewellery are not public goods or merit goods in addition to being luxury goods. Artwork, on the other hand, even if and when it is a luxury good is *often* (and, in principle, *always!*) a public good and a merit good. Even artwork that is a commodity, even artwork that is a luxury good, is never merely a commodity, is never merely a luxury.

Economists are wrong. Artwork is not a commodity and art is not an economic activity. Art hates capitalism even if capitalism loves art. Capitalism loves art because its values are not determined by supply and demand. The reason economists think that art is sacred or artists are 'perverse' is simply due to the fact that artwork is not produced as a commodity for economic exchange. If all production followed the logic of artistic production, capitalism would be history and economists would be out of a job!

Homo Economicus is a shit artist, a blind art critic, a moronic art theorist, a witless art historian and a cynical curator. Homo Economicus is also a dumb collector, a worthless gallerist, and an unreliable dealer. Let's kick the marketplace out of art. And kick the economist up the arse. Are there any economists in the room?

Afterword:

Do We Need a Lab? Capture, Exploitation and Resistance in Contemporary Creative Communities

Agnieszka Kurant, Jan Sowa and Krystian Szadkowski

The surplus labour of the mass has ceased to be the condition for the development of general wealth, just as the non-labour of the few, for the development of the general powers of the human head. With that, production based on exchange value breaks down, and the direct, material production process is stripped of the form of penury and antithesis. The free development of individualities, and hence not the reduction of necessary labour time so as to posit surplus labour, but rather the general reduction of the necessary labour of society to a minimum, which then corresponds to the artistic, scientific etc. development of the individuals in the time set free, and with the means created, for all of them.

Karl Marx (1973: 705-706, emphases in original)

Art and the Capture of Surplus Value in the Social Factory

There is a politically interesting idea in the philosophy of art put forward by Jacques Rancière in his *Politics of Aesthetics* (2004). Going back to Schiller's vision of the 'aesthetic education of man' combined with *The Oldest Systematic Program of German Idealism* (Behler, 2003: 161-163) and filtered through 20th century vanguard movements, Rancière attempts to portray artistic creation as a manifestation of a characteristic specific to the human species, namely the fact that a human being, as opposed to the rest of nature – to put it in an early Marxist perspective – creates its own world (Marx, 1988). Obviously, Marx regarded not art but the labour process as a sort of synecdoche or a symptom revealing this fact, one that is being deeply mystified by capitalist practice and ideology. However, Rancière believes that 'art anticipates work' in this respect (2004: 44), thus manifesting the species-character of humanity in a sort of purer and stronger way.

No doubt there is some truth to this and Rancière's proposition offers insight into the social and political dimension of artistic production. For instance, it makes it easier to understand why contemporary artwork reaches such exorbitant prices. As Diedrich Diederichsen advocates, when we buy art, we are buying something more than just the artwork itself. He argues that we buy petrified time filled with an adventurous and free life (hence the importance of all sorts of myths surrounding a bohemian lifestyle), as opposed to our dull and predictable bourgeois existence. In the Rancièrian perspective, one might say that in buying art, we are buying the petrified essence of humanity – its creativity.

On the other hand, there's a caveat as well. One has to take into consideration the fact that art does not function in an ideal, free, non-alienated, post-revolutionary society, but in a social reality deeply penetrated by capitalist relations and limitations. Whatever art could be in its essence, its social function remains marked by theses relations and limitations. While Rancière's insight could very well describe some sort of ideal type, reality confronts us with a somewhat different and much more sinister process. Art seems to reveal not only the sublime essence of humanity, but also the very treacherous and negative character of contemporary capitalism, namely its parasitic nature. Artistic creativity and value production in art undergo a mystification similar to appropriation of value in the field of immaterial and biopolitcal production. It operates via one of the major common myths surrounding art: the idea of creativity as an individual process. This myth is still rooted quite deeply in art theory, where the concept of an artist-author as a solitary genius taking inspiration from their own personality, life and intellect is still present. *A Joy Forever* tries to question that point of view. We believe that the concept of 'Author' is, to an important extent, a construct created to appropriate the labour of the multitude in order to proclaim it as individual artwork. Mechanisms in the art market and cultural industries lead to the exploitation of the creative general intellect. They are based on the fetishisation and speculation not only of cultural/artistic objects, but also seemingly intangible processes and ideas. We believe that the very figure of an author represents a mechanism of capture devised to appropriate value produced in a dispersed and networked creative process, and thus to make it suitable for spectacular gallery presentations and for trading on the art market, since both require a strong identity to be able to market or even sustain their respective endeavours.

There's a perfect illustration of these processes in artwork pertaining to the field of relational aesthetics. Artists creating relational art work with and through social relations [1]. What is striking is that participants remain mostly anonymous and they rarely accumulate any sort of value as a result of taking part in the project. The artist does. She signs the entire project with her name, gets paid for doing it, adds it to her résumé and, more often than not, carefully documents her work in order to be able to talk about it during conferences, presentations and gallery lectures. The very fact of having a distinguished and renowned identity – as opposed to that of a mere participant – allows for an accumulation of surplus value on the side of the artist. So, yes, everybody is an artist, as Beuys famously claimed, but an artist in the 'social gallery', where his or her creativity is being exploited and captured just like our invisible work is in the 'social factory' described by Mario Tronti several decades ago.

Immaterial Laboratory of Biopolitcal Production

So what to do with art? Does it have any emancipatory or even critical potential? In many circles, art is still conceived as a social laboratory, where innovative ways for organising labour, socialising both for labour and through labour, as well as different types of production, speculation, and generation, accumulation and appropriation of value are continually tested. Art could also be perceived as a field with a potential for the creation of an alternative logic that could inspire the development of alternative economies. Nevertheless, artistic experiments are, like many other things and processes, immediately appropriated and commoditised by creative industries and internal mechanisms in the field of art. Despite this obvious fact, many artists

---

[1] As Nicolas Bourriaud claims, having coined the very term 'relation art'. One can name figures such as Rirkrit Tiravanija, Douglas Gordon, Pierre Huyghe, Liam Gillick or Philippe Parreno. In the Polish context, one could point to Joanna Rajkowska, Paweł Althamer or Roman Dziadkiewicz.

continuously try to play a sort of 'minority game' with creative industries and the rest of the art world. This is surely a way of guaranteeing their own autonomy within the field of cultural production, but it remains unclear whether it could also prove useful in any social struggle undertaken outside of this field.

However, we are aware that there is no ideal type of laboratory, where contemporary cognitive capitalism's experiments with the organisation of labour, valorisation and mechanisms of capture are rooted. There is no single social, cultural or economic sector (which are thoroughly intermingled in the era of the social factory and the real subsumption of life itself under capital) that plays a leading role in the development of so called 'knowledge-based' capitalism, just as there is no single sector that is able to fuel its growth and seize hegemony over the others. However, what seems interesting, and what we have been trying to address in the framework of the Free/Slow University of Warsaw, is an enquiry into how a combination of various sectors of cognitive labour (like art and the academic world) reveals some sort of general tendency in capitalist development. While no single field of immaterial/biopolitical production provides enough data and examples to grasp the contemporary evolution of capitalist economy, all – or at least most of them considered in their similarities, dissimilarities and mutual relationships can tell us something about what is currently happening in the capitalist social factory.

Some scholars like Yann Moulier-Boutang, for example, claim that cognitive capitalism's labour paradigm seeks its models not only in the world of art, but also in the realm of academia. Industrial capitalism favoured *libido sentiendi* – that is, a desire to feel, to enjoy material goods – and *libido dominandi* – i.e. the desire to dominate – as modes of its agents' operations. In cognitive capitalism, *libido sciendi* – the passion for learning and the taste for the game of knowledge, so important in science and art – plays the most significant role in the creative process (Moulier-Boutang, 2011: 75-78).

Indeed, parallel to the abovementioned changes in the contemporary art world, some crucial shifts have occurred in other sectors of immaterial production, for example in higher education and research. As Carlo Vercellone has clearly stated, the struggles of the 1960s and 1970s marked the rise of the development of cognitive capitalism, a system of accumulation where the productive value of creative and knowledge-based activities gain the dominant character, and the processes of valorisation of capital are directly related to the control of knowledge, affects and creative acts, and their transformation into commodities (Vercellone, 2009: 119). Demands for access to universities, democratisation of education, as well as mass refusal of the dull, Fordist monotony of factory work and modes of discipline and control related to it, spread across all Western countries. It gave birth to what Vercellone calls 'mass intellectuality'. This explosion and burst of the creative powers of the working-classes entering higher education systems provoked a response in the development of collective labours' capacities, i.e. the deployment of neoliberal regulation policies, a model of control that, among others, entails processes of precarisation: the multiplication of precarious forms of work (fixed term contract, interim, apprenticeship, subsidised employment, non-voluntary part-time labour, etc.), and a break from standard Fordist full-time and stable employment – both inside academia and in the outside world.

According to Slaughter and Rhoades, authors of *Academic Capitalism and the New Economy* (2004), these practices include, apart from a process of precarisation of academic work, a strong emphasis on intellectual property rights, patent rights, the introduction of managerialism as a form of control over production, and the application and imposition of accountability and effectiveness measurements (a process well described in this volume by Isabelle Bruno in her article about the ubiquitous practice of benchmarking). The abovementioned mechanisms do not *exhaust* capital's instruments of control deployed in the higher education sphere, indeed all of them are, to some extent, implemented in other sectors (art included). The crucial link seems to be, again, the figure of the author and its persistence across a wide range of creative practices. Vanguard visual artists may not have a lot in common with Hollywood movie stars and academic publishers, but they do share one crucial characteristic: a fetishist admiration of signing 'their' work with their name. Zeal in defending copyright seems to be as strong among academics as it is among audio-visual producers. After all, it was not the Record Industry Association of America, but a coalition of academic publishers from Europe that brought down the (in)famous e-book sharing platform Library.nu on the grounds of copyright infringement.

Art and Financial Capitalism

As stated in the introduction by Michał Kozłowski and Kuba Szreder, this book aims to analyse and deconstruct creativity in more ways than one. However, if there is a single topic to sum up and point to as the most inspiring from a socio-political point of view, it would in our opinion be the relationship between contemporary artistic production and the most advanced forms of the capitalist economy. The above mentioned critique of the notion of authorship can very well be transposed to areas of a quite materialist Marxist critique. Figures such as artists or academic publishers, among many others, are widely becoming capital's mechanisms of capture and transformation of the potentia of living creativity into dead creativity, its main source of rent. Mechanisms of capturing and accumulating value very similar to the ones diagnosed in the relational art field are operating in technologically advanced branches of capitalist production like the internet or the academic publishing market. The way Google or Facebook capitalise on the dispersed and networked activity of the multitude of its users, or how huge academic publishing corporations enclose work of scientists and scholars, perfectly corresponds to the practices of relational artists. In both cases, the author/owner doesn't so much produce the final outcome and profits but rather captures the value produced by others and turns it into a sort of rent derived from the author/owner's particular position within the network of cooperation. This is only the first of many striking similarities. The contemporary process of capitalisation is accompanied by the erosion and deregulation of fixed roles and activities. The freer the worker, the more s/he puts herself to work. In response to these processes, the contemporary artist elaborates a perverse series of equivalences: between production time and social time, between discourse and the material conditions of display, between communicative activity and the production of commodities, etc. Artistic praxis starts producing a wider discourse, reaching beyond images and objects towards other forms such as writing and socialising.

Artistic and cultural modes of production (along with scientific ones) are no longer merely supplementary fields of capitalistic social infrastructure: they become central sectors of production to which other fields of social labour remain subordinated in economical as well as symbolic terms. This theme is broached in this volume by several authors. In her article, Marina Vishmidt talks about 'speculation as a mode of production' highlighted in the art world. Art and money as social mediations of labour both depend on the negation of the social form of concrete labour through the modality of 'speculation' – money grows through speculation understood as claims on future value, while art is valued through speculative markets and has been seen as a process of speculative thought since the beginning of Conceptual Art. Whereas speculative thought refers mainly to art and aesthetics, particularly in their connection to re-imagining social relations, 'financial speculation' can be more broadly defined as the self-expanding, or self-valorising, dynamic of capital as such, highlighted in value-form analysis – i.e. speculation as social form. The speculation of art (or, the speculation that is art), measures and dramatises its speculative capabilities through its relation to labour, be it a relation of proximity or negation. In this sense

> art cannot be considered in relation to politics without first being considered in relation to labour – and this is even more the case when artistic subjectivity and modes of production become a supplement to the restructuring of the labour-capital relation away from the wage and its equivalences to the precarious and "infinite" demands of creativity. Art as a model of emancipated labour figures both unalienated activity which is not measured in money, and the infinite unwaged exploitation that capital is imposing on all of us in the drive to find new sources of accumulation. (Vishmidt, this volume)

Similar issues are raised in this book by Luc Boltanski and Neil Cummings who both emphasise the parallel development of contemporary art and financial capitalism. Cummings even points to a remarkable coincidence: the first major public auction of contemporary art happened almost at the same time as the (in)famous abandonment of the gold standard in the US, a move regarded by some as the inaugural moment of financialisation in the world economy. It should come as no surprise that the art market is doing exceptionally well in these times of contemporary financial turbulence. Luc Boltanski, referring to Lucien Karpik's idea of the 'economy of singularity', examines an unexpected link between artistic creation and market speculation: nowadays the most elaborate investment formulas are singular creations of mathematical genius offered to rich investors on individual terms and tailored to their singular demands – exactly like portraits of the rich painted by artists centuries ago. Boltanski argues that by submitting culture to its rule, capital has not destroyed singularity (as was feared by such theorists as Walter Benjamin and other philosophers from the Frankfurt School), but rather learnt to deal with it and adapted itself accordingly. As such it's through contact with art and through the incorporation of the artistic mode of production that capitalism has evolved in the last decades.

We are facing here, again, the same problem of art being a laboratory – not for resistance and emancipation, but rather for exploitation and capture. And not only of art, but an entire sector of immaterial/biopolitical production that represents a dominant tendency in capitalist development.

Artistic Mode of Revolution?

At the same time, the artistic condition has become an illusionary refuge for a lot of disenchanted members of society. In a recent poll, around twenty-five per cent of young German people interviewed by journalists answered the question 'what do you want to do when you're an adult?' by stating that they wanted to be artists. According to Franco Bifo Berardi, they say they want to be artists because they feel that

> being an artist means to escape the future of sadness, to escape the future of precariousness as sadness. They are thinking, well, precariousness and sadness can become something different, something not so sad, not so precarious, if they withdraw their faith, if they withdraw from any expectations of the capitalist future. I don't want to expect anything from the future, so I start my future as an artist. (Berardi, 2012: 43)

Berardi also talks about the general intellect, in its present configuration, as fragmented and dispossessed of self-perception and self-consciousness.

But what does art have to do with social resistance, or moreover, with any kind of social and political revolution? To answer such a question, we could refer back to 2011 – a threshold of social unrest all over the world. In the shadow of the Wall Street occupation of 2011, one of the stages of a very important process came to an end: the march of the Indignados reached Brussels and those involved conducted a mass demonstration on 15th October 2011. A lot has been written on the movements of 2011, but in reference to the activities of the Indignados we should first of all keep in mind it was a process of massive organisational effort – a process of founding, designing and reinventing the frames of autonomous institutions of the common, on a daily basis. The Indignados were thus, first and foremost, a collective effort devoted to the invention of new collective forms of life.

During the last assembly in Brussels there was a discussion concerning the potential next steps that should be taken by the marching Indignados that ended without any strict conclusions. One of the proposals came from the curator of the Berlin Biennale, the well-known Polish artist Artur Żmijewski, famous for his artistic experimentations with excluded and traumatised social groups. Through his representative, he invited a group of Indignados to visit Berlin and become a part of the forthcoming Biennale, granting them full infrastructural support and hospitality. In doing so he simply gave the impression that he would have liked to become a curator of this social event of resistance. In his manifesto, Applied Social Arts, he poses a desperate and at the same time very important question: does contemporary art have any visible social impact? He proposes that the '[i]nstrumentalisation of autonomy makes it possible to use art for all sorts of things: as a tool for obtaining and disseminating knowledge, as a producer of cognitive procedures relying on intuition and the imagination and serving the cause of knowledge and political action' (Żmijewski, 2007). In his view, art must therefore struggle to retain its power to act, also politically. Is the artist or curator, external to a social movement, who presents him or herself as its patron or supporter, able to support the whole process? Is art an open door through which living creativity could escape the mechanisms of capture? We don't really think so. The curator is the ultimate figure of creativity's corruption and contemporary art itself can be approached today as a complex apparatus of the domestication and capture of resistance, transforming it from a living experience into petrified *oeuvres*. The political failure of the Biennale that presented the Indignados movement as a sort of social zoo, reconstructed on the *Kunstwerke* ground level for the bourgeois to watch from the first-floor balcony, epitomises the whole failure of an approach that treats social movements as if they were artistic creations featured in an art exhibition. This is the kind of laboratory we do not need, a laboratory of capture and exploitation signed with the names of its curators. However, like other sectors in society, contemporary art is also a battlefield where the struggle over the control of value is, should and will continuously take place.

The critique of the political economy of social creativity presented in this volume traces multitudinarian paths – as opposed to paths captured by the figure of the author – for surpluses of creativity, as well as for outlining and describing the multiple exploitation mechanisms that capital is always forced to impose in order to prolong its own existence. Nevertheless, the artistic (or biopolitical) mode of revolution is still something that needs to be theoretically and practically worked out and elaborated.

Bibliography

Abbing, H. (2002) *Why are Artists Poor? The Exceptional Economy of the Arts.*
Amsterdam: Amsterdam University Press.

Abbing, H. (2011) 'The Value for artists of work and income: A Rational
interaction explanation of low incomes in the arts', paper presented at the
16th International Conference on Cultural Economics in Copenhagen, 2010,
available at www.hansabbing.nl.

Abbing, H. (forthcoming) *The Art Period. Is Art Becoming Less Special? A Study of
Art, Artists and the Arts Economy.* Amsterdam: Amsterdam University Press.

Adorno, T.W. (1971) 'Spätkapitalismus oder Industriegesellschaft?', in
Aufsätze. Frankfurt a.M.: Suhrkamp.

Adorno, T.W. (1997), Marx und die Grundbegriffe der Soziologie', in
Backhaus, H.-G., *Dialektik der Wertform.* Freiburg: ça ira.

Adorno, T.W. (2007) *Aesthetic Theory*, transl. R. Hullot-Kentor. London:
Athlone Press.

Adorno, T.W. (1991) *The Culture Industry: Selected Essays on Mass Culture*, transl.
various. London: Routledge.

Adorno, T.W. and Horkheimer, M. (1990) *Dialektik der Aufklärung.* Frankfurt
a.M.: Fischer Taschenbuch.

Adorno, T.W. and Horkheimer, M. (2002) *Dialectic of Enlightenment:
Philosophical Fragments*, transl. E. Jephcott. Stanford, CA: Stanford
University Press.

Alberti, L. B. (1966) *On Painting*, transl. J.R. Spencer. New Haven: Yale
University Press.

Alquati, R. (1976) 'L'università e la formazione: l'incorporamento del sapere sociale nel lavoro vivo', *Aut Aut*, 154: 3-96.

Alterman, E. (2012) 'Think again: Is America getting more conservative?', *American Progress*, February 16, online at: http://www.americanprogress. org/issues/2012/02/ta021612.html.

Anderson, K.B. (2002) 'Marx's late writings on non-Western and precapitalist societies and gender', *Rethinking Marx*, 14(4): 84-96.

Anderson, K.B. (2010) *Marx at the Margins: On Nationalism, Ethnicity, and Non-Western Societies*. Chicago: University of Chicago Press.

Appadurai, A. (ed.) (1986) *The Social Life of Things: Commodities in Cultural Perspective*. Cambridge: Cambridge University Press.

Arts Council England (2010) *Annual Equality Report 2009/10*, online at: http://www.artscouncil.org.uk/publication_archive/annual-equality-report-200910/.

Ayache, E. (2010) *The Blank Swan: The End of Probability*. New Jersey: Hoboken.

Ayache, E. (2011) 'In the middle of the event', in R. MacKay (ed.) *The Medium of Contingency*. New York: New York University Press.

Backhaus, H.-G. (1997) 'Theodor W. Adorno über Marx und die Grundbegriffe der Soziologie', in *Dialektik der Wertform*. Freiburg: ça ira.

Badiou, A. (1988) *L'être et l'événement*. Paris: Seuil.

Baker, G. (2007) 'The Artwork caught by the tail: Dada painting', in *The Artwork caught by the tail: Francis Picabia and Dada in Paris*. Cambridge, MA: MIT Press.

Baudrillard, J. (1996) *System of Objects*, transl. J. Benedict. London: Verso.

Baxandall, M. (1991) *Formes de l'intention: Sur l'explication historique des tableaux*. Paris: Jacqueline Chambon.

Becker, H.S. (1982) *Art Worlds*. Berkeley: University of California Press.

Becker, I. (2009) 'Das Bild als Wiedergänger: Retroaktivität und "Remediation" in den Arbeiten von T.J. Wilcox', *Texte zur Kunst*, 76: 83-95.

Bellet, H. (2001) *Le marché de l'art s'écroule demain à 18h30*. Paris: Nil.

Bellet, H. (2011) 'Ce portrait est-il un Léonard de Vinci?: Polémique autour d'un dessin qui aurait appartenu à la famille du duc de Milan', *Le Monde*, September 29.

Bellofiore, R. and Tomba, M. (2009) 'Lesearten des Maschinenfragments: Perspektiven und Grenzen des operaistischen Ansatzes und der operaistischen Auseinandersetzung mit Marx', in M. van der Linden and K.H. Roth (eds.) *Über Marx hinaus*. Berlin: Assoziation A.

Benjamin, W. (2007) 'The work of art in the age of mechanical reproduction', in *Illuminations*, transl. H. Zohn. New York: Schocken Books.

Benkler, Y. (2006) *The Wealth of Networks: How Social Production Transforms Markets and Freedom*. New Haven, CN: Yale University Press.

Berardi, F. (2012) *The Uprising: On Poetry and Finance*. New York: Semiotext(e).

Berger, M. (1989) *Labyrinths: Robert Morris, Minimalism, and the 1960s*. New York: Harper & Row.

Beuret, N. (2011) 'Hope against hope: A Necessary betrayal', *The Paper*, -1, online at: http://libcom.org/news/hope-against-hope-necessary-betrayal-15122010.

Black, B. (1992) 'The refusal of art', *Friendly Fire*. Brooklyn: Autonomedia.

Blum, A. (2003) *The Imaginative Structure of the City*. Montreal: McGill-Queen's University Press.

Boltanski, L. (2009) *De la critique: Précis de sociologie de l'émancipation*. Paris: Gallimard.

Boltanski, L., and Chiapello, E. (2005) *The New Spirit of Capitalism*, transl. G. Elliot. London: Verso.

Boltanski, L., and Thévenot, L. (1991) *De la justification: Les économies de la grandeur*. Paris: Gallimard.

Bonefeld, W. (2001) 'The permanence of primitive accumulation: Commodity fetishism and social constitution', *The Commoner*, 2: 1-15. online at: http://www.commoner.org.uk/02bonefeld.pdf.

Bourdieu, P. (1983). 'The field of cultural production, or: The economic world reversed', *Poetics*, 12: 311-56.

Bourdieu, P. (1984) *Distinction: A Social Critique of the Judgement of Taste*, transl. R. Nice. London: Routledge and Kegan Paul.

Bourdieu, P. (1992) *Les règles de l'art: Genèse et structure du champ littéraire*. Paris: Seuil.

Bousquet, M. (2008) *How the University Works: Higher Education and the Low-Wage Nation*. New York: New York University Press.

Brandt, G. (1990) *Technik, Arbeit und gesellschaftliche Entwicklung*. Frankfurt a.M.: Suhrkamp.

Braverman, H. (1998 [1974]) *Labor and Monopoly Capital: The Degradation of Work in the Twentieth Century*. New York: Monthly Review Press.

Bruno, I. (2008) *A vos marques, prêts… cherchez!: La stratégie européenne de Lisbonne, vers un marché de la recherche*. Paris: Editions du Croquant.

Bruno, I. (2009) 'The "indefinite discipline" of competitiveness: Benchmarking as a neoliberal technology of government', *Minerva*, 47(3): 261-280.

Bryan-Wilson, J. (2009) *Art Workers: Radical Practice in the Vietnam War Era*. Berkeley: University of California Press.

Caffentzis, G. (1999) 'The End of work or the renaissance of slavery? A critique of Rifkin and Negri', *Common Sense*, 24: 20-38.

Caffentzis, G. and Federici, S. (2009) 'Notes on the Edu-factory and cognitive capitalism' in The Edu-factory Collective (ed.) *Toward a Global Autonomous University*. New York: Autonomedia.

Camp, R. C. (1989) *Benchmarking: The Search for Industry Best Practices that Lead to Superior Performance*. Milwaukee: ASQC Quality Press.

Campbell, C. (1987) *The Romantic Ethic and the Spirit of Modern Consumerism*. Oxford: Blackwell.

Carrot Workers' Collective (2001) 'Surviving internships: Counter guide to internships in the creative sector', online at: http://carrotworkers.files.wordpress.com/2009/03/cw_web.pdf.

Cennini, C.A. (1960) *The Craftsman's Handbook*, transl. D.V. Thompson Jr. New York: Dover Publications.

Chakrabarty, D. (2000) *Provincializing Europe: Postcolonial Thought and Historical Difference*. Princeton-Oxford: Princeton University Press.

Chan, A. and Xiaoyang, Z. (2003) 'Disciplinary labour regimes in Chinese factory', *Critical Asian Studies*, 35(4): 559-584.

Clark, T.J. (2001) *Farewell to an Idea: Episodes from a History of Modernism*. Yale: The Yale University Press.

Cleaver, H. (2000) *Reading Capital Politically*. Edinburgh: AK Press.

Colatrella, S. (2011) 'Nothing exceptional: Against Agamben', *Journal for Critical Education Policy Studies*, 9(1): 96-125.

Comrades from Cairo (2011) 'To the Occupy movement – the occupiers of Tahrir Square are with you', *The Guardian*, October 25, online at: http://www.guardian.co.uk/commentisfree/2011/oct/25/occupy-movement-tahrir-square-cairo.

De Angelis, M. (2001a) 'Global capital, abstract labour, and the fractal-panopticon', *The Commoner*, 1: 1-19, online at: http://www.commoner.org.uk/fractalpanopt.pdf.

De Angelis, M. (2001b) 'Market order and panopticism', online at: http://libcom.org/files/Panopticon.pdf.

De Angelis, M. (2005) 'Value(s), measure(s) and disciplinary markets', *The Commoner*, 10: 66-86, online at: http://www.commoner.org.uk/10deangelis.pdf.

De Angelis, M. (2007) 'Measure, excess and translation: Some notes on «Cognitive Capitalism»', *The Commoner*, 12: 71-78, online at: http://www.commoner.org.uk/12deangelis.pdf.

De Waal, E. (1998) *Bernard Leach*. London: Tate Gallery Publishing.

Deleuze, G. (1990) *Logic of Sense*, transl. M. Lester. New York: Columbia University Press.

Deleuze, G., and Guattari, F. (1987) *A Thousand Plateaus: Capitalism and Schizophrenia* 2, transl. B. Massumi. Minneapolis: University of Minnesota Press.

Diederichsen, D. (2008) *On (Surplus) Value in Art*, transl. J. Gussen. New York: Sternberg Press.

Dimon, J. (2012) 'Policies made recovery slower and worse', online at: http://video.foxbusiness.com/v/1450365871001/dimon-policies-made-recovery-slower-and-worse/?playlist_id=87247.

Dussel, E. (1990a) *El ultimo Marx (1863-1882) y la liberacion latino americana*. México: Siglo XXI.

Dussel, E. (1990b) 'Marx's *Economic Manuscripts of 1861-63* and the "concept" of dependency', *Latin American Perspectives*, 17(2): 62-101.

Edu-factory (2010) 'Double crisis', *edu-factory web-journal*, 0.

Ehrenreich, B. (2001) *Nickel and Dimed: On (Not) Getting By in America*. New York: Metropolitan Books.

Elias, N. (1994) *The Civilizing Process. Sociogenetic and Psychogenetic Investigations*, transl. E. Jephcott. Oxford: Blackwell.

Emspak, J. (2011) 'Occupy Wall Street: Why it chose Tumblr', *Discovery*, October 6, online at: http://news.discovery.com/tech/occupy-wall-street-tumblr-111006.html.

Endnotes (2010) 'Communisation and value-form theory', *Endnotes*, 2: *Misery and the Value Form*, online at: http://endnotes.org.uk/articles/4.

Epstein, S.A. (1991) *Wage Labor and Guilds in Medieval Europe*. Chapel Hill: University of North Carolina Press.

ERT (1996) *Benchmarking for Policy-Makers: The Way to Competitiveness, Growth and Job Creation*. Brussels: ERT Publication.

European Commission (2002a) 'Towards a "knowledge" market', *RTD Info*, 34, online at: http://ec.europa.eu/research/news-centre/en/soc/02-07-soc02.html.

European Commission (2002b) 'The age of the researcher-entrepreneur', *RTD Info*, 35, online at: http://ec.europa.eu/research/news-centre/en/pur/02-10-pur01c.html.

European Commission (2004) 'Facing the challenge: The Lisbon strategy for growth and employment', *Report from the High Level Group Chaired by Wim Kok*. Luxembourg: OOPEC.

European Council (2000) 'Presidency conclusions', *Lisbon Summit*, March 23-24, online at: http://www.europarl.europa.eu/summits/lis1_en.htm.

European Council (2002) 'Presidency conclusions', *Barcelona Summit*, March 15-16, online at: http://ec.europa.eu/languages/documents/doc4794_en.pdf.

Fellah, N. (2011) 'The Art of occupation', *New American Paintings*, November 9, online at: http://newamericanpaintings.wordpress.com/2011/11/09/the-art-of-occupation/.

Florida, R. (2002) *The Rise of the Creative Class And How It's Transforming Work, Leisure and Everyday Life*. New York: Basic Books.

Florida, R. (2005) *Cities and the Creative Class*. New York: Routledge.

Florida, R. (2012) 'Why America keeps getting more conservative', *The Atlantic*, February 13, online at: http://www.theatlanticcities.com/politics/2012/02/why-america-keeps-getting-more-conservative/1162/.

Florida, R., Dreher, Ch. (2002) 'Interview with Richard Florida', *Salon*, June 7.

Foresight (2011) 'Technology trends in the financial markets: A 2020 vision', online at: http://www.bis.gov.uk/assets/foresight/docs/computer-trading/11-1222-dr3-technology-trends-in-financial-markets

Foster, J.B. (1998) 'Introduction' in H. Braverman *Labor and Monopoly Capital: The Degradation of Work in the Twentieth Century*. New York: Monthly Review Press.

Foucault, M. (1995) *Discipline & Punish: The Birth of the Prison*. New York: Vintage Books.

Foucault, M. (2008) *The Birth of Biopolitics: Lectures at the Collège de France, 1978-1979*, transl. G. Burchell. Basingstoke: Palgrave Macmillan.

Fraenkel, B. (1992) *La signature: Genèse d'un signe*. Paris: Gallimard.

Fried, M. (2008) 'Introduction', in *Why Photography Matters as Art as Never Before*. New Haven-London: Yale University Press.

Fumagalli, A. and Mezzadra, S. (eds.) (2010) *Crisis in the Global Economy. Financial Markets, Social Struggles, and New Political Scenarios*, transl. J. F. McGimsey. Los Angeles: Semotext(e).

Gambino, F. (2003) *Migranti nella tempesta: Avvistamenti per l'inizio del nuovo millennio*. Verona: Ombre Corte.

Gan, A. (1988) *Russian Art of the Avant-Garde: Theory and Criticism, 1902-1934*. London: Thames & Hudson.

Gell, A. (2009) *L'art et ses agents: Une théorie anthropologique*. Paris: Les presses du réel.

George, S. (2011) 'A coup in the European Union?', *CounterPunch*, October 14, online at: http://www.counterpunch.org/2011/10/14/a-coup-in-the-european-union/.

Gielen, P. (2009) 'The Art scene: A clever working model for economic exploitation?', *Open*, 17, online at: http://www.skor.nl/artefact-4172-en.html.

Gilligan, M. (2008) *Notes on Art, Finance and the Un-Productive Forces*. Glasgow: Transmission Gallery.

Ginzburg, C. (1989) *Mythes, emblèmes, traces: Morphologie et histoire*. Paris: Flammarion.

Glaser, B. (1995) 'Questions to Stella and Judd', in G. Battcock (ed.) *Minimal Art: A Criticial Anthology*. Berkeley: University of California Press.

Glassman, J. (2006) 'Primitive accumulation, accumulation by dispossession, accumulation by "extra-sconomic" means', *Progress in Human Geography*, 30: 608-625.

Gorz, A. (1985) *Paths to Paradise: On The Liberation From Work*, transl. M. Imrie. London: Pluto Press.

Goux, J.J. (1990) *Symbolic Economies: After Marx and Freud*. New York: The Cornell University Press.

Graeber, D. (2011) *Debt: The First 5,000 Years*. New York: Melville House.

Graw, I. (2009) *High Price: Art Between the Market and Celebrity Culture*. New York: Sternberg Press.

Graw, I. (2011) 'Das Wissen der Malerei: Anmerkungen zu denkenden Bildern und der Person im Produkt', *Texte zur Kunst*, 82.

Greenberg, C. (1993) 'Modernist painting', in J. O'Brien (ed.) *The Collected Essays and Criticism* 4: *Modernism with a Vengeance, 1957-1960*. Chicago: Chicago University Press.

Griffin, D. (2011a) 'Pandit says he'd be happy to talk with Wall Street protesters', *Bloomberg Businessweek*, October 12, online at: http://www.businessweek.com/news/2011-10-12/pandit-says-he-d-be-happy-to-talk-with-wall-street-protesters.html.

Griffin, D. (2011b) *'Citi CEO: I'd meet with protesters'*, online at: money.cnn.com/video/news/2011/10/12/n_vikram_pandit_protesters.fortune/.

Gulli, B. (2005) *Labour of Fire: The Ontology of Labor between Economy and Culture*. Philadelphia: Temple University Press.

Haahr, J. H. (2004) 'Open co-ordination as advanced liberal government', *Journal of European Public Policy*, 11(2): 209-230.

Habenundbrauchen (2012) *To have and to need (Manifest)*, online at: http://www.habenundbrauchenll.de/wp-content/uploads/2012/01/HB_web_english_neu.pdf.

Habermas, J. (1981) *Theorie des kommunikativen Handelns*. Frankfurt a.M.: Suhrkamp

Hardt, M. and Negri, A. (2000) *Empire*. Cambridge, MA: Harvard University Press.

Hardt, M. and Negri, A. (2004) *Multitude*. London: Penguin Press.

Hardt, M. and Negri, A. (2009) *Commonwealth*. Cambridge, MA: Belknap Press.

Hartmut, R., (2011) *Accélération: Une critique sociale du temps*. Paris: La Découverte.

Hebdige, D. (1979) *Subculture: The Meaning of Style*. London: Methuen.

Hecker, R. (1987) 'Zur Entwicklung der Werttheorie von der 1. Zur 3. Auflage des ersten Bandes des "Kapitals" von Karl Marx (1867-1883)' in *Marx-Engels-Jahrbuch*, 10: 147-196.

Hegel, G. W. F. (1970) 'Die romantische Kunstform', in *Vorlesungen über die Ästhetik 3*. Frankfurt am Main: Suhrkamp.

Heidegger, M. (2008) 'The origin of the work of art', transl. A. Hofstadter, in D. Farrell Krell (ed.) *Basic Writings*. New York: Harper Collins.

Hilton, R.H. (1969) *The Decline of Serfdom in Medieval England.* London: MacMillan.

Home, S. (1991) *The Neoist Manifestos/The Art Strike Papers.* Stirling: AK Press.

Hudson, M., Sommer, J. (2010) 'Latvia's road to serfdom', *CounterPunch*, February 15, online at: www.counterpunch.org/2010/02/15/latvia-s-road-to-serfdom/.

Huws, U. (2010) 'Expression and expropriation: the dialectics of autonomy and control in creative labour', *ephemera*, 10(3/4): 504-521.

Jaffe, S. (2012) 'Why right-wingers (and media hacks) are totally wrong about what Americans believe – we're becoming less, not more, conservative', *Alternet*, February 17, online at: http://www.alternet.org/election2012/154182/why_rightwingers_(and_media_hacks)_are_totally_wrong_about_what_americans_believe_--_we're_becoming_less,_not_more,_conservative_/?page=entire.

Jameson, F. (2007) *The Modernist Papers.* London: Verso.

Karpik, L. (2007) *L'économie des singularités.* Paris: Gallimard.

Kasher, S. (2010) *Max's Kansas City: Art, Glamour, Rock and Roll.* New York: Abrams.

Kok, W. et al. (2004) *Facing the Challenge: The Lisbon Strategy for Growth and Employment.* Luxembourg: OOPEC.

Kolinko (2002) 'Hotlines', online at: http://www.nadir.org/nadir/initiativ/kolinko/lebuk/e_lebuk.htm.

Krauss, R. (1977) 'Notes on the index: Seventies art in America', *October*, 3: 68-81.

Krauss, R. (1993) *The Optical Unconscious.* Cambridge: MIT Press.

Krauss, R. (2000) *A Voyage on the North Sea: Art in the Age of the Post-Medium Condition.* London: Thames & Hudson.

Krugman, P. (2011) 'Lats of lack', *New York Times*, July 18, online at: http://krugman.blogs.nytimes.com/2011/07/18/lats-of-luck/.

Kuhn, T. and Giles, S. (eds.) (2003) *Brecht on Art & Politics (Brecht's Plays, Poetry and Prose)*, transl. L. Bradley, S. Giles, T. Kuhn. London: Methuen.

Lazzarato, M. (1996) 'Immaterial labour', transl. P. Colilli, E. Emery, in M. Hardt and P. Virno (eds.) *Radical Thought in Italy. A Potential Politics.* Mineapolis: University of Minesota Press.

Lazzarato, M. (2011) 'The Misfortunes of the "artistic critique" and of cultural employment', transl. M. O'Neill, in G. Raunig, G. Ray and U.

Wuggenig (eds.) *Critique of Creativity: Precarity, Subjectivity and Resistance in the "Creative Industries"*, online at: http://mayflybooks.org/wp-content/uploads/2011/05/9781906948146CritiqueOfCreativity.pdf.

Le Chevallier, M. (2008) *L'audit*. Paris: Courtesy Galerie Jousse Entreprise, online at: http://www.martinlechevallier.net/audit.html.

Leach, B. (1940) *A Potter's Book*. London: Faber & Faber.

Lefebvre, H. (2000) *Everyday Life in the Modern World*, transl. S. Rabinovitch. London: Athlone Press.

Levitt, T. (1984) 'The Globalization of markets', *The McKinsey Quarterly*, Summer: 2-20.

Lieber, E. (2000) *Willem De Kooning: Reflections in the Studio*. New York: Abrams.

Lüthy, M. and Menke, C. (2005) 'Einleitung', in *Subjekt und Medium in der Kunst der Moderne*. Zürich/Berlin: Diaphanes.

MacKay, R. (ed.) (2011), *The Medium of Contingency*. London: Urbanomic and Ridinghouse.

Malle, B. (2004) *How the Mind Explains Behavior: Folk Explanations, Meaning and Social Interaction*. Cambridge: MIT Press.

Marazzi, C. (2010a) *Il comunismo del capitale: Finanziarizzazione, biopolitiche del lavoro e crisi globale*. Verona: Ombre Corte.

Marazzi, C. (2010b) *The Violence of Financial Capitalism*, transl. J.F. McGimsey, K. Lebedeva. New York: Semiotext(e).

Marin, L. (2003) *Die Malerei zerstören*. Berlin: Diaphanes.

Marini, R.M. (1991), *Dialéctica de la dependencia*, México: Ediciones Era.

Marion, J.-L. (1982) 'L'idole et l'icône', in *Dieu sans l'être*. Paris: Fayard.

Martin, R. (2011) 'Taking an administrative turn: Derivative logics for a recharged humanities', *Representations*, 116(1): 156-176.

Marx, K. (1972) *Capital: A Critique of Political Economy*. Volume 3. London: Lawrence & Wishart.

Marx, K. (1973) *Grundrisse: Foundations of the Critique of Political Economy*, transl. M. Nicolaus. London: Penguin.

Marx, K. (1976) *Capital: A Critique of Political Economy*. Volume 1. London: Penguin.

Marx, K. (1979a) *Das Kapital 1*, Marx Engels Werke. Berlin: Dietz Verlag.

Marx, K. (1979b) *Das Kapital 3*, Marx Engels Werke. Berlin: Dietz Verlag.

Marx, K. (1979c) 'The future results of British rule in India' (*New York Daily Tribune*, 8.08.1853), MECW 12. Moscow: Progress Publishers.

Marx, K. (1986) *Economic Manuscripts of 1857-58*, MECW 28. Moscow: Progress Publishers.

Marx, K. (1987) 'Preface to a Contribution to the Critique of Political Economy', in *Collected Works, Vol. 29*. New York: International Publishers. (1857-1861)

Marx, K. (1988) *Economic and Philosophic Manuscripts of 1844*, transl. M. Mulligan. New York: International Publishers.

Marx, K. (1989) 'Marginal notes on Adolph Wagner's *Lehrbuch der Politischer Oekonomie* (1881-82)', MECW 24. Moscow: Progress Publishers.

Marx, K. (1990) *Ökonomisches Manuskript 1861-1863* 1, MEW 43. Berlin: Dietz Verlag.

Marx, K. (1996) *Capital* 1, MECW 35. Moscow: Progress Publishers.

Marx, K., Engels, F. (1976) *The German Ideology*, MECW 5. London: Lawrence & Wishart.

Marx, K. and Engels, F. (1983) *Letters 1856-59*, MECW 40. Moscow: Progress Publishers.

Marx, K. and Engels, F. (1986) 'Marx to Engels, 2nd August 1862', MECW 41. Moscow: Progress Publishers.

Marx, K. and Engels, F. (1996) *Manifeste du partii communiste*, Paris: Mille et une nuits.

Marx, K. and Michajlovskij, N.K. (1989) 'Letter to editor of *Otecestvennye Zapiski*, November 1877', MECW 24. Moscow: Progress Publishers.

McNally, D. (2009) 'From financial crisis to world-slump: Accumulation, financialisation, and the global slowdown', *Historical Materialism*, 17: 35-83.

McNally, M. B. (2010) 'Enterprise content management systems and the application of Taylorism and Fordism to intellectual labour', *ephemera*, 10(3/4): 357-373.

Mezzadra, S. (2006) *Diritto di fuga: Migrazioni, cittadinanza, globalizzazione*. Verona: Ombre Corte.

Mohri, K. (1979) 'Marx and "underdevelopment"', *Monthly Review*, 30(11): 32-42.

Morris, W. (2007) *Signs of Change*. Gloucester: Dodo Press.

Moulier-Boutang, Y. (2002) *Dalla schiavitù al lavoro salariato*. Roma: manifesto libri.

Moulier-Boutang, Y. (2011) *Cognitive Capitalism*, transl. E. Emery. New York: Polity Press.

Moulin, R. (1992) *L'artiste, l'institution et le marché*. Paris: Flammarion.

Murray, P. (2000) 'Marx's "truly social" labour theory of value: Part II, How is labour that is under the sway of capital actually abstract?', *Historical Materialism*, 7(1): 243-273.

Murray, P. (2004) 'The social and material transformation of production by capital: Formal and real subsumption in *Capital, Volume 1*', in R. Bellofiore and N. Taylor (eds.) *Capital, The Constitution of Capital: Essays on Volume I of Marx's "Capital"*. Basingstoke-Hampshire: Palgrave Macmillan.

National Union of Journalists (2008) 'NUJ Work Experience Survey', online at: http://www.nuj.org.uk/getfile.php?id=559.

Naville, P. (1953) *Le nouveau Léviathan* 1. Paris: Anthropos.

Nef, F. (2000) *L'objet quelconque: Recherches sur l'ontologie de l'objet*. Paris: Vrin.

Negri, A. (1991) *Marx beyond Marx: Lessons on the 'Grundrisse'*, transl. H. Cleaver, M. Ryan, M. Viano. New York: Autonomedia/Pluto.

Negri, A. (1998) *Marx oltre Marx*, Roma: manifesto libri.

Negri, A. (2004) 'A contribution on Foucault', transl. A. Bove and D. Skinner, online at: http://www.generation-online.org/p/fpnegri14.htm.

Negri, A. (2006) *Goodbye Mr Socialism*. New York: Seven Stories Press.

Negt, O. und Kluge, A. (1993) *Geschichte und Eigensinn*. Frankfurt a.M.: Suhrkamp.

Neumann, A. (2010a) *Kritische Arbeitssoziologie*. Stuttgart: Schmetterling.

Neumann, A. (2010b) *Conscience de casse: La sociologie critique de l'Ecole de Francfort*. Paris: Burozoïques.

Neumann, A. (2014) *Après Habermas*. Paris: Editions Delga.

Ngai, P. (2004) 'Women workers and precarious employment in Shenzen special economic zone, China', in M. Keating (ed.) *Gender and Development*. Vol 12(2). (29-36)

Ngai, P. (2005) *Made in China: Women Factory Workers in a Global Workplace*. Durham: Duke University Press.

Parry, A. (1960) *Garretts & Pretenders: A History of Bohemianism in America*. New York: Cosmo.

Pasquinelli, M. (2008) *Animal Spirits: A Bestiary of the Commons*. Rotterdam: NAi Publishers/Institute of Network Cultures.

Peirce, C. S. (2000) 'Die Kunst des Räsonierens', in C. J. W. Kloesel and H. Pape (ed.) *Semiotische Schriften* 1. Frankfurt am Main: Suhrkamp.

Pétré-Grenouilleau, O. (2004) *Les traites négrières: Essai d'histoire globale*. Paris: Editions Gallimard.

Pomian, K. (1987) *Collectionneurs, amateurs et curieux*. Paris: Gallimard.

Pomian, K. (2003) *Des saintes reliques à l'art moderne: Venise – Chicago XIIIe - XXe siècle*. Paris: Gallimard.

Precarias a la Deriva (2003) 'First stutterings of Precarias a la Deriva', online at: http://www.makeworlds.org/node/61.

Precarias a la Deriva (2004) 'Adrift through the circuits of feminized precarious work', online at: http://www.republicart.net/disc/precariat/ precarias01_en.htm.

Precarias a la Deriva (2005) 'A very careful strike: Four hypotheses', online at: http://zinelibrary.info/files/A%20Very%20Careful%20Strike.pdf.

Precarias a la Deriva (2010) 'Close encounters in the second phase', online at: http://caringlabor.wordpress.com/2010/12/14/precarias-a-la-deriva-close-encounters-in-the-second-phase-the-communication-continuum-care-sex-attention/.

Preziosi, D. (2001) *Brain of the Earths Body. Art, Museums, and the Phantasms of Modernity*. Minnesota: The University of Minnesota Press.

Rancière, J. (2004) *Politics of Aesthetics*, transl. G. Rockhill. London: Continuum Books.

Read, J. (2003) *The Micro-Politics of Capital: Marx and the Prehistory of the Present*. Albany: State University of New York Press.

Ricoeur, P. (1990) *Soi-même comme un autre*. Paris: Seuil.

Rigby, D. and Bilodeau, B. (2009) 'Management tools and trends 2009', online at: http://www.bain.com/management_tools/Management_Tools _and_Trends_2009_Global_Results.pdf.

Roggero, G. (2011) *The Production of Living Knowledge: The Crisis of the University and the Transformation of Labor in Europe and North America*, transl. E. Brophy. Philadelphia: Temple University Press.

Rosa, H. (2013) *Social Acceleration: A New Theory of Modernity*, transl. J. Trejo-Mathys. New York: Columbia University Press.

Rosler, M. (2010) 'Culture class: Art, creativity, urbanism, part I: Art and urbanism', *e-flux*, 21, online at: http://www.e-flux.com/journal/culture-class-art-creativity-urbanism-part-i/.

Rosler, M. (2011a) 'Culture class: Art, creativity, urbanism, part II', *e-flux*, 23, online at: http://www.e-flux.com/journal/culture-class-art-creativity-urbanism-part-ii/.

Rosler, M. (2011b) 'Culture class: Art, creativity, urbanism, part III', *e-flux*, 25, online at: http://www.e-flux.com/journal/culture-class-art-creativity-urbanism-part-iii/.

Ross, A. (2003) *No-Collar: The Humane Workplace and its Hidden Costs.* Philadelphia: Temple University Press.

Rottmann, A. (2011) 'Netewerke, Techniken, Institutionen: Kunstgeschichte in offenen Kreisläufen', *Texte zur Kunst*, 81: 67-71.

Roubini, N. (2011) 'The Instability of inequality', *EconoMonitor*, October 14, online at: http://www.economonitor.com/nouriel/2011/10/14/from-project-syndicate-the-instability-of-inequality/.

Ruskin, J. (1854a) *True Functions of the Workman in Art.* London: Smith, Elder & Co.

Ruskin, J. (1854b) *The Stones of Venice.* London: Smith, Elder & Co.

Ruskin, J. (2006) *A Joy Forever and Its Price in the Market.* Online at: http://www.gutenberg.org/ebooks/19980.

Sacchetto, D. (2004) *Il Nordest e il suo Oriente: Migranti, capitali e azioni umanitarie.* Verona: Ombre Corte.

Salmon, C. (2007) *Storytelling: La machine à fabriquer des histoires et à formater les esprits.* Paris: La Découverte.

Sander (2011) 'Will China save global capitalims?', *Mute*, July 27, online at: http://www.metamute.org/en/articles/will_china_save_global_capitalism

Schiller, F. (1794) 'Letters upon the aesthetic education of man', online at: http://www.fordham.edu/halsall/mod/schiller-education.asp.

Schott, J. and Vaughn, E.J. (1973) *America's Pop Collector: Robert C. Scull – Contemporary Art at Auction.* 16mm film. New York: MoMA.

Schwendener, M. (2011) 'What does Occupy Wall Street mean for art?', *Village Voice*, October 19, online at: http://www.villagevoice.com/2011-10-19/art/what-does-occupy-wall-street-mean-for-art/.

Sciardet, H. (2003) *Les marchands de l'aube: Ethnographie et théorie du commerce aux puces de Saint-Ouen.* Paris: Economica.

Searle, J. (1998) *La construction de la réalité sociale*, transl. C. Tierceline. Paris: Gallimard.

Searle, J. (2005) 'What is an institution?', *Journal of Institutional Economics*, 1: 1-22.

Sennett, R. (2008) *The Craftsman*. London: Allen Lane, Penguin.

Shell, M. (1995) *Art and Money*. Chicago: The University of Chicago Press.

Slaughter, S., Rhoades, G. (2004) *Academic Capitalism and the New Economy: Markets, State, and Higher Education*. Baltimore-London: John Hopkins University Press.

Sohn, T. (2012) 'Field trip: Brooklyn detention complex housewarming', February 16, online at: http://urbanomnibus.net/2012/02/field-trip-brooklyn-detention-complex-housewarming/.

Stallabras, J. (2004) *Art Incorporated: The Story of Contemporary Art*. Oxford: Oxford University Press.

Strange, A. (2011) 'Occupy Wall Street protesters used alternative social networks', *PC Magazine*, October 3, online at: http://www.pcmag.com/article2/0,2817,2394043,00.asp.

Terranova, T. (2000) 'Free labor: Producing culture for the digital economy', *Social Text*, 18(2): 33-58.

Thoburn, N. (2003) *Deleuze, Marx and Politics*. London: Routledge.

Tilly, C. (2006) *Why?* Princeton: Princeton University Press.

Tomba, M. (2013) *Marx's Temporalities*, transl. P.D. Thomas and S.R. Farris. Leiden, Boston: Brill.

Tronti, M. (2008) 'Classe', in LUM, *Lessico Marxiano*. Rome: manifesto libri.

Van der Linden, M. (2007) 'Warum gab (und gibt) es Sklaverei im Kapitalismus?: Eine einfache und dennoch schwer zu beantwortende Frage', in M.E. Kabadayi and T. Reichardt (eds.) *Unfreie Arbeit: Ökonomische und kulturgeschichtliche Perspektiven*. Hildesheim: Georg Olms Verlag.

Vaneigem, R. (1982) *The Revolution of Everyday Life*, transl. D.N. Smith. Oakland: PM Press.

Vaneigem, (1996) 'Postface: Observations sur le Manifeste' in K. Marx and F. Engels *Manifeste du Parti Communiste*. Paris: Mille et une nuits.

Vercellone, C. (2005) 'The hypothesis of cognitive capitalism', paper presented at the *Historical Materialism Annual Conference*, London, online at: http://hal-paris1.archives-ouvertes.fr/halshs-00273641/.

Vercellone, C. (2007) 'From formal subsumption to general intellect: Elements for a Marxist reading of the thesis of cognitive capitalism', *Historical Materialism*, 15(1): 13-36.

Vercellone, C. (2009) 'Cognitive capitalism and models for the regulation of wage relations: Lessons from the anti-CPE movement', in The Edu-factory Collective (ed.) *Towards a Global Autonomous University*. New York: Autonomedia.

Vincent, J.-M. (1987) *Critique du travail*. Paris: PUF.

Vincent, J.-M. (1998) *Max Weber ou la démocratie inachevée*. Paris: Le Félin.

Virno, P. (2004), *A Grammar of the Multitude. For an Analysis of Contemporary Forms of Life*, transl. I. Bartoletti, J. Cascatio and A. Casson. New York: Semiotext(e).

Virno, P. (2009) 'The Dismeasure of art: An Interview with Paolo Virno', online at: http://classic.skor.nl/article-4178-nl.html?lang=en.

Wainwright, J. (2008) 'Uneven developments: From *Grundrisse* to *Capital*', *Antipode*, 40(5): 879-897.

Wikipedia (2013) 'Art Treasures Ehibition', online at: http://en.wikipedia.org/wiki/Art_Treasures_Exhibition,_Manchester_1857.

Wills, J. (2011) *Intervention at the Self- Organising and the Community Seminar Series*, Queen Mary, University of London.

Wouters, C. (2007) *Informalization, Manners and Emotions since 1890*. London: Sage.

Zukin, S. (1989) *Loft Living: Culture and Capital in Urban Change*. New York: Rutgers University Press.

Žmijewski, A. (2007) 'Applied Social Arts', online at: http://www.krytykapolityczna.pl/English/Zmijewski-Applied-Social-Arts/menu-id-240.html.